China's transformation into a technologically advanced nation has been the most remarkable economic and geopolitical phenomenon of the past 50 years. Economists and political scientists have explored many of the forces behind this extraordinary process; yet, the momentous changes in the country's financial system have not received as much detailed attention. This book provides that needed focus.

Professor Jolly, who has many years of experience in China as an academic researcher and business consultant, has undertaken a detailed and thorough examination of the Chinese financial system, its institutions, mechanisms, actors, and policies, in terms of four themes: the financial underpinning of the nation's economy; its essential role in the development of infrastructure; its support for the international expansion of Chinese firms; and the introduction of advanced technologies to the financial sector.

The Central Government's controlling role in the financial sector has been dominant. China's success is "not simply the product of market forces... The State Council can be viewed as a conductor and financial and economic actors as performers." Chapters 1 to 4 explain the development of the financial system, government policy with the state as the controlling force, regulation, and the key financial actors. These include the five major banks and a myriad of small ones (a "fringed oligopoly") plus the local government financing vehicles. Jolly notes the exclusion of foreign banks, the later development of the stock exchanges, and the key role of the three policy banks in funding infrastructure.

Chapter 5 analyses the role of the Central Government in financing its "Go Global" strategy. Its encouragement of foreign direct investment by Chinese companies demonstrates the primacy of geopolitics over business when it comes to investing abroad.

Chapter 6 describes the evolution of advanced technologies in the consumer finance sector, initiated by private companies and rapidly adopted by consumers. Although innovative private companies introduced these advanced technologies, the firms have increasingly come under central control.

Importantly, this book investigates the major societal and demographic issues confronting China and their impact on finance, dealing with the aging population, the lasting impact of the one-child policy, financing of pensions, real estate bubbles, and burgeoning debt.

This book concludes by looking to the future, in which China is entering into a transition phase with a slowing growth rate. Positive factors include the impact of the Belt and Road Initiative on China's global influence, the possible admission of foreign banks, and the potential globalization of the currency.

Readers will find this book of great interest, due to the breadth of its coverage and the detailed examination of policies, institutions, and actors, and its informed and authoritative perspective. It is even-handed in its judgments, considering (as the author says) both the *yin* and the *yang* of each issue. It will be a valuable resource for business executives, policy makers, researchers, and students of China.

Bruce McKern, Professor of Chinese Business
UTS Business School, Sydney, Australia

Dominique Jolly's *The Chinese Financial System: Sino-centricity and Orchestrated Control* is an insightful, detailed, and masterful treatment of a complex topic neglected in the Western literature on Chinese business and economics. It therefore joins the ranks of excellent books on China as this country pulls out of the COVID-19 crisis and resumes its more traditional rates of growth. Readers will deepen their knowledge of the complexities of China's financial policies, institutions, and regulatory environment. The book is an excellent reference tool for Chinese financial enthusiasts because of Jolly's thorough research and knowledge. Pulling back the veil on how "Sino-centricity" affects China's financial system, Jolly argues that market forces do not drive China's financial policies. Understanding China's financial regulation and its variegated impacts on the global financial system precisely requires a fresh treatment at a time when the Chinese currency and financial system are increasingly considered as a possible challenger to the existing order. *The Chinese Financial System: Sino-centricity and Orchestrated Control* is therefore essential reading for anybody interested in China's global standing at this juncture in a post-Bretton Woods world. Jolly's straightforward writing style makes the book accessible both to experts and novices. Enthusiasts of finance, economics, and China's global role will find this text rewarding and that it opens new vistas for future research and policy action.

John R. McIntyre, Professor of Management,
Executive Director, Georgia Tech CIBER,
Scheller College of Business, Atlanta, GA, USA

An extremely comprehensive guide to understand how China's financial system evolved, the roles it served in the economy, and the underlying logic it is designed. Read it if you want to know more about doing business in China.

Timothy (Jun) Lu, Associate Professor,
Emlyon Business School, Shanghai Campus, China

THE CHINESE FINANCIAL SYSTEM
Sino-centricity and Orchestrated Control

World Scientific Series in Chinese Business, Innovation, Investment and Economic Growth

Series Editor: Jiatao Li *(The Hong Kong University of Science and Technology, Hong Kong)*

Published:

Vol. 1: *The Chinese Financial System: Sino-centricity and Orchestrated Control*
by Dominique Jolly

World Scientific Series in Chinese Business, Innovation, Investment,
& Economic Growth – Volume 1

THE CHINESE FINANCIAL SYSTEM
Sino-centricity and Orchestrated Control

Dominique Jolly

 **World Scientific**

:W JERSEY · LONDON · SINGAPORE · BEIJING · SHANGHAI · HONG KONG · TAIPEI · CHENNAI · TOKYO

Published by

World Scientific Publishing Co. Pte. Ltd.

5 Toh Tuck Link, Singapore 596224

USA office: 27 Warren Street, Suite 401-402, Hackensack, NJ 07601

UK office: 57 Shelton Street, Covent Garden, London WC2H 9HE

Library of Congress Cataloging-in-Publication Data

Names: Jolly, Dominique R., author.

Title: The Chinese financial system : Sino-centricity and orchestrated control / Dominique Jolly.

Description: New Jersey : World Scientific, [2024] | Series: World scientific series in
   Chinese business, innovation, investment, & economic growth ; vol. 1 |
   Includes bibliographical references.

Identifiers: LCCN 2023016733 | ISBN 9789811276255 (hardcover) |
   ISBN 9789811276262 (ebook for institutions) | ISBN 9789811276279 (ebook for individuals)

Subjects: LCSH: Finance--China. | Financial institutions--China. | China--Economic policy

Classification: LCC HG187.C6 J65 2024 | DDC 332.0951--dc23/eng/20230605

LC record available at https://lccn.loc.gov/2023016733

British Library Cataloguing-in-Publication Data

A catalogue record for this book is available from the British Library.

For any available supplementary material, please visit
https://www.worldscientific.com/worldscibooks/10.1142/13409#t=suppl

Desk Editors: Sanjay Varadharajan/Kura Sunaina

Typeset by Stallion Press
Email: enquiries@stallionpress.com

Printed in Singapore

Preface

This book offers a strategic and geopolitical view of the financial system in China, its stakeholders, and its recent evolution. Four roles are distinguished and evaluated. The first key mission has been the financing of the domestic economy. The second is the financing of infrastructures (transportation, energy, and telecommunication) so as to offer proper production conditions for developing manufacturing facilities. A third role has been supporting Chinese international investment strategies once the domestic economy was established. A fourth additional role, much more recent, is the active use of technology in finance and investment; it should prepare China for the future by changing the rules: the finance industry's core mission is less and less to collect money, and more and more to collect big datasets. The financial impact of several societal challenges is analyzed, and new perspectives are offered and assessed.

The first thesis of this book is that finance and investment in China are not simply the product of market forces. They are the output of several dimensions including regulation, geopolitics, technology, and internal governance. The second thesis is that the Chinese State Council can be viewed as a conductor and financial and economic actors as performers who imperatively have to follow the track decided by the conductor. In this context, geopolitical decisions provide the structure for any domestic and international strategy. And the third thesis is that the Sino-centric perspective adopted by the Chinese authorities impedes foreign entries. Contrary to other industries that largely opened to foreign companies (for example, the car industry), the Chinese government half-opened the door of the banking industry to foreign competitors – making foreign banks a marginal actor in this system.

As such, the book is of interest for academics studying the finance business in China, business students curious to learn about China, consultants looking for references, and business people who want to know more about the place where they want to conduct business.

About the Author

 **Dominique Jolly** is a business strategy expert and an independent advisor on foreign business with China. He works as a consultant for several large companies. He also advises international organizations and foreign governments in the areas of innovation and technology. His assignments have taken him to over 20 countries in Europe, Asia, North America, South America and Africa. He has 35 years of experience as a Professor of Business Strategy. He worked as the dean and associate dean for Webster University Geneva (Switzerland), SKEMA Business School (Sophia-Antipolis, France), and Grenoble Ecole de Management (Grenoble, France). He has been an invited Professor at the Center on China Innovation at CEIBS (Shanghai, China), and HEC Montréal (Montréal, Canada).

Acknowledgments

I want to thank a group of highly qualified professors and bankers who kindly helped me in the process of writing this book by answering my questions and reviewing chapters. They did a great job by giving meaningful comments and suggestions, identifying errors and mistakes, challenging slippery developments or weakly convincing explanations, and suggesting deletions of other incongruities. Yet, this volume might still show some discrepancies which are all my sole responsibility. All views expressed in this book are mine and only mine. A big thank you to the following people:

ALBOUY Michel, Professor, Université Grenoble Alpes (France)
BANKS Marcia, Consultant (Switzerland)
BANKS Ronald, Steering Committee Member of the Association of American Clubs (Switzerland)
BEDUNEAU-WANG Laurent, Professor, Africa Business School (Morocco)
CHEN Shukang, Banker, Crédit Agricole (China)
DU Yong, Banker, China Development Bank (China)
FONTAINE Patrice, Professor, Eurofidai, CNRS (France)
GAULARD Mylène, Professor, Université Grenoble Alpes (France)
ISAAK Robert, Professor, University of Mannheim (Germany)
LACOSTE Denis, Professor, Toulouse Business School (France)
LU Jun (Timothy), Professor, EM Lyon, Shanghai Campus (China)
MARQUES Joseph, Professor, Institut de Hautes Etudes Internationales et du Développement (Graduate Institute), Geneva (Switzerland)

PHAN Nhko, Banker, Banque de Chine, Paris (France)
RUDSTRÖM Lennart, Director, Bikmis Consult Ltd. (China)
SCHIRMAN Chalom, Professor, University of Haifa (Israel)
SHEN Liqiong, Banker, BNP Paribas (France)
SPIGARELLI Francesca, Professor, University of Macerata (Italy)
WU Ramon, Banker, SEB China (China)
YANG Huihui, SKEMA Business School (France)
ZHU Fuquan, Consultant (China)

Contents

List of Figures

List of Tables

List of Vignettes

Introduction

The Chinese banking industry did not exist at the beginning of the 20th century. The following quote from a book published in 1902 is very illustrative of the situation: "There isn't a single big Chinese bank: Chinese banks are small institutions that lend at usurious rates among people who know each other. The Hong Kong and Shanghai Banking Corporation, where the big Chinese capitalists have placed their funds, is absolutely in European hands" (Weulersse, 1902, p. 217).

Today, the situation is incredibly different from the fragmented industry which was observed by Georges Weulersse when he visited imperial China in 1900. After a long period of absence, China made a remarkable comeback over the last 40 years on the economic, political, and technological scenes. On the economic scene, China moved from a marginal position (a GDP less than the one of Italy at the beginning of 2000) to become the second economy in the world since 2010 (and even the first one if you take into account the purchasing power parity). The country now has a strong impact on the world economy: According to the International Monetary Fund, China's contribution to global GDP growth between 2013 and 2018 was more than double the contribution made by the USA. On the political scene, the economic success of the regime legitimated its existence: Chinese citizens supported the regime because it offered to a large majority of them a remarkable improvement in their standard of living. Political leadership increasingly presents its regime as a successful alternative model to the West (it has yet to face mounting

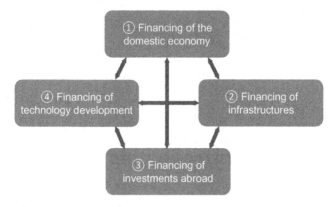

Figure 1.   The Four Roles of the Chinese Financial System

societal pressures inside the country[1]). And on the top of this, on the technological scene, China has forged a solid national system of innovation which is starting to produce tangible results thanks to the bundling of all the required ingredients (universities, research centers, science and technology parks, companies investing strongly in R&D, etc.). The country is no more a place for low labor cost, but is becoming a respectable place for technology creation – as illustrated by the 5G, the electric car, and the space station. China is even threatening the US leadership. We are witnessing a geopolitical confrontation between the existing superpower and the aspiring superpower (Allison, 2017).

While the economic, political, and technological aspects are well documented, the Chinese financial system is still not well known, and the overall aim of this book is to cast a light on this system. As illustrated by Figure 1, the Chinese financial system can be depicted along the following four lines:

- The first role has been the financing of the domestic productive economy. This came as a driver since 1978 with the open door policy of President Deng Xiaoping. This worked through the emergence of five leading banks and the creation of a large network of smaller banks scattered all over the country.

---

[1]The Chinese political leadership was challenged at the end of 2022 because of the constraints imposed by the zero-COVID strategy from 2020 to 2022, and the economic consequences of this policy.

- The second role has been the financing of infrastructures. The Chinese government has always placed strong emphasis on providing the economy with the proper infrastructures for transportation, energy, and telecommunications (this came before 1978). Three institutional banks were created to be devoted to this role.
- The third role resulted from the "Go Global" strategy started by Beijing two decades ago. As the economy developed along with its consequent ramifications over a large part of the Chinese territory, the government came up with the idea that Chinese companies should also invest outside the country.
- The fourth and latest role is technology. The challenge was not only to finance the now well-established Chinese system of innovation but also to foster the specific segment dealing at the interface between technology and finance – the so-called FinTech, which is step by step transforming the financial industry. The more impactful effect is yet to come: a modification of the very nature of the industry. Finance is less and less about collecting money and more and more about collecting huge datasets. This could well be a future competitive advantage for China.

The book is structured into eight chapters, each with the following synopsis:

- Chapter 1 presents how *the Chinese financial system* is regulated. The overarching and compelling conductor role of the Chinese State Council, and the roles of the Central bank, and the different commissions put in place, are emphasized. Some specific features of the Chinese financial system, such as its immaturity, emerge when compared to established systems. Furthermore, the financial strategy of the government is summarized.
- Chapter 2 analyzes *the performers of the financial system in China*. The banking industry is defined as a fringed oligopoly, with five big banks and several thousands of small banks. Banks have historically been the only source for financing the economy. The creation of three stock market platforms came to complement that financing capacity. Some elements are given on the recently launched or reopened stock exchange platforms. Size is presented as a key variable which is usually seen as a strength but which could also quickly turn into a nightmare.

- Chapter 3 examines *the recent evolution of the financial system*. Three aspects are considered: the controversial shadow banking system, the parallel entities created by local governments known as "local government financing vehicles" (LGFV), and the timid emergence of private banks.
- Chapter 4 is about *the financing of infrastructures*. The development of transportation, energy, and telecommunications infrastructures played a key role since 1978; infrastructures have been a strong booster to economic development. The functions of the three institutional banks in charge of the financing of infrastructures are described. The evolution of their missions since their creation in 1994 from a domestic focus to a tool for foreign policy is depicted. And, the recently founded Asian Infrastructure Investment Bank (AIIB) is introduced.
- Chapter 5 demonstrates *the primacy of geopolitics over business when it comes to investing abroad*. It analyzes the emergence, since 2004, and the evolution of Chinese companies' outward Foreign Direct Investments, and their motives. And, it describes the role of the recently created China Investment Corporation (CIC).
- Chapter 6 is dedicated to *the power of technology in finance*. It shows how technological forces are strongly impacting the financial system because they are turning the game from money collection to data collection. Two aspects are distinguished: the financing of the high-tech Chinese sectors and the use of technology to revolutionize the banking industry, i.e. FinTech (including the generalized use of smartphones for digital payment).
- Chapter 7 looks at *three major domestic societal challenges* which will impact the Chinese financial system in the near future and challenge its equilibrium: the Chinese real estate industry which is under threat, the financing of future retirement pensions, and the worrisome increasing public and private debt. The chapter examines how these endogenous threats hurt the system and shows the associated risks and consequences.
- Chapter 8 is about *the new refreshing perspectives* coming from the Belt & Road Initiative, the opening to foreign banks, and the future of Chinese currency outside China.

Regarding the perspective of this book, 25 years since my first trip to China and now more than 50 visits to the mainland, Hong Kong, and

Taiwan, I was inspired by the yin/yang model.[2] Even if this introduction gives an enthusiastic picture, I am not naive and I see some discrepancies and challenges (as Chapter 7 will show). As such, the aim of the book is to give a picture with the yang (the sunny side), but also with the yin (the cloudy side), i.e. the positive as well as the negative aspects of the situation.

This book gives a picture of the financial system in China, its potential to support China's future economic development, and the problems the system is facing. We will see that this picture generates some questions such as the overwhelming role of banks over the stock exchange platforms and the limited role of private banks and foreign banks; I will suggest some hypotheses to explain these situations. We will see that the financial system in China is Sino-centric. It is a bit like the Chinese Internet – often regarded as a big Intranet. There is a kind of self-sufficiency. The system is Sino-centric, i.e. it works by itself, almost not open to foreigners. We will see as well that the financial strategy of the Chinese government is totally linked to a very specific context, i.e. being the largest country in the world by population, having a recent economic restoration, and being under the control of a strong political institution (i.e. which has not changed since 1949). That is, the State and the Chinese Communist Party, not the market forces, have the final say in the financial sector.

After four decades of intense development, China is entering into a transition phase: The growth rate has started to decrease for a decade, as well as the economic opportunities attached to it. The years of frantic growth are behind. This means that segments of the population with low revenues are going to suffer. The strong revenue discrepancies which prevail cannot be hidden anymore by positive perspectives. The hope that poor people will find some opportunities will fade. As this might be a trigger to social unrest, this is going to be an important input to the strategy of the Chinese Communist Party, including the financial aspects, as the party is afraid of social tensions and obsessed with maintaining social stability.

---

[2] Yang and yin refer to the dialectic of opposition and complementary of many phenomena. Opposites are seen as complementary and not exclusive of each other; the Chinese culture emphasizes the inseparability between the proposition "there is" and the proposition "there is not" more than the opposition between the two propositions. The poles are complementary: without the top, there is no bottom, and vice versa.

Bibliography

Allison Graham (2017), *Destined for War: Can America and China Escape Thucydides's Trap?*, Houghton Mifflin Harcourt, Boston, New York, 350 pages.

Dominique Jolly (2022), *The New Threat: China's Rapid Technological Transformation*, Palgrave Macmillan, Asian Business Series, 154 pages.

International Monetary Fund, World Economic Outlook.

Thomas W. Pauken II (2019), *US vs China: From Trade War to Reciprocal Deal*, World Scientific, 344 pages.

Weulersse Georges (1902), *Chine Ancienne et nouvelle, impressions et réflexions*, Librairie Armand Colin, Paris – reedited by Bibliothèque nationale de France and Hachette France, 366 pages.

Chapter 1

The Financial System in China: Ruled by the State

This first chapter presents how the Chinese financial system is regulated. The first section stresses the overarching and compelling role of the Chinese State and the Chinese Communist Party. One fascinating characteristic is the newness of the framework. The transformation of the Communist system into a "socialist market economy" came with the creation of new institutions as well as the revitalization of organizations which were operating before the 1949 victory of the Communists over Chiang Kai-shek and the nationalists. The second section of the chapter benchmarks the Chinese system with some other international systems. Missions of central banks are quite similar from one country to another. But, the economic profiles of the banks and the stock exchange platforms differ significantly. Finally, the third section presents the financial strategy of the government.

1.1. The Chinese Central Bank and the Other Regulatory Bodies

1.1.1. *Capitalism with "Chinese Characteristics"*

Western capitalism, European or American, became financially dependent on emerging countries – especially China. While the USA, Europe, and Japan were accumulating debt, China was accumulating capital. If there is one place in the world where capital accumulation and the pursuit of profit have become the norm it is China. It was Mao's children who invented capitalism with "Chinese characteristics". The Chinese authorities are the champions of syncretism: Marrying communism and capitalism has been more than an oxymoron – it came with economic and financial performance. The 1980s and 1990s correspond to a phase of pre-capitalism; the Chinese companies learnt from companies abroad. Since 2000, and in particular 2001 when China joined the WTO, capitalism has been in full swing.

On the Communist side, there is the legacy of planning. China turned it into an advantage. In fact China is almost run like a business: Plans are defined (since 1953!) and implemented within a hierarchical system with impressive efficiency if you look at the results achieved. In China, every five-year plan has been set up with defined vision and targets. The so-called "socialist market economy" develops guidelines, which help to avoid disordered competition and unnecessary resource usage. The State is the great conductor of the economy. Bureaucrats are not obstacles to growth, but almost engines of it.

For example, the 11th five-year plan (2006–2010) set the course: 20% improvement in energy efficiency as an objective, followed by the implementation of a program targeting the thousand most energy-consuming companies, and then execution! More recently, Chinese leaders have promised carbon neutrality for 2060, and thus the government set up the corresponding policy to promote the carbon-neutral industries and will stimulate more talent development in the upstream and downstream industries, investment guidance in the related sectors, and banking support to the related companies. In order to achieve the carbon neutrality objective by 2060, the Chinese government will largely promote a green and ecological economy via detailed laws and has also raised a very precise quantitative index, for example, to increase the total installed capacity of solar power and wind power to achieve 1.2 billion kilowatts. The clear-defined requirement helps to avoid ineffective investment and swarming investment. From the banking industry, under the guideline of the 14th five-year plan (2021–2025), carbon neutrality has been incorporated into the risk evaluation system. Chinese banks will gradually strengthen the divestment of energy-intensive and high-emission assets and fossil-fuel-related projects will be excluded from the green bond financing list.

1.1.2. *The Regulated Public Inherited from the Communist Years Still Dominates*

Regulated public is again a heritage of the Communist history. As illustrated in Table 1.1, the core of the reactor of China has so far remained under State control: big banks, energy, shipbuilding, car manufacturing, aircraft construction, maritime transport, air transport, rail transport, and telecommunications are dominated by state-owned enterprises (SOE). They have been widely defended by the state. China maintained protected access to a huge internal market, and preferential financing. There are thus hundreds of millions of consumers who depend on firms in very largely cartelized sectors.[1]

The Chinese economy is based on autocratic capitalism, with its state-owned firms. There were 98 Chinese firms in the Fortune 500 ranking in 2015; only 22 were private and the first 12 were all public. According to the 2021 Fortune 500 ranking, China continues to rank first for the second consecutive year with 135 companies (including Hong Kong) among the top 500 vs. 122 from the USA. There are nine Chinese banks among the

Table 1.1.   Very Few Private Companies in the Core of the Reactor

Industry Type	Extent of Private Presence among Competition in the Industry
Banks	China Minsheng, Ping An Bank, and some online retail banks
Energy	Few private companies as Hengli
Shipbuilding	Very few shipbuilding companies such as Yangzijiang
Car manufacturing	Geely, BYD, Greatwall, and some start-ups in the electric car segment such as NIO or XPeng
Aircraft construction	No private manufacturer – except Airbus in a joint venture
Shipping	No private competitor
Air transport	Limited competition from private operators
Rail transport	No privately owned railway company
Telecommunications	No private operator

---

[1] Two concrete examples: To fill up their car with gasoline, Chinese drivers have only two options, i.e. Sinopec or Petro-China. To sign up for a telecommunication subscription, Chinese citizens have only three options, i.e. China Mobile, China Telecom, or China Unicom.

135 companies, including the big five and CMC, Industrial Bank, SPDB, and Minsheng Bank. The ranking of these banks has risen almost for all. This growth has no doubt reflected the quick economic recovery after the COVID crisis where China was the only key economy to gain positive growth in 2020.

A 2022 ranking identifies no less than four Chinese companies in the top 10 and all are state owned. And, the biggest four banks in the world (by asset size) are Chinese state-owned banks: the Industrial & Commercial Bank of China (ICBC), the China Construction Bank (CCB), the Bank of China (BoC), and the Agricultural Bank of China (ABC) – which will be presented in Chapter 2.

Besides this autocratic capitalism, there is also democratic capitalism – with its private firms like Alibaba, BYD, Huawei, and Sany. The licenses granted by public authorities are considered as a mandate given by the community to a private entrepreneur (see the vignette on Payment Service Providers). The State can also be very generous, like when supporting the electric car. The invisible hand of the market acts only where the hand of government leaves it open.

Liberal economic theorists from the Western world, sure of the virtues of their models, are at the very least challenged by a vibrant economy largely controlled by the State which itself is embodied by a single party. And it's been working for over 40 years! Authoritarian capitalism has certainly had precedents (for example, in Latin America), but not with the same success. Liberal economists worry that China's reemergence on the world stage will be seen as a threat to liberal values on the planet.

Yet, state-owned enterprises are starting to show their limits. The Chinese State is, first of all, present in economic fields which embody the

---

Vignette: The Ruling of Payment Service Providers (PSP) by the People's Bank of China

In 2011, the People's Bank of China (PBoC) granted licenses to a first batch of 27 payment service providers (PSP), including Ant Financials, which is the arm of Alibaba Group in charge of all the finance-related aspects, and Tencent with WeChat. The PBoC granted licenses to a new batch of 27 additional companies in 2013. They are all under the regulation of PBoC. Until May 2021, the PSP licenses numbered to 232, and due to

(Continued)

the strict regulatory requirement, there may be more licenses revoked by PBoC.

In 2015, PBoC even initiated with Tencent, Alibaba, and six other institutions a program to assess the creditworthiness of borrowers based on the behavior of individuals on the Internet. However, two years later, after detailed evaluation of the platform capacity, PBoC judged that none of the eight institutions were qualified as individual creditworthy institutions mostly because they were owned by the big companies, and they had their own lending and borrowing business. Using their own platform could lead to a lack of transparency and fairness, which could result in completely different data in each of the platforms, leading to complexity for the lenders in making the right decision.

Under the fast development of the market, especially with the emergence of many Internet-based new technologies in the financing industry, the regulator judged the necessity to try new means and did not hesitate to correct and adjust the new policy in order to control the risk and maintain the steadiness of the financial market.

growth model of the past (steel, coal, shipbuilding, heavy equipment, etc.) and much less the future trends like the Internet, health, technology, education, and recreation. In addition, there are still state-owned enterprises known as "zombie" enterprises, crushed by overcapacity production facilities and characterized by a longstanding deficit situation, with debt greater than their assets and with no other prospect than filing for bankruptcy.

1.1.3. *An All-Powerful Regulator at the Order of the Government*

The Central Bank (People's Bank of China or PBoC) plays the role of setting up the monetary policy and maintaining the stability of the financial system (see the vignette). It had the same governor, Zhou Xiaochuan (75 in 2023), from 2002 to 2018 – when Yi Gang succeeded him. He was placed under the authority of Guo Shuqing, appointed Party Secretary – a post previously held by Zhou Xiaochuan. The PBoC is not independent like the FED or the European Central Bank. The Chinese governor does not have the freedom of speech like Christine Lagarde of the European

Central Bank or Jerome Powell of the US Federal Reserve. The Chinese Central Bank is technically only an advisory body of the Council of State (headed by the Prime Minister).

The control was held by the Central Bank, i.e. the People's Bank of China (PBoC), until 2003 when the control was transferred to the newly created Chinese Banking Regulatory Commission (CBRC). In April 2018, CBRC and Insurance Regulatory Commission were merged to form the CBIRC as the main regulatory body to oversee and govern the banking system and insurance system.[3] As illustrated in Figure 1.1, all banks are

---

Vignette: The People's Bank of China

The People's Bank of China or PBoC[2] was first established in 1931, long before the CCP took over the whole state. Between 1949 and 1983, PBoC operated as both a central bank and a commercial bank. It has been statutorily the only bank in the country until 1978; it sets interest rates and defines the required reserve ratio. PBoC also regulates the lending activities, oversees the payment and settlement system of the country, and supervises the State Administration of Foreign Exchange (SAFE).

The People's Bank of China is in charge of the injection of liquidity or quantitative easing to keep pace with the growth of the economy. Chinese monetary policy is now adjusting to the expected economic slowdown and the risk of deflation: It is targeting lower rates. The key rate has been reduced several times.

The People's Bank of China controls the foreign exchange reserves, i.e. holds the foreign currencies (dollar, euro, pound sterling, yen, won, etc.). It is the Central Bank that gives the yuan to Chinese exporters in exchange for the dollars, euros, or yen they have collected. The composition of Chinese foreign exchange reserves is kept secret, but the current assumption is that two-thirds are made up in dollars, one-quarter in euros, and the rest in Japanese yen and British pounds. This stock can therefore only be used abroad. China has suddenly become the banker of the USA.

---

[2]The People's Bank of China (PBoC) is the Central Bank of the PRC. It should not to be confused with the Bank of China (BoC) – which effectively played the role of the Central Bank in the past when the Republic of China was created. The BoC was created in 1912 by Sun Yat-sen to replace the Imperial Bank of China. It operated as the Central Bank until the end of the civil war in 1949.

[3]Hong Kong is apart and has its own regulator.

(Continued)

Those reserves are under the control of the State Administration of Foreign Exchange (SAFE). They make it possible to protect China against external shocks. They are fueled by foreign investment and especially by the country's trade surplus.

One of the reasons why the Chinese government does not authorize the full convertibility of the yuan is that it is afraid to see part of the Chinese public savings leave and go where they would be better remunerated.

---

overseen by the China Banking and Insurance Regulatory Commission (CBIRC) – which reports to the PBoC, itself under government orders.

Consequently, political instructions often take precedence over risk analysis: allocation of credits is less the product of a risk analysis than the directives defined by the authorities. The careers of public company managers depend on their loyalty and dedication to the Chinese Communist Party (CCP). In the banking sector, the first factor explaining the performance of banks is not so much their management but the government decisions that open or close options: capital ratio, interest rate ceilings, limits on the remuneration of deposits, etc.

If Chinese banks are performing well, it is because, with the blessings of the CBIRC, they remunerate individuals poorly (less than 0.5%) on the money they lend to large state-owned enterprises. Banks are under stringent regulations (in the whole world) because of their systematic importance. Hence, banks usually have their hands tied in providing riskier loans such as to SMEs. In the Chinese context, this means that a vast majority of bank credits are going to state-owned enterprises, especially the larger ones, while the very fast-growing privately owned SMEs cannot tap into this funding source in most situations. Banks prefer to lend to enterprises that have the implicit support of the government. Their margins are nevertheless likely to decline in the future due to competition from new players, such as Alibaba, already in retail banking but possibly also in investment banking and private banking in the future.

The main functions of the CBIRC are the regulation and the supervision of banks and insurance companies in the country. Regulation means drafting laws. It looks at the protection of financial customers. It issues

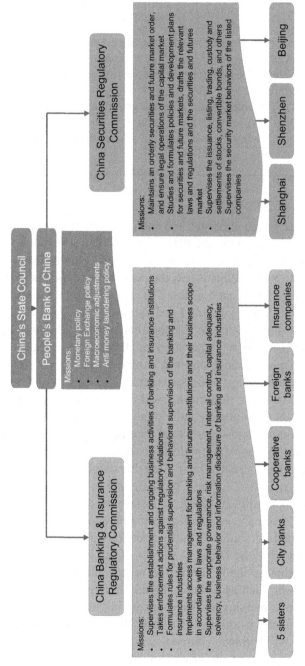

Figure 1.1.   China's Financial System Regulatory Framework

licenses to banking and insurance institutions. Supervision means the control of corporate governance, risk management, solvency, compliance, and information disclosure. Headquartered in Beijing, it has local offices in all provinces and large municipalities.

To bridge with governmental agencies, banks and other financial institutions created representative associations. The China Banking Association (CBA) was created in 2000. It is based in Beijing; it has more than 760 members from the banking sector and other financial institutions. It conducts in-depth research on the industry. There are also local associations like the Shanghai Banking Association (SBA); created in 1992 to represent banks and financial institutions in Shanghai, it has about 250 members.

1.2. The Chinese Financial System Compared to Other Systems

The Chinese financial system is aligned with foreign systems regarding the generic missions of the Central Bank. The scope is always along two dimensions: (a) the monetary policy and (b) the regulation of financial actors. Yet, as detailed in Table 1.2, the Chinese system exhibits several differences when compared with other foreign systems. It exhibits five specific aspects:

1. The State acts as a conductor, and market forces have limited impact.
2. Most of the institutions are new. Consequently, the system is not mature and still subject to changes.
3. Banks play a much larger role than the stock exchange platforms.
4. There are very few private banks.
5. The system is Sino-centric: there are very few foreign banks, as the entry of foreign banks is hampered by the Chinese government. And, there isn't any foreign company listed on a Chinese stock exchange platform.

1.2.1. The State as a Conductor

The central role of the government appears at different levels. The first obvious feature is that almost all the banks are publicly owned: the largest ones are state-owned banks and the others are under the control of local governments. The second feature relates to the extent of regulations and the power of regulators – the point appears when the question is raised of foreign bankers working in China (see the vignette).

Table 1.2.   Comparing Four Banking Systems in Leading Countries

Countries	USA	China	Japan	United Kingdom
Regulation level	Federal and state levels	Central	Central	Central and countries' level
Central Bank	The Federal Reserve System (created in 1913)	People's Bank of China (established in 1948)	Bank of Japan (founded in 1882) and the Financial Service Agency	Bank of England (nationalized since 1946)
Missions of the central bank	• Conducts nation's monetary policy • Supervises and rules financial institutions • Keeps the system stable • Gives financial services to the government	• Formulates and implements the monetary policy • Issues the yuan and administers its circulation • Supervises financial institutions	• Defines Japanese monetary policy • Maintains financial stability • Provides clearing services	• Maintains monetary and financial stability • Set official interest rate • Defines prudential regulation for banks in the UK
Governance	A board of governors is accountable to the Congress	Reports to the State Council (i.e. the central government)	Governors are appointed by the government	A Court of Directors answers to the people of the UK through Parliament
Largest banks	JP Morgan Chase Bank of America Wells Fargo Citi Group Goldman Sachs	Industrial & Commercial Bank of China China Construction Bank Bank of China Agricultural Bank of China Bank of Communications	Bank of Tokyo-Mitsubishi Sumitomo Mitsui Bank Mizuho Bank	HSBC Lloyds NatWest Barclays Standard Chartered Royal Bank of Scotland National Building Society

Number of banks	About 5,000	About 4,000	About 1,400	About 350
Number of brokerage companies	About 3,400 (e.g. Charles Schwab)	Less than 200 (e.g. Citic Securities)	1,000 securities firms (e.g. Nomura)	About 5,600 (e.g. Vanguard)
Economic profile	Highly fringed oligopoly: Some tens of large banks and a huge number of small banks	Fringed oligopoly (see Chapter 2)	Fringed oligopoly: the three largest banks represent 30% market share	Fringed oligopoly
Stock exchange platforms	More than 500 foreign companies are registered on the New York Stock Exchange, including 120 Chinese companies[a]	No foreign company is listed in Shanghai nor in Shenzhen, or the newly Beijing place	2,400 companies are listed on the Tokyo stock exchange; the number of foreign companies listed went down from 120 to close to zero since the bursting of the economic bubble	More than 1,000 companies (from 100 countries, including 5 from China) on a total of 2,500 companies listed[b]
Maturity of the places	NYSE originated in 1817; Nasdaq was established in 1971	Shanghai reopened in 1990. Shenzhen opened in 1990. Beijing reopened in 2022	Tokyo stock exchange was first opened in 1878	The history of the LSE can be traced back more than three centuries

Notes: [a]Due to tensions with the USA, this number started to decline.
[b]The number of foreign companies listed in London went up; but, it went down in Paris and in Frankfurt.

Returnees who previously worked in Wall Street or in a big US bank had some knowledge, and came back to China with liberal experience and fresh ideas. But, to attain success in China, they had to cooperate with the system that was in place and consequently were not able to convince the authorities that competition is always better and to give more space to private institutions. The culture resulting from a long-lasting history of government controlling everything cannot be changed overnight!

Vignette: Dealing with China's Regulation When You Are a Foreign Bank

Being accepted to join the orchestra is hard for a foreign bank. It has to read the music sheet carefully, learn how to play the music along the defined lines, and overall follow the directions and orders of the conductor.

When they enter in China, foreign practitioners face a highly regulated banking system they are not used to. They report that the main difference between working in China and working in Europe or in the USA is that Chinese authorities intervene intensively – formally and informally – and the regulatory framework can also be modified very rapidly.

Beyond the existing formal regulatory framework, regulators such as the China Banking and Insurance Regulatory Commission (CBIRC) or the State Administration of Foreign Exchange (SAFE) send messages to banks. Those messages are presented as "window guidance" – but, everyone understands that those counseling notes are more than simple recommendations; they are rules you need to comply to.

In addition, the role of regulators encompasses a spectrum of domains much larger in China than in Europe or in the USA markets: Interest rates, currency exchanges, and acquisition abroad are domains strongly regulated or requiring abundant paperwork to be compliant. In Europe or in the USA, when foreign banks develop products on their market, they define a pricing for those products, and then the pricing is accepted or rejected by the client. In China, it is not only the client you have to convince but also the regulators, who are used to giving their opinion to banks on their pricing. Regulators might claim changes in products, pricing, structure, or even fees. And decisions are not always fully explicit. Since 2021, the situation of Evergrande has still been vague when observed by non-Chinese actors.

(Continued)

Finally, on the basis of one single rule or guideline, interpretation might differ from one administrative bureau to another; for example, one decision made in Beijing can be followed by different interpretations in different provinces. Yet, contrary to practices in Europe, even when the rule has been defined, there is frequently some room for discussion with the regulator. In China, you have what is allowed, what is not allowed, and what can be discussed.

From a practical point of view, this means that foreign managers need to demonstrate some very specific capabilities. They need to know to operate in gray areas, to navigate in blurred contexts, and to manage by trial and error; if they are inflexible, they will be destabilized and they will not survive.

Source: Interviews with industry leaders.

1.2.2. *A Lack of Maturity and a Minor Role for the Stock Exchange*

Another difference emerges when you start to benchmark with what exists in Japan, Europe, or in the USA. Structures have been established in Japan, Europe, or the USA a long time ago. Central banks and stock exchange platforms are older. For example, the Tokyo Stock Exchange opened in 1878 and the Bank of Japan was founded in 1882. To go further, simply note that the so-called Bâle regulatory framework[4] emerged in the eighties before the China Banking Regulatory Commission was formed in 2003. Simply note as well that the "Export–Import Bank of the United States" was founded in 1934, and the Chinese equivalent was established in 1994.

The specificity of the Chinese financial system is also that it heavily relies on the banking sector; this is the fundamental basis of the system. Banks play a major role compared to Chinese stock exchange platforms

---

[4]Banking supervision in the West is guided by Bâle agreements. The first one came in 1988; it required banks to demonstrate a minimum solvency ratio of the credits offered to equity of 8%. It was followed by Bâle 2 in 2004 putting emphasis on transparency. Bâle 3 came in 2010 requiring equity to reach a minimum of 3% of assets.

which play a limited role: China's stock market accounted for 3% of China's total outstanding credit stock at the end of 2019 (according to PBoC) vs. 52% in the USA. Compared to the USA or the UK, where stock exchange platforms play a major role, China's situation is very different. Chinese companies are less likely to use equity financing than US companies. They prefer to rely on bank loans and retained earnings.

1.2.3. *Few Private Banks*

When comparing the banking industry in China and the banking industry in the USA, Japan, or Europe, another difference is that there are very few private banks in China because the Chinese government does not allow private financial institutions. The Chinese authorities have not been keen to open to privately owned banking considering the safety and importance of the financial industry. The power system in China is very different from what prevails in the West: The Chinese authorities exert strong control over what happens in the society. China Minsheng Bank[5] has long been the only exception, the only really significant privately owned bank – it is a large bank (50,000 employees). Yet, it might not be a good example as it is now facing serious trouble because it lent a lot to the Chinese real estate industry – especially to the falling Evergrande. The private insurance company Ping An, now known as Ping An Bank, is another private bank since it took over the Shenzhen Development Bank in 2012 – see the vignette below. Alibaba, Tencent, and some other Internet players also received licenses for retail banking – at that time, traditional regulators had to face something new and high-tech.

This situation in the banking sector is totally different from the situation which prevails in the Internet sector where most of the companies are private. Yet, the dichotomy between private and public in China is not as sharp as it is in the West. The equity might be under the control of private individuals, but the governance is strongly influenced by the Chinese authorities. Those private entrepreneurs have to follow the decisions of the authorities like managers of state-owned companies. The decision of

---

[5]The China Minsheng Bank Corp. (CMBC) should not be confused with the China Merchants Bank (CMB), established in 1987 in Shenzhen – as both have close acronyms. With 90,000 employees, China Merchants Banks operates in the wholesale finance business, retail finance business, and other business segments.

Vignette: Ping An – Competition from the Insurance Business

The core business of the Ping An company is insurance (life and non-life). Ping An operates across the whole of the People's Republic of China, and in Hong Kong and Macau. In its core business, it not only faces state-owned competitors, like China Life Insurance (second largest in China), the People's Insurance Company of China (PICC), China Pacific Insurance, New China Life Insurance, and Huaxia, but also faces private competitors, like Anbang, and some foreign competitors, like Axa and Allianz, predominantly in the form of joint ventures.

Ping An has several subsidiaries such as Ping An Life, Ping An Property & Casualty, Ping An Health, Ping An Asset Management, and Ping An Bank. Ping An Bank has 38,000 employees. Ping An is also the second largest shareholder of HSBC. In 2013, the authorities allowed insurance companies (such as Ping An) to enter the mutual fund business – thus increasing competition in this business. It remains focused on the insurance market with its 1.4 million insurance agents and 228 million customers. But, it aims to become a global leader in retail financial services.

The company was founded in 1988. It is headquartered in Shenzhen. The Group is listed on the Hong Kong and Shanghai stock exchanges. With a capitalization of $118 billion (July 2022), the insurance company Ping An has become the first in the world in terms of market value ahead of Axa, Allianz, and AIG. As of December 31, 2021, according to its annual report, the company employed 356,000 employees, of which 189,000 were in the insurance business. Ping An ranked 17th in the Forbes Global 2000 list in 2022 and ranked 25th in the Fortune Global 500 list in 2022.

Even in the insurance sector, which is not strictly speaking high-tech, Ping An adopted a somewhat marginal strategy: It invests heavily in technology. The Ping An insurance company devotes 1% of its turnover to R&D ($1.5 billion in R&D in 2018). It has heavily automated its activities. It is engaged in artificial intelligence in the medical field, big data to serve its customers, easy recognition, traffic flow evaluation, etc. It employs 23,000 people in R&D and has a portfolio of 8,000 patents – in 2019 alone, it filed 1,700 patents.

the authorities to cancel the IPO of Ant Financial (Alibaba) in Hong Kong in late 2020 after Jack Ma publicly attacked the government has been a strong signal (see a vignette on Alibaba in Chapter 6). It illustrates that the ultimate boss in China is always the State.

1.3. The Financial Strategy of the Chinese Government

The financial strategy of the Chinese government is embedded into four equally important principles of action:

(a) The first and obvious rule is that China and Chinese companies come first. This principle prevails not only for banking but also for all the sectors of the Chinese economy.

(b) The full control of the State over banking, finance, stock exchange, and currency exchange is another clear posture; despite the strong message given by Xi Jinping in Davos in 2017 where he delivered a vibrant speech in favor of the market, those forces are still absent from the banking industry in China. The Chinese financial system is a legacy of a very recent past. The rationale of the Chinese authorities to explain this situation is that the mission of banks is to support the economy, and this mission is intrinsically related to public interest. As such, private banks will favor their own interests if there is some conflict, and not favor public interests.

(c) The third point is progressiveness. As usual in China, reforms take place gradually, tests are conducted, and decisions are made to pursue or not in the direction explored. The Chinese authorities are always moving progressively with a prudent or conservative approach. This is fully in line with the step-by-step expansion of the Special Economic Zones during the 1980s. China's policy keywords are frequently caution and wisdom.

(d) The last point relates to stability. The Chinese authorities are always looking for social and financial stability.[6] And the search for equilibrium includes the budget, as well as the monetary policies, such as, the tracking of non-performing loans.

---

[6]It is because of social pressures that the Chinese government did two major surprising U-turns in 2022. The first one happened in November when it asked banks to refinance the real estate sector after putting severe pressure on it in August 2020 with the famous three "red-lines". The second one, which made headlines, is the brutal cancellation of its "zero-COVID" strategy that it firmly stuck to for almost three years.

The financial strategy is developed along three dimensions:

(a) The consolidation of the banking system is the first target. The government wants the banks to reinforce their equity and serve the real economy.
(b) The government will continue to give more power to regulators of the banks, the insurance, and the stock exchange. There will be more and more rules in the future.
(c) The internationalization of the yuan is the third aim. China's economic success relied on export of its goods. If the government wants foreign countries to use the yuan, the Chinese currency might fluctuate more than today and may depreciate. And, China will need to issue more yuan to buy more foreign goods. One of the first efforts to internationalize the yuan has been the Qualified Foreign Institutional Investor (QFII) program (see Chapter 2). The CNY is the onshore currency used in China while the CNH is the offshore currency (traded on the HKSE). The latter can be used outside China; it is a kind of intermediate step between the CNY and a foreign currency (euro, dollar, etc.).

1.4. Conclusion

This chapter puts the emphasis on the conductor role played by the Chinese government (and its single-party driver). The government put in place different regulatory bodies which report directly to the party. The role and the impact of the market forces are rather limited. This central role of the authorities is not a surprise when you remember that from 1949 to 1978, the State was the deciding authority for almost everything.

The legacy, combined with the newness of institutions and rules, is the main difference when comparing the Chinese system with other international systems. Interestingly, Chinese banks play a much more important role than stock exchange platforms – once again, relatively young. And, privately owned banks, as well as foreign banks, look like an anomaly in an environment dominated by state-driven organizations and rules.

Chinese financial authorities operate along very clear lines. They are guided by the interests of the country, the willingness to control the financial system, implement reforms gradually, and maintain financial stability.

And, on the top of this, they have to also maintain social stability. As the Chinese authorities are challenged both by foreign countries and Chinese citizens, the risk of social upheaval has increased and the financial system is expected to support government action.

Takeaway from Chapter 1

1. From 1949 and the victory of Chairman Mao Zedong over Chiang Kai-shek and the nationalists to 1978 and the "open door policy" of Deng Xiaoping, the Chinese economy was under the full direction and control of State planning, without any market forces impacting the economy. Because of a chaotic economic development, and limited interactions with foreign countries, the Chinese financial system was consequently very limited during Mao's years.

2. The major achievement of President Deng Xiaoping has been a progressive opening of the country to foreign economies and to capitalism, to which he attached the concept of "socialist characteristics". The so-called "open door policy" acted as major agent of economic change in the country. This came with the creation of new financial regulatory bodies, and the revitalization of structures and regulations previously erased by the Maoist experiences. This makes the Chinese financial system relatively new (quite a contrast with a country which claims a multi-millennial history). And banks are playing a much more important role than the stock exchange platforms.

3. The Chinese financial system accomplishes the same range of functions as any other financial system in the world, i.e. basically the monetary policy and the regulation of financial actors. But a long-lasting history of government control over everything makes it very different.

4. The legacy of the communist years is felt as wide sections of the economy are still under State control and are Sino-centric. This is especially true for banks. Contrary to what we see in mature economies, the Chinese financial system is fully under government control: the largest banks are all publicly owned companies, and smaller banks belong to provinces, municipalities, districts, or rural

cooperatives. Chinese authorities view banking as a sovereign activity, and with limited export potential.

5. Private companies have developed very significantly in some sectors such as the Internet – some firms became renowned multinational companies (like Alibaba, Tencent, Baidu, ByteDance, and Jingdong). The big difference with what we are used to in the West is that those private companies can be viewed as having a "mandate" granted by the State to private entrepreneurs to undertake some economic ventures. But this mandate can be withdrawn at any moment if the State decides to do so.

6. The power of the State lies in the public ownership of almost all the banks; a very limited number of banks are privately owned. But, it is also reflected by the overwhelming power of the regulator. This starts with the Central Bank, i.e. the People's Bank of China (or PBoC), under government orders, and it goes with the China Banking and Insurance Regulatory Commission (CBIRC), the China Securities Regulatory Commission (CSRC), and the State Administration of Foreign Exchange (SAFE).

7. Metaphorically, the State (and its single party driver, the Chinese Communist Party) acts as the conductor of an orchestra, that is, the boss. The banks, the stock exchange platforms, and the other companies of the financial industry are the performers of the orchestra. The conductor is the master and performers have to follow "the music sheets". They have to be fully compliant with the directions, the orders, and the style of the conductor. And this conductor is extremely powerful. Joining the orchestra is especially challenging for a foreign bank.

Bibliography

China Banking Association, www.China-cba.net.

Cousin Violaine (2011), *Banking in China* (Second edition), Palgrave, New York, 334 pages.

Deloitte (2020), *China Market Opportunities for Foreign Insurance Companies Under the New Opening-Up Policies*, 20 pages.

Jin-Kai Feng (2017), *Rising China in a Changing World: Power Transitions and Global Leadership*, Palgrave, London, 192 pages.

Marlene Amstad, Guofeng Sun, and Wei Xiong (2020), *The Handbook of China's Financial System*, Princeton University Press, Princeton & Oxford, 504 pages.
Stent James (2016), *China's Banking Transformation: The Untold Story,* Oxford University Press, New York, 304 pages.

Chapter 2

Performers of the Chinese Financial System

Banks are an essential part of the Chinese financial system. The first section of this chapter characterizes the Chinese banking system as a "fringed oligopoly", meaning that it is made up of several big fish and thousands of small fish. The big fish are the five well-established commercial banks covering the whole country and the small fish are the more recently created local banks. As already stressed in the first chapter, this financial system is under powerful regulation by the state. As such, banks prefer to lend to companies that enjoy government support, i.e. state-owned companies.

The second section is dedicated to the stock exchange platforms. The creation (or the reopening) of stock market places came as a way to complement the financing capacity of banks. Three aspects will emerge from this presentation of Chinese stock exchange platforms: The lack of maturity, the predominance of retail investors (more than 200 million accounts), and the small window opened to foreign investors. The last section of this chapter examines the impact of size – a constantly overwhelming dimension in the Chinese context.

2.1. A Fringed Oligopoly: Five Established Banks and a Myriad of Smaller Banks

The Chinese banking system exhibits different categories of institutions: a few leading commercial banks, some main joint stock commercial banks,[1] a large number of city commercial banks, rural commercial banks, rural credit cooperatives, a few private banks, and a group of three policy banks. As explained in the previous chapter, in total, there are over 4,000 banks and other financial institutions, while the top 100 banks account for over 90% of the assets according to statistics based on the 2019 annual reports.

Beyond banks, there are also diverse financial institutions, such as mutual fund companies, financial leasing companies, auto-finance companies, money brokerage companies, consumer finance companies, financial assets management companies, and a few foreign financial institutions. The mutual fund market, for example, attracted more than 1,000 competitors. This includes large established banks which operate joint ventures with foreign companies. This is, for example, the case with the joint ventures between Industrial and Commercial Bank of China (ICBC) and Blackrock, between Shanghai Pudong Development Bank (SPDB) and Axa, and between Agricultural Bank of China (ABC) and Amundi (a subsidiary of the French Crédit Agricole). But, the mutual fund market includes small Chinese companies as well (publicly or privately owned).

2.1.1. *A Sino-centric Sector Where the Public Dominates*

According to the World Bank, 95% of the Chinese banking sector is under government control; the same figure drops to 74% in India and 40% in Russia. China has five very large banks with outlets scattered all over the country: The Industrial and Commercial Bank of China (ICBC) – the world's largest bank in terms of assets – the China Construction Bank (CCB), the Agricultural Bank of China (ABC), the Bank of China (BoC), and the Bank of Communications (Bocom). These so-called "five sisters" are all state-owned (at its lowest, the central government owns 59% of CCB) specialized banks. All are headquartered in Beijing (except Bocom which is headquartered in Shanghai). They represent 45% of bank assets. Table 2.1 offers a brief overview of those five mastodons. The top Chinese

---

[1] They hold 21% of the total commercial banks assets. The group includes Bocom, China Merchants Bank, CITIC Industrial Bank, and Shanghai Pudong Development Bank.

Table 2.1.   The Five Sisters

	ICBC	CCB	ABC	BoC	Bocom
Vocation	Specialized in business loans to manufacturers, retailers, power companies, and other businesses	Services corporate business: corporate credit loans, trade financing, international financing, enterprise equity, and corporate deposits	Originally specialized in financing enterprises in rural China, it diversified into corporate and consumer banking services and products	Corporate banking, personal banking, treasury operations, investment banking, and insurance	Consists of commercial banks, securities, trusts, financial leasing, fund management, insurance, and offshore financial services
Total assets (trillion US$)[a]	5.537	4.762	4.576	4.207	1.836
Creation	1984	1954	1951	1912	1908
Employees	460,000	347,000	503,000	309,000	90,000
Outlets	16,200	15,000	22,800	23,000	3,270
Retail clients (million)	704	726	878	327	185
Corporate clients (million)	3.6	3.5	2.7	10	na
Listed on Hong Kong Stock Exchange (HKSE) since	2006	2005	2010	2006	2005
Listed on Shanghai Stock Exchange (SSE) since	2006	2007	2010	2006	2007
Overseas subsidiaries	400	29	<20	Operates in >60 countries	68

Notes: [a]As a benchmark, at the beginning of 2022, the biggest American bank, JP Morgan Chase, had $3.7 trillion total assets. Bank of America had $3.2 trillion. BNP Paribas had $3 trillion (see Table 2.2).
Source: Published documents.

bank rankings sometimes include the sixth bank, i.e. the Postal Saving Bank of China (PSBC) – opened in 2007 – or the China Merchants Bank (CMB).

As shown in Table 2.1, all the established banks have been on the stock exchange in mainland China and Hong Kong since 2005. For example, 15% of the Bank of China is on the stock exchange. So the equity of those banks is no more 100% under the control of the State. Yet, the common thread to the five sisters is that the State always remains the first undisputed, dominant shareholder.

Table 2.2 shows that the top banks in China are also the top banks in the world. The five biggest banks in China have been ranked together with Mitsubishi UFJ, BoA, HSBC, BNP Paribas, Crédit Agricole, and JP Morgan Chase as the 2022 World's Largest Banks by Standard & Poor.

The banks' financial strength is improving continuously as demonstrated by the core tier-one capital ratio.[2] In 2019, there were eight commercial banks that successfully raised capital via A-share listing in China, raising over 65 billion yuan ($9.5 billion). Until 2020, there were 54 listed banks in China, where the total assets of the six big banks accounted for 62% of the total assets of the listed banks. The average asset growth was 10.20% in 2020. Since 2018, the banks could issue perpetual bonds[3] to supplement the core capital, which stimulated the insurance of perpetual bonds, especially for mid-sized and small-sized banks. Until the end of June in 2021, there were in total 28 banks issuing 32 perpetual bonds, reaching 310.5 billion yuan ($45 billion). The solid tier-one ratio has demonstrated the anti-risk capacity in the competitive international environment. The listed banks, no matter if part of the big five or six, the joint stock commercial bank, or the city commercial banks, have all shown steadiness and strong growth momentum in the past few years.

One possible hypothesis to explain this high level of performance is that the Chinese government has protected Chinese banks from foreign competition. Chinese authorities offer Chinese banks proper conditions to profit. Chinese banks outperform because they operate in a closed environment where they are protected from their deficiencies.

The key Chinese banks have all gone through innovation and several rounds of reforms to strengthen core competitiveness during the last

---

[2]The core tier-one capital ratio is the ratio of the equity capital and disclosed reserves to the total risk-weighted assets (Basel 3).

[3]Perpetual bonds are a fixed income security with no maturity date.

Table 2.2.   The World's 30 Largest Banks

Rank	Bank	Headquarters	Total Assets (US$ Billion)
1	**Industrial and Commercial Bank of China**	**China**	**5,537**
2	**China Construction Bank**	**China**	**4,762**
3	**Agricultural Bank of China**	**China**	**4,576**
4	**Bank of China**	**China**	**4,207**
5	JP Morgan Chase and Co.	US	3,744
6	Mitsubishi UFJ Financial Group	Japan	3,177
7	Bank of America	US	3,169
8	HSBC Holdings	UK	2,954
9	BNP Paribas	France	2,906
10	Crédit Agricole Group	France	2,674
11	Citigroup	US	2,291
12	Sumitomo Mitsui Financial Group	Japan	2,177
13	Japan Post Bank	Japan	1,999
14	**Postal Savings Bank of China**	**China**	**1,981**
15	Mizuho Financial Group	Japan	1,956
16	Wells Fargo	US	1,948
17	Barclays	UK	1,874
18	**Bank of Communications**	**China**	**1,836**
19	Banco Santander	Spain	1,815
20	Groupe BPCE	France	1,724
21	Société Générale	France	1,665
22	Deutsche Bank	Germany	1,506
23	The Toronto Dominion Bank	Canada	1,486
24	The Goldman Sachs Group	US	1,464
25	**China Merchants Bank**	**China**	**1,456**
26	Royal Bank of Canada	Canada	1,377
27	**Industrial Bank**	**China**	**1,354**
28	**China CITIC Bank**	**China**	**1,266**
29	**Shanghai Pudong Development Bank**	**China**	**1,251**
30	Crédit Mutuel Group	France	1,249

Note: Chinese banks are indicated in bold.
Source: Standard & Poor's Global Intelligence, The world's 100 largest banks, 2022.

decade. In the past, Chinese banks were known as bureaucratic places where standing in the long queue was the norm. This is no more the case since banks have invested in computing, and the Internet and the smartphone have percolated into all sections of the Chinese society. Chinese clients do not go physically to their banks. Almost all transactions are made on the Internet predominantly with smartphones – including buying mutual funds. All small transactions are realized with Alipay or WeChat pay – "small" depends on the client's revenue, but it can go up to 10,000 euros. All big transactions are conducted on the websites of banks.

In China, the banks have been reformed to promote digital service, especially due to the fierce competition from FinTech competitors in various domains (see Chapter 6). In 2020, the total banking investment in information and technology reached 207 billion yuan ($30 billion) in China, especially from the six biggest banks, whose investment accounted for almost half of the total investment. It is obvious that those who could profoundly increase the efficiency and reduce the cost by digitalizing the internal process and provide the omni-channel service model will benefit from those investments.

But it's not just the five or six sisters. Table 2.2 shows that competition comes also from city commercial banks such as well: Bank of Shanghai, Bank of Beijing, Bank of Dalian, Bank of Ningbo, Bank of Nanjing, and Shenzhen Development Bank – which are themselves owned by local governments. Given the size of the Chinese market, even these regional banks can grow to respectable sizes: The Bank of Beijing, for example, has ten million customers. But, they remain very dependent on the local economy.

2.1.2. *The Issue of Bad Banks*

The system has come a long way because, from 1998 to 2002, under the effect of non-performing loans representing 25% of their accounts, Chinese banks laid off employees and closed branches on a large scale. The accounts could only be cleared with the creation of defeasance companies,[4] the recapitalization by the state holding company Central

---

[4]Four defeasance companies were created at the end of the 1990s by the Chinese Ministry of Finance to take over the bad debts of the four largest Chinese banks (ICBC, CCB, BoC, and ABC): China Huarong Asset Management, Cinda, Orient, and Great Wall. Cinda went

Huijin Investment,[5] and a partial opening of capital to foreign banks. Chinese banks have since reached the largest capitalization levels in the world. They are now confident that they are too big to fail. Despite their large size, Chinese banks are fragile. They still lack expertise in risk management. Credits are allocated more accordingly to the government's orders than accurate research studies. It will take 10 or 20 years to make changes in this domain.

The bad debt ratio (bad debts to total loans) of Chinese commercial banks was around 1% at the end of December 2013 (1.02%); it has since continued to increase to reach 1.96% in September 2020 and then dropped to 1.84% at the end of 2020. This can vary significantly from one bank to another (see the last column in Table 2.3). The capital-to-risk weighted asset ratio increased to 14.41% in September 2020, compared to 12.19% in 2013.

There has been a belief in the past that the Chinese government will always take care of investors when a financial structure turns insolvent. The only bank which went bankrupt recently was the Shantou Commercial Bank in 2001. Yet, several more recent cases have shown that the Chinese authorities do not provide implicit guarantee of the State anymore and want to clean the banking system by reducing the overall level of debt. One illustration is Baoshang – another private bank. The case of Baoshang (see the vignette) shows how the Chinese authorities behave when one bank becomes insolvent. Chinese authorities took control of the bank and drove it to bankruptcy; this move was the first since the takeover of Hainan Development Bank in 1998.

2.1.3. *China Union Pay: The Monopoly Challenged Not Only by Competitors*

When it comes to payment cards, there is only one system: China Union Pay. It was created and is majority owned by the Central bank, and this

---

public in Hong Kong. Rather than cutting back, the asset managers of these institutions raised more than $100 billion on the markets between 2013 and 2018. In early 2021, Huarong struggled to repay its debts and its stock market value literally collapsed. Cinda took 20% of Ant Financial's consumer finance entity at the end of 2021.

[5]Central Huijin is a wholly state-owned company which represents the government as an investor in key state-owned financial institutions.

Table 2.3.   2021 Top 30 Banks in China (Based on the 2020 Annual Reports)

Ranking	Bank Name	Tier 1 Net Capital (100 mil RMB)	Total Asset (100 mil RMB)	Net Profit (100 mil RMB)	Cost/ Revenue Ratio (%)	Bad Loan Ratio (%)
1	ICBC	26,530.02	333,450.58	3,176.85	22.30	1.58
2	CCB	22,614.49	281,322.54	2,735.79	25.12	1.56
3	ABC	18,753.72	272,050.47	2,164.00	29.23	1.57
4	BOC	17,047.78	244,026.59	2,050.96	26.73	1.46
5	BoCom	7,276.11	106,976.16	795.70	28.29	1.67
6	CMB	6,100.92	83,614.48	979.59	33.30	1.07
7	PSBC	5,423.47	113,532.63	643.18	57.88	0.88
8	Industrial Bank	5,284.52	78,940.00	676.81	24.16	1.25
9	SPDB	5,192.68	79,502.18	589.93	23.78	1.73
10	China CITIC Bank	4,712.51	75,111.61	495.32	26.65	1.64
11	China Mingsheng Bank	4,619.21	69,502.33	351.02	26.19	1.82
12	China Everbright Bank	3,460.22	53,681.10	379.05	26.38	1.38
13	Ping An Bank	2,737.91	44,685.14	289.28	29.11	1.18
14	Huaxia Bank	2,222.30	33,998.16	215.68	27.93	1.80
15	Beijing Bank	1,982.78	29,000.14	216.46	22.07	1.57
16	China Guangfa Bank	1,710.08	30,279.72	138.12	28.66	1.55
17	Shanghai Bank	1,663.45	24,621.44	209.15	18.93	1.22
18	JiangSu Bank	1,400.46	23,378.93	156.20	23.46	1.32
19	China Zheshang Bank	1,163.78	20,482.25	125.59	25.96	1.42
20	NingBo Bank	1,032.63	16,267.49	151.36	37.96	0.79
21	Bank of Nanjing	969.25	15,170.76	132.10	28.46	0.91
22	Chongqing Rural Commercial Bank	937.27	11,363.67	85.65	27.09	1.31
23	Bohai Bank	831.04	13,935.23	84.45	26.52	1.77
24	Shengjing Bank	Q792.93	10,379.58	12.32	29.76	3.26
25	Shanghai Agricultural & Commercial Bank	784.04	10,569.77	84.19	28.86	0.99
26	HuiShang Bank	702.71	12,717.01	99.21	23.71	1.98
27	Hengfeng Bank	697.95	11,141.55	52.03	39.47	2.67
28	Beijing Agricultural & Commercial Bank	645.05	10,192.84	74.15	36.88	0.90
29	Hangzhou Bank	630.11	11,692.57	71.36	26.35	1.07
30	Guangzhou Agricultural & Commercial Bank	603.99	10,278.72	52.77	31.95	1.81

Source: China Banking Association.

Vignette: Baoshang Filing for Bankruptcy

Baoshang was a commercial bank created in December 1998 in the industrial city of Baotou (Inner Mongolia). The bank was among the top 50 Chinese banks. It served almost five million clients with 10,000 employees. Sino-Canadian billionaire Xiao Jianhua, owner of Tomorrow Holdings (a diversified investment company), took a dominant stake of 89% in the equity of the bank right at the beginning. It was the most important financial arm of the tycoon. His wife, Zhou Hongwen, was born in Baotou.

In 2016, the bank's outstanding debt went higher than $20 billion, a significant part of which was to serve subsidiaries of Tomorrow Holdings. At that time, the bank stopped publishing its financial accounts. In 2017, Dadong, a respected Chinese rating agency, revealed some risky real estate investments in the portfolio of the bank. Cancellation of several projects by the municipality of Baotou induced an increased deficit. Moreover, corruption issues emerged involving Xiao Jianhua[6] and local public leaders who were linked to the bank. A potential systemic impact was envisioned with the associated risk of a general collapse.

In reaction, the People's Bank of China decided in May 2019 (for the first time since 1998) to put the assets of Baoshang under the control of the CBIRC. And, the China Construction Bank was entrusted the responsibility of commercial operations. The major decision of Chinese authorities was to guarantee only a small part of the inter-bank debts of Baoshang; the rest was reputed insolvent. One year later, in 2020, Baoshang filed for bankruptcy and its remaining assets were liquidated. A new commercial bank, the Mengshang Bank, was created to replace the defunct Baoshang.

---

monopoly applies to 85 Chinese banks. Interestingly, the main threat to China Union Pay was not competition, but new entrants using new technologies, i.e. mobile payment (see Chapter 6). China Union Pay, which sees its dominant position challenged by Alipay and WeChat Pay, has chosen international diversification. Outside of China, over 100 million China Union Pay cards were issued, mainly focused in Asia but also in North America and Russia. China Union Pay constitutes the largest

---

[6] Xiao Jianhua was abducted from the Four Seasons hotel in Hong Kong in 2017 by Chinese security police from the mainland. His trial for corruption took place in 2022 in Shanghai. Xiao Jianhua was sentenced to 13 years in prison, and his company was sentenced to a 55 billion yuan ($8 billion) fine for bribery and illegal taking of public funds.

purchase volume among the different card schemes and continues to grow progressively.

The China Union Pay monopoly was not challenged until 2020 by Mastercard, Visa, and American Express – after pressure from the US administration. In February 2020, Mastercard obtained approval from PBoC after years of effort to enter the card payment and clearing arena with China Union Pay as well as with the two wallet giants. Amex was also given the green light to operate in China afterward, and both US card giants are collaborating with local partners. They are operating under PBoC regulation; as China has entered the digital payment era in the past 10 years, traditional card players will surely need to find new ways to serve the Chinese consumers who have high dependence on the technology innovation.

2.2. The Chinese Stock Exchange Platforms

The Chinese mainland stock exchange platforms are much younger than US ones. There are only 140 securities houses in China, i.e. much less than in developed countries (e.g. 1,000 in Japan). Those firms are mostly state owned such as CITIC Securities, Huatai Securities, and Guotai Junan Securities. And, China stock exchange platforms attract more retail investors than US markets where institutional investors play a dominant role: retail investors make only 10% of the daily trading value in the USA while they represent 70% of the daily volume on onshore exchange in China.

2.2.1. The Three Mainland Stock Exchange Platforms

As explained in Chapter 1, stock exchange platforms in Shanghai, Shenzhen, and Beijing operate independently under the supervision of the China Securities Regulatory Commission (CSRC); this commission does not have the independence of the Securities and Exchange Commission (SEC) in the USA. The Hong Kong Stock Exchange (HKSE) has remained outside its purview, and is independent of mainland China.[7] The HKSE has its own rules. It is supervised by the Hong Kongese Securities and Futures Commission (SFC). Its index is the well-known Hang Seng index which tried to buy the London Stock Exchange (LSE) in 2019.

---

[7]In view of the strong political takeover by the mainland of Hong Kong's governance, the next step might be to reinforce Beijing's control over the HKSE.

Established in 1990, Shanghai (SSE) is the largest stock exchange market in China. It has two trading boards: the main board and the Science and Technology Innovation board, i.e. known as the Star Market (see the vignette in Chapter 6). On the main board, more than 2,100 companies were listed in 2022; the number was only 870 in 2009. At the end of September 2022, the Shanghai market's capitalization was US$7.05 trillion (NYSE is at US$28.8, Nasdaq at 27.8, and HKSE at 35). Most of the market capitalization is made up of formerly state-run companies like major commercial banks and insurance companies.

The Shanghai Stock Exchange lists Class A shares in yuan of companies incorporated in mainland China, with Kweichou Moutai, Ping An Insurance, Fosun Pharmaceuticals, and Midea among the well-known stocks. Class A shares are open to a limited number of foreign beneficiaries as part of the so-called Qualified Foreign Institutional Investor (QFII) program launched by the CSRC in 2002. Since 2016, China has been rolling out a series of measures to encourage foreigners to invest in Chinese bond markets. The American asset manager Vanguard actually moved to Shanghai in 2017 (it was established in Hong Kong in 2011). As of December 2021, 670 institutions outside China obtained this qualification; these approved institutions are mainly banks, insurance companies, securities companies, pension funds, and sovereign wealth funds. UBS currently holds the largest position. The strongest representation comes from Hong Kong, the USA, Singapore, the UK, South Korea, Taiwan, Japan, and France. The long period of growth in China has attracted foreign investors. But, decline of the growth rate combined with tensions with the USA and a potentially emerging societal crisis in the low-revenue segment in China's population might conversely impact investment in the future.

The Shanghai Stock Exchange also lists in US dollars, the so-called preferred Class B shares, for companies incorporated in mainland China; they are also traded in Shenzhen. They can be traded by international investors and PRC residents with a foreign currency dealing account. Finally, H shares for companies incorporated in mainland China are listed on the HKSE and traded in the Hong Kong dollar.

In Shenzhen[8] (SZSE), about 2,700 companies are listed (there were more than 2,100 firms listed at the end of 2018). It has two trading

---

[8]Shenzhen is probably the fastest growing city in the world. The city had only 20,000 inhabitants in 1979. It grew to 300,000 inhabitants in 1980. The figure reached more than three million in 1993 and six million in 2004. Since 2009, the megalopolis had more than 10 million inhabitants, and reached 15 million in 2017. It is therefore a city of migrants.

boards: the main board and the Growth Enterprise Market (GEM) board, also known as ChiNext. The ChiNext board was opened in 2009 for innovative companies and start-ups. Shenzhen Stock Exchange lists Class A shares and Class B shares. The exchanges mainly relate to local actions. But big groups like Vanke or Midea are listed as well. Market capitalization at the end of September 2022 was US$4.5 trillion.

A third stock exchange platform exists now on the mainland. Closed in 1952, the Beijing Stock Exchange (BSE) was reopened in 2021. It will be dedicated to innovative SMEs, reproducing the "Star Market" model set up in Shanghai in 2019, offering investors and savers an alternative to real estate investment. It could accommodate 200 to 300 introductions per year.

Shanghai is the most open market to the outside world. Chinese stock exchange platforms are strongly dominated by domestic investors and internationalization is progressing slowly, with only 5% of the Chinese stock market owned by foreigners. In April 2022, China's market capitalization was $11.1 trillion with foreign investors holding over $600 billion in Chinese stocks (according to Investopedia). Although the ceiling for foreign investment was raised from 30 to 80 billion dollars in 2012, then to 300 billion at the start of 2019, this amount remains low. State Administration of Foreign Exchange (SAFE) officials finally decided in September 2019 to remove quotas on foreign investment programs hitherto imposed on QFIIs to encourage capital inflows.

2.2.2. *Introductory Phases Interspersed with Periods of Freezing*

The pace of introduction of new titles has never been constant. IPO was very active in 2007 when several state-owned companies went public: China Mobile, Shenhua, Petro China, China Railway Group, and China Pacific Insurance. Then, the introductions were frozen from September 2008[9] to May 2009 by order of Beijing. In 2009, it was the turn of China State Construction Engineering Corporation (CSCEC) and Metallurgical Corporation of China to enter. In 2011, the cases of Sinohydro and New China Life Insurance were noted. Introductions were again suspended by

---

Shenzhen with all its satellites, Guangzhou, and Hong Kong form the "Greater Bay Area" which may one day rival the San Francisco Bay Area.

[9] Just after Lehman Brothers went bankrupt.

the CSRC between November 2012 and January 2014. In early 2016, new entries were allowed in Shanghai and Shenzhen by the CSRC. The authorities have appointed a new boss for the CSRC.

2.2.3. *A Stunning Volatility*

Chinese stock markets are characterized by volatility, to say the least: Stock market debacles follow periods of exuberance. The composite index of the Shanghai Stock Exchange, for example, soared to a maximum (6,900 points) at the end of 2007 before collapsing. It oscillated between 2,000 and 3,000 points from 2008 to 2014. The second half of 2014 included the rebound of Chinese equities: The index doubled in one year and went back above 4,000 points and even 5,000 points – a development unquestionably uncorrelated from the fundamentals of the Chinese economy as the growth rate was structurally declining. And, in June 2015, it crashed again: The Shanghai stock market fell 13% in one week and 28% over three weeks (between 12/6 and 3/7) – the largest drop recorded since 1992 – to descend below 3,700 points. Between mid-June and early July 2015, the Shenzhen Stock Exchange index also (mostly a reflection of technology stocks) lost a third of its value. The rise in the stock market that had been hailed as a sign of confidence in the economy ended in the bursting of a bubble.

These discrepancies can be explained by the fact that markets are dominated by unsophisticated retail investors who tend to blindly follow the herd. Markets are violent and unpredictable – it feels like being at a baccarat table. In other words, small Chinese stockholders invest in the stock market like people bet on horse races.

When firms increase their results by 150%, there is nothing shocking if the stock market is progressing by 150%. In China, if the stock market gains 150% in one year, it is not necessarily because companies have increased their performance by 150% (or are expected to do so). These corrections are explained by the slowdown in the Chinese economy and the crisis in the real estate market – hysterized by the gregarious movement of retail investors who are not necessarily very well informed. The fact that the government allowed the purchase of shares with borrowed money did not calm that matter down. In absolute value, the market capitalization of Shanghai melted in less than a month by $3,000 billion. For comparison, with the bursting of the dot.com bubble at the end of the 1990s in the USA, $5,000 billion had evaporated. At the beginning of 2022, prices fell again under the effect of the war in Ukraine and the rebound of the epidemic.

Things are nevertheless changing as there is a growing share of institutional investors with better knowledge of stock markets.

2.2.4. *A Tough Backlash*

With the exception of a few investors who had correctly anticipated and withdrawn before the crash, there were many unhappy people. And this involved not just the brokers, but also small shareholders, who number not in millions but in tens of millions – a hundred million in total.[10] One thinks in particular of the stockbrokers who entered the market in May 2015; they are the ones who suffered. Hundreds of companies suspended their listings. The Chinese government stepped in to calm things down – including suspending new entries and banning big players (i.e. holding 5% or more) from intervening in the market until the index returns above 4,500. The authorities also hunted down investors speculating on the downside. There were many interventions where the Chinese authorities deviated from the promise to give more room to market forces. The government also multiplied investigations to flush out opaque practices.

Such movements of the composite index are akin to a roller coaster; they are not likely to strengthen the already limited confidence that one can have in the Chinese stock market and by extension in the Chinese economy. One thinks in particular of the rare foreign players who have been granted a license to operate in the Chinese market. If foreigners are little exposed, there is however reason to worry about the impact of such a slump on Chinese banks when we know that they have refinanced brokers. And still in 2017, the Chinese regulator was questioning the practices of three investment banks (Citic, Guosen, and Haitong) and imposing fines of several tens of millions of euros on them.

2.2.5. *Technology Boards Were Created*

Since 2009, Shenzhen has also been home to ChiNext – a platform dedicated to technology stocks, inspired by the Nasdaq. Launched with 28 companies, the figure of 500 listed firms was achieved in 2015. It reached 734 at the end of 2018 and bypassed 800 in 2020. Shanghai launched the "Star Market" in July 2019, dedicated to science and

---

[10]Here is one sad aspect of size effects which will be developed in the next section.

technology companies with the promise of reducing administrative delays of entry (see hereafter in Chapter 6). This creation was in tune with the "Made in China 2025" plan in the sense that the activities targeted by the Star Market largely overlap those of the plan. And this launch consolidates the position of new actors of technological creation in China. Star Market is made for Chinese tech companies and Chinese investors (again, the question of reciprocity or rather the lack of reciprocity arises). 140 companies were registered as of October 1, 2019 (cf. Chapter 6). The development of activity in Shanghai and Shenzhen has been accompanied by the emergence of Chinese players such as China Securities and CITIC Securities. In 2018, New York-based financial services firm MSCI included more than 200 Chinese companies in its emerging markets index.

2.2.6. *A Bridge with Hong Kong*

The Shanghai Stock Exchange has been connected since the end of 2014 with the Hong Kong Stock Exchange. A similar link was established between Shenzhen and Hong Kong in mid-2016. Regulators expect it to be possible to distribute Hong Kong-domiciled funds in mainland China and vice versa (initially within a daily limit of 13 billion yuan to the north and 10 billion to the south, quotas were abolished in 2016). Wealthy mainland Chinese citizens can therefore invest directly in Hong Kong without individual approval. They have a choice of 266 stocks listed in Hong Kong, and foreigners have access to 568 A shares listed in Shanghai. CATL (batteries) and Moutai (baijio) were the two most traded securities. The connection also works in the Hong Kong–Shanghai direction. As mentioned previously, foreign banks and funds that wanted to invest in Shanghai have until now to be selected by the Chinese regulator under the QFII program. After Hong Kong introduced the so-called "dual-class" shares in 2018 (where the shares of the founders have more voting rights at the expense of ordinary shareholders), after some discussion, the mainland exchanges authorized Chinese investors' access to these securities.

2.3. The Issue of Size

In line with my introductory comment about the dichotomy between yin and yang, I will start with the sunny side and carry on with the cloudy side.

2.3.1. *The Advantages of Size: A Barrier to Foreign Banks*

China's surface area (9.6 million square kilometers) is twice that of the European Union. Population-wise, China is more than four times the size of the USA. The weight of numbers is immediately perceived by the visitor in the streets, buses, train stations, and other public places. China's first strength is that of numbers. The effects of size are an extraordinarily powerful engine.

The point is obvious in telecommunications and the Internet. Firms can put several hundreds of engineers on a given R&D project – which small countries like Switzerland or Israel cannot. The same goes for equipment: By 2014, China had built and erected many more base stations and 4G masts than the whole of Europe. By the end of 2020, China had already finalized 720,000 5G bases, which accounted for 70% of 5G bases in the world. According to China's Ministry of Industry and Communication, another 600,000 5G bases will be built in the country. It reflects the scale economy of the whole industrial chain, with the population size, engineers, researchers, and scientists in all related industries continuing to grow in China, which results in a resilient economy that is able to resist against economic change and various external factors. In addition, with nearly a billion cell phone carriers (they were less than 100 million in 2000), China is sure to have an impact on future formats and standards. The simple deployment of a standard on Chinese territory has the potential to have an impact beyond this territory. The size advantage also applies to activities with low technological intensity: The Taiwanese Yue Yuen Industrial is one of the world's largest shoe producers, producing a fifth of the sports shoes on the planet (notably supplying Nike, Adidas, Puma, Converse, and Asics).

Section 2.1 of this chapter stressed the leading position of Chinese banks by assets as well as other criteria such as the number of employees and the number of branches. China's banking industry has been dominated for a long time by the four biggest banks (ICBC, CCB, ABC, and BoC). Till Q3 of 2020, the four big banks all had very high capital adequacy ratio, much higher than the Basel accord requirement. ICBC even registered 17.01% in the 2021 first half-year financial report, which shows improved corporate governance and strong resilience due to the changed environment. As shown previously, the five largest Chinese banks are among the largest companies in the world. As of Q3 2020, the total assets of the big four banks totaled 113.8 trillion yuan, which was around one-third of the national financial industry assets and 1.12 times the total national GDP in 2020.

Size is a key success factor of the banking industry, whatever the type of banking activity. Retail banking benefits from geographical coverage to gain access to clients. And large volumes help to amortize the cost of information systems and to offer attractive prices of banking services or lending conditions. The existing distribution networks of Chinese banks, and their intimate knowledge of Chinese clients' behavior, impede foreigners from entering the Chinese market from scratch. That's why entries can only come through takeovers. Corporate banks use size as a way to balance uncertainties and large geographical scope allows one to support clients in different locations. And finally, private banking is driven by the amount of assets under management. Size is an obvious advantage for China.

Credit expansion also contributes to the utilization of the size advantage, as large parts of traditionally underdeveloped sectors or areas can now be funded for investment due to those new credits. Of course, this is a double-edged sword as many of those investments are highly risky and the returns often cannot match the risk, leading to potential future problems.

2.3.2. The Limits of Size: Mastodons Are Not Agile

There is a downside. The benefits of size are not automatic; they must be managed proactively. If nothing is done, you can have millions of clients, and yet the processes in place or the service offered may never improve. Another big drawback is the extravagance of means.

China may display staggering numbers when it comes to the number of new engineers trained each year. Demographically, the size ratio is also overwhelming compared to its neighbors – Vietnam (93 million), Laos (7 million), Cambodia (16 million), Mongolia (3 million), and South Korea (51 million) – with the exception of India and Japan. However, having numbers is not the same as having power. Size doesn't always determine success. Small countries such as Switzerland, Luxembourg, Sweden, Norway, Finland, Israel, and Singapore are doing very well with populations below 10 million. Switzerland was also the first country in continental Europe to have signed a free trade agreement in 2013 with China.

Size poses the challenge of gigantism. China is like an ocean liner in terms of maneuverability and therefore changes of course are difficult. Politically, size is a challenge because of difficulty in maintaining the unity of such an ensemble. Economically, the size advantage can become a liability if, for example, bad debts turn out to be larger than expected. China benefits from scale effects when it builds huge real estate complexes. But these size effects are turned against the juggernaut when the demand for housing no longer meets the supply, when millions of square meters remain vacant, and even ghost towns, develop – we know in particular the cases of Ordos/Kangbashi (Inner Mongolia) or Zhengzhou New District (Henan) with major consequences on the financial sector (cf. Chapter 7). The stock market also offers an illustration of the negative face of the size effects: during the stock market crash of the Shanghai Stock Exchange in June 2015, it was not millions but tens of millions of small shareholders who paid the price.

Chinese banks have a strong advantage thanks to their very large networks. Despite their overwhelming size, they nevertheless have their own fragilities. The limits of size are that large Chinese banks are not agile. In addition, size comes with constraints induced by administrative processes and rigidities, making it difficult to implement change. These banks still have to make progress in risk management, in the use of derivative products, and in service delivery (which is a problem in one of the state-owned banks), and most of the branches will find it challenging to make a money transfer.

China must be careful not to hurt its partners. Size ratios can indeed be overwhelming. The case of Ecuador is illustrative. Chinese banks have already loaned $11 billion to the country and will probably lend another seven billion for the construction of an oil refinery. This is well over half of the inward FDI. Ecuador is a country of only 16 million people whose income depends up to 40% on oil – which is to say an extreme dependence on their Chinese partner.

2.4. Conclusion

The history of Chinese banking is short. The Chinese financial system is based on structures which were recently created or reinstated from structures that existed in the past, i.e. before Communists came to power in 1949. Similarly, most of the rules governing this framework were issued recently and tend to favor state-owned enterprises to private firms. This immaturity is tangible in stock markets with a growing number of companies listed or in the unsophisticated behavior of retail investors on the stock market platforms. It can explain why regulators have to adjust rules frequently.

All stakeholders are learning quickly. Contrary to the car industry where learning from industrialized countries took place through the channel of joint ventures, in the banking industry, learning took place through repeated visits to Western banks and also due to some returnees. They observed in-depth examples of many other countries from not only one-shot visits but also the Chinese diaspora (in the USA and in Europe) who came back home with an intimate knowledge of the practices they had been observing for 10 or 20 years. More specifically, stock exchange platforms are less like casinos as retail investors leave room to more professional investors. The good news is the system is moving toward a standardization of patterns.

The system is under full control of the Chinese government, and market mechanisms are quite limited. For example, most of the large banks in China are listed on Chinese stock exchange platforms; yet, only part of the equity is on the stock exchange and the majority is always under the control of a public body (State, province, municipality, district, etc.). There is still a long way to go regarding privatization and internationalization. Opening to foreign banks and foreign investors is very limited (this point will be developed in Chapter 8); like in the Internet sector, the Chinese government has limited the entry of foreign competitors. It is possible, under several conditions, to invest in Shanghai or Shenzhen; but, it is impossible for a foreign company to be listed in Shanghai or Hong Kong.

Finally, as a constant in the history of China, size has always been one of the most impactful variables. Size effects that China is able to mobilize not only come with scale benefits but also with some limitations such as the lack of agility.

Takeaway from Chapter 2

1. The banking sector in China is a "Sino-centric fringed oligopoly", i.e. it has several big fish and thousands of small fish. The big fish are the five well-established commercial banks covering the whole country (ICBC, CCB, ABC, BoC, and Bocom) and the small fish

are the local banks (city banks and rural banks) that were more recently created and are usually focused on a regional area. There are over 4,000 banks in China, but the top 100 represent 90% of the assets. And almost all those banks are Chinese (with very limited foreign involvement).

2. Like the Internet sector, Chinese government has protected Chinese banks from foreign competition; this protection ended in 2001 when China was accepted into the World Trade Organization. And, market mechanisms are quite limited. Even when they are listed on the Chinese stock exchange platforms, Chinese banks are publicly owned, i.e. the equity is under the control of a public body (State, province, municipality, district, county, etc.). They lend money preferentially to state-owned companies as they need to satisfy their indisputable owner.

3. Beyond the Hong Kong Stock Exchange – which has its own rules and its own regulatory body – there are three stock exchange platforms in mainland China which operate under the control of the China Securities Regulatory Commission (CSRC). Shanghai Stock Exchange was closed by the Communists in 1949 and restarted in 1990. Beijing Stock Exchange was closed in 1952 and reopened in 2021. And, Shenzhen Stock Exchange was created from scratch in 1991. As such, all the three mainland platforms are much younger than their North American or British counterparts.

4. Another big difference, when compared to the USA or the United Kingdom, is that Chinese stock exchange platforms are dominated by retail investors; institutional investors are growing, but still make up a much smaller part. Again, as for banks, a very limited role is entrusted to foreigners. A few lucky ones were accepted into the so-called "Qualified Foreign Institutional Investor" (QFII) program launched by the CSRC. And, there is no single foreign company listed on the different Chinese mainland stock exchange platforms.

5. Because the authorities decided to put the emphasis on technology creation, the financing of technology start-ups and unicorns became very popular in financial institutions. Each of the three stock exchange platforms put in place a Nasdaq-style board dedicated to technology companies: ChiNext in Shenzhen, Star Market in Shanghai, and the equivalent of the Star Market in Beijing.

6. In their short life, Chinese stock markets have already experienced several bubbles and violent crashes. Volatility, one key feature of the Chinese stock exchange platforms, is due to the gregarious behavior of unsophisticated retail investors. Unsurprisingly, the pace of IPOs is defined by the authorities.

7. One irresistible characteristic of China at large has always been the size. This impacts the financial world as well. Because of China's size, Chinese banks are naturally among the biggest capital institutions in the world. Yet, beyond the fascination for scale effects, size also comes with downsides. Size poses the challenge of gigantism. Behemoths are rarely agile. And, when the stock exchange market crashes, tens of millions of Chinese citizens are bluntly impacted.

Bibliography

Chen Chien-Hsun and Shih Hui-Tzu (2002), *The Evolution of the Stock Market in China's Transitional Economy*, Edward Elgar Publishing, Cheltenham (UK), 187 pages.

China Banking Association: www.China-cba.net.

China Industrial Map Editorial Committee, China Economic Monitoring & Analysis Center, and Xinhua Holdings (2012), *Industrial Map of China's Financial Sectors*, World Scientific, Singapore, 296 pages.

Dezan Shira & Associates (2021), *China's Stock Markets – An Introductory Guide for Foreign Investors*, China Briefing. www.Investopedia.com.

Securities Association of China, www.sac.net.cn.

U.S.–China Economic and Security Review Commission (2020), *China's Banking Sector Risks and Implications for the United States*, 28 pages.

World Bank: China Overview: Development News, Research, Data | World Bank.

Chapter 3

Evolution of the Chinese Financial System

The financial system and the economic system seem inseparable in that the first one makes it possible to finance the second. The massive economic transformation of China since 1978 required some changes in the financial system. Over the last 20 years, three alternative financing sources appeared:

(a) the development of shadow banking, i.e. of not-approved banks exploiting the mismatch between assets with long-term maturity and short-term funds collected on money markets;

(b) the creation of "Local Government Financing Vehicles" (LGFV);

(c) the slow emergence of private banks.

3.1. The Development of Shadow Banking

As traditional financial institutions operate under well-defined rules, shadow banking refers to unregulated activities as illustrated in Figure 3.1. The scope of shadow banking depends on the way it is defined. A narrow definition focuses on credit institutions in banks which are not approved banks, i.e. informal and non-recognized banking mechanisms and organizations. An extended view encompasses new financial institutions, formally recognized, like LGFV, real estate, or Internet finance. It can even cover shadow banking practices undertaken by banks themselves.

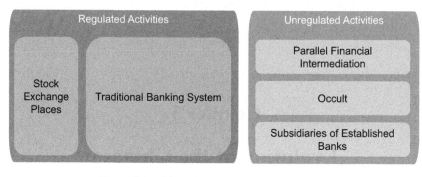

Figure 3.1.   Financing Sources of the Economy

3.1.1. *Shadow Banking in Western Countries: A Temporal Mismatch*

In the USA, the term "shadow banking" emerged during the 2007–2009 financial crisis. According to the economist Paul McCulley,[1] it refers mainly to non-bank financial institutions that engaged in what economists call "maturity transformation", i.e. creating a temporal unbalance between assets and liabilities. Commercial banks engage in maturity transformation when they use deposits, which are normally short term, to fund loans that are longer term. Shadow banks do something similar. They raise short-term funds on the money markets and use those funds to buy assets with longer-term maturities. But because they are not subject to traditional bank regulation, in case of emergency, they cannot – as banks can – borrow from the Federal Reserve (the US central bank) and do not have traditional depositors whose funds are covered by insurance; they are in the "shadow".

With the development of hedge funds, securitization funds, or money market funds, the shadow banking system has become an important source of funding worldwide for the real economy over the last two decades. According to the Financial Stability Board,[2] non-bank financial intermediation bypassed the $200 billion bar in 2021.

---

[1]Paul McCulley is an American economist who worked as managing director at PIMCO – an American investment management firm.

[2]The Financial Stability Board (FSB) is a multilateral financial institution which was established in 2009 after the G20. Its role is to monitor the world financial system and

For example, besides providing traditional insurance services, some insurance corporations may also enter into derivative transactions or underwritten collateralized debt obligations to invest their cash. Some pension funds invest in securities issued in securitization processes, such as asset-backed securities and collateralized debt obligations. In Europe, shadow banks are much smaller than in the USA. Shadow banking is generally believed to be less resilient than traditional banking due to dense interconnection, liquidity and maturity mismatches, credit enhancement, significant leverage, a highly runnable funding base, and missing access to public backstops.

Shadow banking can contribute to financial instability and systemic risk, as shadow banks do not (usually) have access to central bank funding and are denied access to deposit guarantee schemes. They are therefore very vulnerable to shocks and can accelerate a systemic crisis.

3.1.2. *The Notion of Shadow Banking in China*

Figure 3.2 illustrates a sharp increase of shadow banking from 2003 to 2017 followed by a relative decline. Why has shadow banking developed so fast? The development of shadow banking in China can be traced back to the creation of the central bank in 1983. Shadow banking developed on the one hand because the traditional banking system in China was not able to offer enough financing. China's financial markets were underdeveloped with regard to its economic scale, and hence most credit demands had to go through the so-called "indirect financing channel", i.e. bank loans. On the other hand, because the regulation was too stringent, preventing SMEs from finding sources of funding, it stimulated the creation of trusts and securities firms. Those credit organizations developed from 2000 to 2017 because the Chinese authorities agreed to give them some financial freedom. But their number increased after the 2007 financial crisis (as shown in Figure 3.2) because of a tough regulation impacting credit.

Shadow banking not only involves new financial institutions but also new financial instruments, many of which were in the "gray" area of regulation, particularly during 2013–2018 when the Chinese government was promoting "financial innovation". Examples include "With funding"

---

suggest recommendations. It is an extension of the Financial Stability Forum initially created by the G7 countries in 1999.

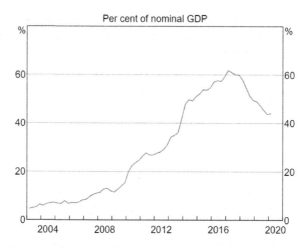

Figure 3.2.   China's Shadow Financing

Notes: Includes trust loans, entrusted loans, undiscounted bank-accepted bills, alternative financing and non-standard debt assets.
Source: CEIC Data; RBA; WIND Information.

("PeiZi" in Chinese) on stock market investment during the 2014–2015 market boom and bust as well as "Down-payment loan" and "Business loan" (actually used for household real estate purchasing but pretended to be business loans of an SME) which were used in real estate speculation. All of these expand credit provision, and increase leverage of the economy, leading to higher financial risks in the future.

Experimentation was conducted, but the government was unsatisfied with the output. Shadow banking usually has a complex business structure, layers of operators, excessively high leverage, incomplete information disclosure, and low transparency. Some of those institutions created chaos, variation, quality imbalance, and even had fraudulent behaviors. Opaqueness prevails financially through shadow banking. Shadow banking has become a hotbed of hidden credit growth and non-performing assets, which pose a serious threat to financial security and stability. That's why those structures were targeted by the Chinese government. The establishment of the "Financial Stability and Development Committee" in 2017 came as a means of oversight on shadow banking. The CBRC made new directives to control shadow banking in 2018. The government cracked down on most of the problematic institutions, thus provoking their disappearance.

Estimating the size of the shadow banking system is difficult because many of the entities do not report to government regulators. Since 2017, China has significantly reduced the shadow banking sector as part of a massive de-leveraging campaign. At the end of 2019, China's shadow banking sector as defined broadly shrank to 84.8 trillion yuan ($13 trillion) from a peak of 100.4 trillion yuan in 2017. By a narrower definition, the sector also declined by 12 trillion yuan from 39.1 trillion yuan. Those numbers are most likely underestimating the size of shadow banking, as many underground financial activities are difficult to detect.

3.1.2.1. *When commercial banks do shadow banking*

In China, shadow banking is still in a great part led by commercial banks. The traditional commercial banks are subject to strict regulations by the PBoC in deposit and loans. The deposit rate is strictly framed by the PBoC guided rates, but people tend to seek for higher-yield deposit financial products.

This has gradually become the funding origin of shadow banking. In terms of deposit resource, commercial banks or other financial institutions attract funds by creating higher-rate trust or high-yield financing products, usually without guarantee on the capital, although not always acknowledged by the individual investors. After 2009, the so-called Wealth Management Products ("LiCai" in Chinese) boomed and quickly emerged as the main types of products that the depositors could invest in. The underlying investments of those products are generally opaque to the investors. Yet, the banks typically provide a "guaranteed rate of return" to those products (prohibited in 2020). The guaranteed rates are generally significantly higher than the typical deposit rates.

Before the pandemic, it was easy to find a return rate above 5% for a one-year LiCai product, while one-year deposit rates were at 3% or lower. This created a subtle "handshake agreement" between the banks and the depositors. By law, banks are not allowed to "guarantee" such a high rate, yet because of the economic development and credit boom, most of the underlying investments were relatively safe (just like in the earlier stages of the subprime loans in the USA), and hence the banks are not worried about the risk of breaking those promises, i.e. the "guaranteed rates". On the depositor's side, most are uninformed individuals who do not have adequate financial knowledge, but who trust the government and the banking system. When they see "guaranteed rates", they believe that those are hard promises that are not to be broken, and hence opt for it. The risks undoubtedly became non-negligible when the pandemic era began and the economy slowed down. Hence, in 2020, the government started to crack down on those guaranteed rates, publicly announcing that all LiCai product returns are non-guaranteed. As a consequence, many of those products saw significantly lower returns than their promised rates, with some even recording negative returns.

Over a long period of time, the individual investors may consider that the risk could be minimal with good and regular interest return brought by such kind of products. For commercial loans, due to the capital being heavily and strictly regulated by the central bank, the normal loans could only be granted to high-quality corporates which have various sources of lending such as bond issuance.

The commercial banks, usually actively working with some non-financial institutions to select the projects to lend to, mostly related to real estate, infrastructure, and construction projects in the form of investment projects, cause the financial flows to be out of balance. As it is considered off-balance sheet, it could help the commercial banks to extend their financing size and it indeed stimulates the economy by injecting the financial to those companies which could otherwise hardly obtain the traditional loans. The financial assets will usually be packaged by financial institutions, and hidden risk brought about by the mismatched term between the deposit end product and loan project could be enlarged when economy's growth is slowed down.

3.1.2.2. *Shadow banking by non-recognized entities*

Some financial institutions that do not register as banks may also have used complex structures to evade regulatory controls. The risk is high for savers who entrust their savings to these structures; in the event of bankruptcy, since these are not banks, the authorities have no reason to compensate for a creditor's default. Shadow loans are profitable as long as the economy is strong. When the economy is slowing, they are more vulnerable because borrowers are more fragile. When defaults occur, one can see the anger of investors. The Chinese government is aware of the scale of the phenomenon. It seeks to use shadow finance for profit by opening or closing the floodgates.

With the growth of Internet online financing, shadow banking has been growing by combining the commercial banks and some high-tech companies such as Ant Financials, which is the financial arm of the Alibaba group. The convenience brought about by Internet online deposit financing, typically like Yuebao of Ant Technology (previously Ant Financials) with no minimum limit of deposit, has largely changed the usual banking deposit conception. Yuebao attracted nearly two trillion yuan at the end of 2018 with an attractive high interest rate (7%) to become the world's number one money market fund; the interest rate went down and is now in the range 1.7–2%. Yuebao is registered as a money market fund ("TianHong" fund) which is not under strict regulation like a bank. This type of financial activity worries the government, which probably contributes to the famous IPO suspension of Ant Financials in 2020, as the government was seeking more strict regulation and monitoring on such businesses. There are many other Internet financing institutions that were created during the financial innovation era (2013–2018). Unlike Yuebao, most of those institutions committed highly risky financial speculations or even financial frauds, and the government cracked down on many of them in the past several years. Their activities have largely contributed to financial market instability (stock market boom and bust, real estate market boom) during those years.

Internet loans are of smaller amounts but they amount to huge numbers of lenders, who usually cannot obtain banking loans under strict conditions. The PBoC has tightened its control over the Internet loan business. In early 2021, CBIRC urged that commercial banks must jointly contribute funds to issue Internet loans with a partner and also stipulated the proportion of capital from the partner to limit the possible risk brought about by the downside economy and slow growth impact.

3.2. The Case of Local Government Financing Vehicles

Until 2015, most of the local governments in China were not allowed to borrow money directly from public or running fiscal deficits. That's why they had to create special entities to raise money. The so-called "Local Government Financing Vehicles" (LGFVs) are public establishments which sell bonds on bond markets to finance real estate (such as new residential areas) and/or infrastructure projects (highways, railways, metro, airport, utilities, etc.). Beijing Infrastructure Investment, Changde Economic Construction Investment, Shandong Land Development and Construction Investment, and Chengdu High-Tech Investment Group are some examples. There might be 10,000 LGFVs all over China.[3] They can be found in all Chinese provinces with a geographic focus – from the rich ones (Jiangsu, Zhejiang, Shandong, etc.) to the poor ones (like Guizhou). Funds are mostly raised with institutions and marginally with retail investors. Figure 3.3 shows the evolution of LGFV onshore bonds from 2017 to 2021. LGFVs have also issued some offshore bonds.

LGFVs are SPVs (Special Purpose Vehicles) which operate like investment funds. They sell bonds known as "municipal investment bonds" ("chengtou" in Chinese). But, since they do not have the status, they are not bound by the same rules. They don't fit into the fiscal budget. They work closely with banks (particularly the local banks who are under political pressure to cooperate with the local governments) to issue their Chentou bonds, where the banks are typically the main buyers of those bonds (i.e. providing loans to the local governments). Banks in turn package those bonds into their LiCai products and sell to the depositors. Local governments also "collaborate" with credit rating firms to have them issue high ratings to those bonds.

Most LGFV borrowing is classified as corporate debt. The activities of these platforms are concentrated in real estate – with the risks attached to this area (cf. Chapter 7). They provide loans to local governments (provinces, cities, and counties) – loans guaranteed by their land reserves. Local governments use their political credit to guarantee repayments of those debts and to secure lower interest rates which do not correctly reflect their underlying risks. Most of those debts are used in investments of public products like infrastructure, which may have public benefits, but have highly susceptible economic returns. The "political credit" also appears to be unreliable – as local governments are restricted by central government policies – and is further tied up by the overall economic conditions.

Some LGFVs are defaulting. Lenders frequently believe that these loans are risk free and that the Chinese government will guarantee if something goes wrong. In fact, when the repayments are not on point, it is the lenders who will suffer casualties. When Yunnan Provincial

---

[3] They were 7,200 LGFVs in 2015.

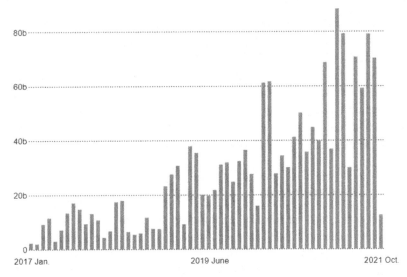

Figure 3.3.   China's Outstanding LGFV Onshore Bonds

Source: Bloomberg

Highway Development and Investment Co. defaulted on the principal, in 2011, this created fear among investors. After this event, investors understood that the Chinese Central government was not implicitly guaranteeing these institutions. State Council intervened in 2014 to reinforce rules.

In 2015, in an effort to help local governments, the Central government tripled the quota of bonds that local governments could issue so that they can access better rates. And since 2015, local governments (mostly provincial) have been allowed to issue bonds directly. The weight of LGFVs should be reduced in proportion. In 2018, Chinese authorities restricted guarantees of these vehicles and their scope. This doesn't mean that defaults stopped. For example, Yongcheng Coal and Electricity Holding Group (Henan) defaulted in 2020 for $150 million. However, these shortcomings have so far remained isolated cases.

Today, as the real estate market suffers both on the demand side and the supply side, there are some fears about the ability of LGFVs to reimburse. Investors had better follow evaluations from Standards & Poor's, Moody's, or Fitch.

3.3. The Emergence of Private Banks

For any type of business in China, the entrepreneur needs a certificate from the government. And this applies to the financial industry. You need a certificate to open a hedge fund, to open a mutual fund, to open a security company, etc. The system does not encourage individuals or companies to start their own financial business. In the near future, the Chinese government is not going to change its position. The trend is probably toward stricter rules – especially as the current political regime was renewed in 2022 for the next five years.

3.3.1. *The Omnipresence of the State*

Market forces are far from being unleashed in many sectors. Banking is a prominent example with energy, steel production, telecommunications services, shipbuilding, and transport. State-owned enterprises, under the control of the government, are the masters of those sectors. The Chinese communist party will always give preference to state-owned enterprises.

The march toward a market economy has however been initiated, whether through the continent's three stock exchange platforms, the entry into the WTO in 2001, or the timid opening to the private sector of industries such as banking. The law on non-competitive practices of 2008, aligned with the anti-monopoly laws of the USA and Europe, testifies to the willingness of the authorities to control market forces.

In 2001, China was denied market economy status by the WTO. The exception had to be lifted before the end of 2016 (i.e. 15 years after accession). But in 2017, both the European Union and the USA refused to give China the market economy status within the WTO on the grounds that China did not carry out the reforms promised in 2001. The State today still very much interferes in the choices of companies. More interference from the government has led to big crackdowns in several important industries like education and training, online gaming, and internet finance. Most of the large private-owned firms have made subtle changes of the actual controllers from the initial entrepreneurs to people with strong ties to the government. The market is notoriously absent from the financing of state-owned enterprises by banks – which are themselves state-owned. This change in status should have facilitated low-cost Chinese imports. And Westerners would have been legally restrained from raising anti-dumping or anti-subsidy taxes.

It is undoubtedly to counter this image that President Xi Jinping came to Davos in 2017 and made a strong impression by taking part in globalization and by establishing himself as the champion of economic free trade (in total opposition to protectionism claimed at that time by President Trump). The debate within the WTO is also about China's status as a developing country, which Europeans and Americans contest.

3.3.2. *A Burgeoning Private Sector*

There were hardly any private commercial banks in China for a long time, with China Minsheng Bank being the only private bank.[4] China Minsheng Bank, founded in 1996 by Jing Shuping, a fairly connected Chinese businessman who was able to obtain a bank license from the authorities, has long been an exception in the Chinese banking landscape. It has been listed in Shanghai since 2000 and in Hong Kong since 2009. After this first case, between 2014 and 2017, the Chinese regulatory authorities (the CBRC) approved the formation of 15 private commercial banks and in particular the demands from Alibaba, Baidu, Tencent, Fosun, and Juneyao. It is therefore very little in proportion considering that there are around 4,000 banks in China ($[1 + 17]/4,000 = 0.0045$).

Private investment is gaining more and more space – it is a political development announced by President Xi Jinping, although the theme remains a subject of debate in China. Thus, since 2014, energy sectors, a traditional public preserve, have been opened to private financing. The same movement affects the financing of infrastructure and telecommunications. In the petroleum business, Sinopec sold $17.5 billion (i.e. 30%) of its distribution subsidiary. China National Nuclear Corporation (CNNC), the Chinese nuclear giant, did open its capital on the Shanghai Stock Exchange. The same goes for the conglomerate Citic, 20% of the capital of which was sold to Japanese Itochu (a trading house) and Thai Charoen Pokphand in 2015.

This is called "mixed reform" ("HunGai" in Chinese), an attempt to involve more private capital and management capability in SOEs that are deemed to be systematically important. A recent example is Tencent's investment in China Unicom. However, this type of reforming

---

[4]Technically, Baoshang (cf. Chapter 2), since it was owned by Xiao Jianhua, was also a private bank.

is considered by most as just utilizing the capital power of the private sector, but not impacting the state-owned characteristics of those firms. Hence, private firms are mainly financiers in those cases but not true owners who can impact strategic decisions.

Revitalizing the economy by supporting private companies will be one of the key factors to maintain the growth of the economy in China. With China's 14th five-year plan (2021–2025) and its vision toward the year 2035, we will surely witness another leap of the economy with more innovative technologies including artificial intelligence, semiconductors, and cloud computing in different application areas. The central government is focusing on those so-called "hard technology" sectors such as semiconductors, high-end manufacturing, and pharmaceuticals. China announced its aim to have the digital economy account for about 10% of China's newly added economic output, which could be accelerated with the rapid growth of 5G network and infrastructural investment.

3.4. Conclusion

This chapter has examined three financial effects of the massive economic transformation of China. The first relates to actions taken by banks and other financial institutions developing shadow banking, i.e. financial intermediaries in deregulated zones in parallel to the traditional regulated banking system. The second one has been the creation by local governments of parallel entities, the LGFVs, to sell bonds on bond markets. The third move has been the emergence of private banking.

This chapter has shown again how powerful the authorities in China are. Regarding shadow banking, we saw that the Chinese regulators undertook several measures to reduce its opacity and financial risk. The same attitude prevailed when local governments started to establish their own financing vehicles (the LGFVs). Chinese central regulators, after letting shadow banking develop over 15 years or so, took action when LGFVs defaulted to reinforce rules. On the top of this, in a country where the State interferes in the choices of companies and in the banking industry where almost all actors are public, i.e. belong to the Central state, a province, a municipality, or a district, the authorities are faintly opening to private interest, as the regulators maintain the option of going back to the initial position.

Takeaway from Chapter 3

1. As a consequence of China's rapid economic growth since the "open door policy" of President Deng Xiaoping in 1978, the financing needs of economic actors (public and private companies) have strongly risen. In parallel to the development of banks and stock exchange platforms, alternative financing sources have appeared in deregulated zones. And the regulator has marginally permitted the development of the private financial sector.

2. As a consequence of the inability of the system to provide enough financing to the private part of the economy, shadow banking developed in China (from 2000 to 2017). Shadow banking refers to informal and non-recognized banking mechanisms and organizations. These unregulated financial activities use deposits from agents, which are normally short term, to fund loans which are longer term, creating a maturity mismatch.

3. There is an increased risk of creditors entrusting their savings to those parallel financial structures. This is why new rules were issued by the Chinese regulator in 2018 to curb the development of shadow banking.

4. As municipalities were not allowed to borrow money from the public, they created specific public establishments called "Local Government Financing Vehicles" (LGFVs) with the purpose of raising funds. They use those parallel structures to sell "municipal investment bonds" ("chengtou" in Chinese) on the bonds markets, mostly to banks, to finance real estate and infrastructure projects. About 10,000 of those specific structures were created. Yet, the law was changed in 2015 to give more slack to municipalities.

5. For a long time, China Minsheng Bank, thanks to the political connections of its founder, had been the only privately owned bank in China. There is now a burgeoning private sector. Between 2014 and 2017, the Chinese regulatory authorities (the CBRC at that time) gave a mandate, i.e. approved the formation of 15 private commercial banks and in particular the demand from a subsidiary of Alibaba, Baidu, Tencent, Fosun, and Juneyao.

6. The State is the great conductor of the economy. It acts to regulate and reinforce rules in unregulated zones, and it proceeds to slightly

open the sector to private banks. The Chinese authorities have their "music sheets". They produce and disseminate many road maps on a regular basis: The five-year plan has been uninterrupted since 1953, the foreign direct investment policy is regularly revised, the "Go Global" policy was launched in 1999, the "Made in China 2025" project was launched in 2015, the Belt & Road Initiative policy started in 2013 with the New Silk Road, etc.

Bibliography

Bloomberg website, https://www.bloomberg.com/.

Financial Stability Board (2021), "Global Monitoring Report on Non-bank Financial Intermediation", 85 pages.

Franklin Allen, Jun "QJ" Qian, and Xian Gu (2015), China's Financial System: Growth and Risk, *Foundations and Trends in Finance*, Vol. 9, No. 3–4, pp. 197–319.

Jianjun Li and Sara Hsu (editors) (2009), *Informal Finance in China: American and Chinese Perspectives*, Oxford University Press, New York.

Jun Lu (2021), Thoughts about the Chinese Corporate Debt Market, *Breakthrough and Renascence – Exploration of the Development of the Globe and China*, Economic Press China, Beijing, pp. 42–45.

McMahon Dinny (2018), *China's Great Wall of Debt: Shadow Banks, Ghost Cities, Massive Loans, and the End of the Chinese Miracle*, Houghton Mifflin Harcourt, Boston.

Sheng Andrew and Ng Chow Soon (2016), *Shadow Banking in China: An Opportunity for Financial Reform*, Wiley, Hoboken, 284 pages.

Chapter 4

Financing Infrastructures

In 1973, Alain Peyrefitte[1] wrote, "Public transport remains rare, and always overloaded. Trains are neither numerous, nor fast: 50 km per hour on average on the Beijing–Shanghai line. Airplanes, which are so necessary in large countries, remain an exceptional luxury. In three hours, at the Shanghai airport, a metropolitan area of 10 million people, we did not hear any planes take off or land" (p. 359). We can see how far we've come in five decades!

More recently, when I first visited China in 1998, many infrastructures were just under construction. 25 years after, China now has a dense network of roads and highways, the largest high-speed train network in the world, a large number of brand-new airports, ... China reached a point where first- and second-tier cities are now quite well equipped. The country even implemented a 5G network much better than many countries around the world – including Europe and the USA. Yet, there are still investments in infrastructures to be made in small cities and rural areas.

Section 4.1 explains how infrastructures have been the driving force of the Chinese economy; the government aligned on the common assumption that a modern economy runs on reliable roads, modern

---

[1] Former French diplomat, member of the French Parliament, and minister in the French government over several terms. He conducted one of the first in-depth analyses of the reemerging China in the seventies.

railways, regular electricity supply, performing telecommunications, and efficient ports to import and export goods. Section 4.2 depicts the financial system put in place by the Chinese authorities to finance those infrastructures, i.e. the three so-called policy banks: the China Development Bank (CDB), the Export–Import Bank of China (Exim Bank), and the Agricultural Development Bank of China (ADBC) – not to be confounded with the Agricultural Bank of China (ABC) which is a commercial bank. We will see that financing of infrastructures is 99.9% Chinese; foreign banks are absent. China has put in place a strong network of infrastructures of transportation, power, and telecommunication – at least in the coastal regions, and in large and medium-sized cities in the hinterland. To keep Chinese construction companies active, the Chinese leadership is pushing for the internationalization of those firms. This is one of the reasons for the creation of the Asian Infrastructure Investment Bank (AIIB), described in Section 4.3. Figure 4.1 offers an overall picture of the chapter.

The prevalent view in economics is that a high level of investment in infrastructure is a precursor to economic growth. This doesn't mean that all investments are successful. China has several examples of unproductive or overcapacity projects. And, this infrastructure development came with a severe increase of public debt (cf. Chapter 7).

4.1. 40 Years of Domestic Experience

There are several factors like the abundant and non-expensive labor, the under-evaluated yuan, the export-friendly trade and investment policies, sound macroeconomic management, and political stability which explain China's economic success. Yet, infrastructure is probably the first keyword that would come to the mind of most of China's observers. Infrastructures are at the core of the government's action. China's achievements in infrastructure are recognized by the entire world. The World Economic Forum Global Competitiveness report ranked China 36th in terms of infrastructure quality in 2018–2019, improving from 46th overall in the 2017–2018 report. China has overtaken the USA and Europe to become the world's largest investor in infrastructures. And, this has been quite visible for regular travelers to China over the last three or four decades.

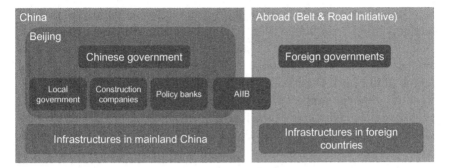

Figure 4.1.   Stakeholders of the Chinese Infrastructure Strategy

4.1.1. *The Chronological Sequence*

I view infrastructure development along two parallel dynamics. The first dimension is a move toward modernization. And, the second one is a geographical expansion as the country is so vast.

The first dimension is a change in nature. China started 40 years ago with basic manufacturing, incorporating a strong labor force component to benefit from the low labor cost which was prevalent in those times. Then, step by step, manufacturing was improved and modernized to encompass more sophisticated production means. To deal with the labor cost increase, the Chinese leadership pushed for incorporating more and more automation with a large investment in robots: Since 2013, China has become the world's largest buyer of robots.[2] Launched in 2015, the "Made in China 2025" plan offers guidance toward more autonomy and more quality in manufacturing. And, after years of effort in bundling the different components of a national system of innovation, China is now well established in technology creation, and high-tech production.

---

[2]In 1997, only 11 robots for 10,000 employees were installed in China vs. a ratio of tens or even hundreds in the most advanced industrial nations at the time. In 2017, with 97 robots per 10,000 employees, China surpassed the global average of 85 robots per 10,000 employees. The ratio is still much higher in several countries: 710 in South Korea, 658 in Singapore, 322 in Germany, and 308 in Japan (where the number has decreased). But, ultimately and because of its size, China now has the largest robot fleet in the world.

Three steps can be identified in this move for modernization of the economy. Step 1 started in 1978. The issue was to fill the gap compared to industrialized nations as existing production equipment, as well as product models, in China were outdated. This corresponded with the launch of the Open Door Policy by President Deng Xiaoping, and the creation of a limited number of Special Economic Zones (SEZs) – including Shenzhen (Guangdong) – where foreign companies were allowed to operate in joint ventures. Step 2 came since 2000. The aim was the reproduction of Western infrastructures. This encompassed the construction of metro lines, high-speed trains, high-tech parks, new airports, the densification of the Internet network, and the Beidou navigation satellite system. Beidou (Big Dipper), the "Chinese GPS", is a less visible investment initiated in 1983 to overcome dependence on American GPS. This satellite navigation system now covers an area from Russia to Indonesia. A total of 35 satellites have been operational since 2020 – the impact to be expected will be significant. Applications are expected in particular in the fields of transport, fishing, hydrological use, weather forecasting, and forest fire prevention. The system will also serve the New Silk Road project (see Chapter 8). Step 3 is the outpacing of the West. This outpacing, i.e. the implementation of advanced infrastructures at a much larger scale than anywhere else, already took place in different domains: payment using mobile phones has pervasively penetrated all spheres in China thanks to Alipay and WeChat pay, 5G networks largely cover the country thanks to Huawei, and similar investments were made for charging stations for electric vehicles, cloud computing, renewable power generation units, etc.

The second dimension is geographical expansion. Three parallel moves can be distinguished. The first move was from the coast to the hinterland: The story started in SEZs which were initially all located on the coast, and then developed inside the country. It continued with the "Go West" Policy of President Jiang Zemin (from 1993 to 2003) aiming for the development of infrastructures in the poorest provinces of the Chinese national territory. The second move was from large cities to smaller cities. For example, development started in the megalopolis of Shanghai before reaching its neighboring city Suzhou, and the development of Suzhou came before the development of infrastructures in satellite cities like Wuxi. Finally, the third move was regional integration. This took shape thanks to the development of highway networks, high-speed trains, and airports. One example is the train connection from Lhasa (Tibet) to Xian (Shaanxi), and the high-speed train

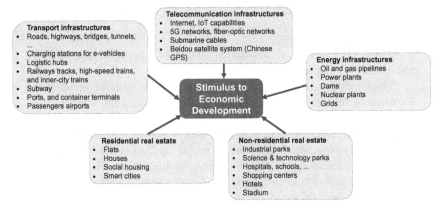

Figure 4.2.   The Spectrum of the Infrastructures Strategy

connection from Urumqi, the capital of Xinjiang, to Xian through Lanzhou (Gansu).

4.1.2. *The Range of Infrastructures*

Real estate (residential and non-residential) has considerably improved the standard of living for most Chinese citizens. With real estate, infrastructures are the achievements that constitute tangible proof of the progress made by China: metros in major cities, road infrastructure, high-speed trains, port facilities, airports, nuclear plants, dams, etc. As shown in Figure 4.2, these infrastructures cover a large spectrum.

Vignette: The Chinese High-Speed Train – From Local to Global

The Chinese high-speed train is one of the most tangible illustrations of the Chinese concept of "technological digestion": The Chinese local teams studied the various high-speed train programs of the world, analyzed all the inputs, and produced their own trains. The track construction program started recently: Before 2007, there was no high-speed train in China. Since 2017, the country has had the largest network in the world, i.e. close

(Continued)

(Continued)

to 40,000 km. Rail is an illustration of China's potential size effects (mentioned in Chapter 2).

The Chinese program experienced a sad episode with the accident in Wenzhou in July 2011. Although this crash undermined the international ambitions of the program managers, China still managed to sell its train to Laos (for the link between Kunming and Vientiane) in exchange for deliveries of potash and copper ore. A project in Turkey was completed. A contract was also signed with Indonesia for the Jakarta–Bandung line. The Chinese authorities also signed a contract with Thailand (a north–south project linking Kunming to Singapore). The Chinese high-speed train could one day find an outlet in connections between major African capitals, in Argentina, and even in the USA on the project between Las Vegas and Los Angeles, which has however been denounced. Similarly, projects in Venezuela, Libya, Mexico, and Myanmar have been abandoned.

By order of the State Council, the two Chinese entities which produce high-speed trains, CNR (China Northern Rolling Stock) and CSR (China Southern Rolling Stock), were merged in 2015 to make a single entity capable of positioning itself globally. The Chinese government wants to prevent any destructive competition. The new China Railway Rolling Stock Corporation (CRRC) represents a company of 170,000 employees with a turnover of more than $30 billion.

One of the most visible investments for foreign visitors is the high-speed train. China has built the world's most extensive high-speed rail network in record time. See the above vignette.

Another impressive investment is the 82 airports which have been built as part of the 12th five-year plan (2011–2015). In Beijing, the construction of the third terminal of Beijing Capital Airport was not enough (more than 80 million passengers in 2013 – making it the second airport in the world after Atlanta). Traffic went up to 100 million passengers in 2019 before crashing to 30 million due to COVID. Authorities have started the construction of a new airport in Daxing in the south, on the edge of Hebei province, to keep up with the explosion in air traffic; with seven airstrips, and more than 80 billion yuan ($11.6 billion) in investment, it should be able to accommodate 70 million passengers by 2025 (that will not reduce the smog in the capital or make China more ecologically sustainable). The Chinese air transport market could have displaced the USA from its world leadership in 2022, according to IATA (International Air Transport Association). Yet, the zero-COVID policy dramatically restrained the recovery of the sector.

Building infrastructure is a business dominated by state-owned enterprises. There are, however, a few big private companies like China Pacific Construction Group (CPCG) – a company with a turnover of $60 billion. Over the years, China has thus forged a competitive advantage in building infrastructure that it can exploit outside its territory.

4.1.3. The Rationale for Investing in Infrastructures

The Chinese authorities have not discovered the benefits of infrastructure in the last 50 years. The Sui and Tang dynasties (i.e. from the sixth to the tenth centuries), contributed to the digging of the Grand Canal to foster exchanges. Infrastructures were traditionally viewed as a boost to the economy. Poor transport infrastructures are considered a major obstacle hindering economic growth. The expected advantages are presented in Table 4.1.

Starting at the beginning of the 1990s, inward foreign direct investment (FDI) came to China massively from industrialized countries (cf. Chapter 5). Compared to other destinations like Africa or India, China has been preferred by developed countries not only because of the low labor cost but also because Chinese industrial parks were offering all the required conditions to run manufacturing activities and ports were offering all the facilities to carry out export–import activities. To maintain the momentum since these inward FDI started to penetrate the country, Chinese authorities had to continue to improve conditions offered to foreign investors.

Table 4.1.   Investing in Chinese Infrastructures: The Pros

Pros
• Attracting inward Foreign Direct Investments
• Stimulus to production
• Stimulus to job creation
• Stimulus to demand
• Science & Technology parks to foster technology creation
• Opening up of rural areas
• Size effects
• Virtuous circle
• Progressive and uninterrupted implementation

The creation of infrastructure has stimulated production and demand. Infrastructures are first a stimulus to production. Industrial parks which were created along the coast, but also in the hinterland later on, have played this role. Among the most significant projects is the Suzhou Industrial Park (SIP). The place offers good roads, reliable utilities, power supply units which allow regular energy distribution and consumption, urban development for employees, and educational institutions to provide the park with educated employees. All those infrastructures have fostered economic activity in Suzhou. Nearby ports support the logistics of manufacturing activities and exports. The 800,000 people attracted by the SIP are an illustration of the positive return on the infrastructure investment made by the authorities.

A good example of the stimulus of infrastructures to demand is the car industry. In 2000, China was a tiny market compared to its size: about 600,000 private cars per year, i.e. about the same production as India (or Iran). In 2018 (before COVID), production in China bypassed 23.5 million while production in India was about four million. Such a difference (×6) can be due to the extent and the quality of roads and highways. China made a tremendous effort to develop a dense and good-quality transportation network while India still suffers from a weak network. Why would you buy a car if you cannot use it? As such, the development of the road network has had a positive effect on the demand for cars.

Regarding technology creation, China put in place all the required components: research universities, public research centers, science and technology parks, incubators, financing sources, etc. There are now more than 200 science and technology parks all over the country. Among the most important are the Zhangjiang high-tech park in Shanghai for chemicals, pharmaceuticals, and semiconductors, Zhongguancun in Beijing for information technologies, spatial technology, and bio-technology, and Shenzhen (Guangdong) for telecommunications, electronics, pharmaceuticals, and bio-technology – which all house major high-tech companies such as SMIC in Zhangjiang, Baidu in Zhongguancun, and Huawei, ZTE, BYD, DJI, BGI, and Tencent in Shenzhen.[3]

Once again, the size factor plays in favor of China. Infrastructures are more easily amortized. The deep sea port of Yangshan, close to Shanghai,

---

[3] Shenzhen per capita GDP bypassed $22,000 in 2019 (160,000 yuan) compared to the average $11,000 in China. Shenzhen's economy surpassed Hong Kong's in 2018. The city has the highest minimum wage in China.

is not only there to serve Shanghai but also the Jiangsu, Zhejiang, and Anhui neighboring provinces.

Finally, investments in infrastructure carried out by the government gave China the opportunity to build an engineering and construction market that is a recognized force, and which is now used outside China thanks to the Belt & Road Initiative (cf. Chapter 8).

4.1.4. *The Limits of the Infrastructure Strategy*

The infrastructure strategy developed in China also has several downsides. Table 4.2 gives a snapshot of those cons.

The question of the effectiveness of these investments in infrastructures is regularly raised: In 2014, a report by the Planning Agency suggested that half of the investments made between 2009 and 2013 were inefficient (useless steelworks, ghost towns, empty stadiums, uncrowded highways, etc.). The specific case of ghost cities has been heavily publicized. The lack of quality construction has also been reported. The 2011 crash of the Chinese high-speed train in Wenzhou regrettably illustrated the negative externalities of development programs implemented at a very high rhythm.

Another negative aspect is the ecological challenge. For example, China is sitting on a pile of coal, and that coal became the norm for guaranteeing the electricity supply of the industry. Unfortunately, coal power stations are disseminated all over the country. And this energy supply has had a huge negative impact on the air quality. Even the Three Gorges dam, one of the most impressive power infrastructures built in China, supposed to be the utmost ecological solution for electricity production, in fact had serious impacts on the environment of the Yangzi Jiang.

Table 4.2.   Investing in Chinese Infrastructures: The Cons

Cons
• Oversized and inefficient infrastructures
• Deficient quality
• Ecological impact
• Crisis of residential real estate
• Non-exportable model
• Increase of public debt

The excesses of Chinese real estate – skyrocketing prices, runaway debt, dependence of municipalities on income from the sale of land, corruption, properties vacant for years, and even ghost towns – were already known. The ticking time bomb was in place and the Evergrande case might be one of the signs signaling the end of the Chinese economic miracle (see appendix). We are at a pivotal moment. What has been the main engine of the Chinese economy has been frozen for at least a decade. And if real estate is to crash, what will be the future engine of China's economic growth? The Chinese real estate industry has caused hardship for many – but the problem should not go far beyond China's borders even if future off-shore bond issuers will reduce their confidence in Chinese borrowers. The real estate activity is Chinese, with land under the control of Chinese local authorities, developments made by Chinese promoters, customers who are Chinese citizens, constructions built by Chinese construction companies, and financing coming largely from Chinese banks. The activity therefore cannot be compared to the threat hanging over the Taiwanese production of semiconductors, which is a global product, which requires suppliers throughout the world, which finds customers across the planet, etc.

Finally, this infrastructure model is very specific to China. Can China's practice of infrastructure governance bring fresh experience for other developing countries? It is difficult to derive some "best practices". It should not be duplicated in other countries as China is too vast. Because of its size, there is a bias at inferring lessons from the Chinese experience for developing countries. It is probably more relevant for policy makers, practitioners, and researchers to look at experiences at the provincial level where the size is more comparable. And, as will be discussed in Chapter 7, investments in infrastructures came with a significant increase in the public debt. Tensions regarding an increase in public debt are also likely to slow down the pace of investment in the future.

4.2. The Three Policy Banks for the Financing of Infrastructure

There are three state-owned banks in China responsible for financing infrastructure: the China Development Bank (CDB), the Export–Import Bank of China (Exim Bank), and the Agricultural Development Bank of China (ADBC). All three were created in 1994 – making them relatively new institutions. Their scope goes beyond China, as CDB and Exim Bank are also operating in foreign countries. They are all called policy (or institutional) banks because they are chartered to implement state economic policies: They are in charge of medium- and long-term lending to support the development of China's national economy. Their combined assets equaled about $4 trillion at the end of 2021. Table 4.3 offers a picture of their profile.

They are all headquartered in Beijing. They are all unlisted. They are all directly supervised by the State Council of China. All debts issued are owned by local banks; they do not use funds from individuals. All three are under the supervision of the China Banking and Insurance Regulatory Commission (presented in Chapter 1). All three have received excellent appreciation from the three non-Chinese rating agencies because they are supported by the Chinese Central government in cases of stress. CDB and China Exim Bank have recently sought to collaborate with foreign counterparts such as the European Bank for Reconstruction and Development (EBRD).

CDB was founded to finance major infrastructure projects in mainland China. It was designed to deploy resources in infrastructure projects:

Table 4.3. The Three Institutional Banks

	China Development Bank	Export-Import Bank of China	Agricultural Development Bank of China
Shareholders	Ministry of Finance of China (37%), Central Huijin (35%), SAFE (27%)	Wholly state-owned	Wholly state-owned
Total assets ($ billion)	2,356	609	996
Equity ($ billion)	186	54	110
Number of employees	9,000	4,300	50,000
Number of offices	37 branches in China and 5 offices overseas	21 in China	No significant position outside China
Ratings Standard & Poor's	A+	A+	A+
Fitch	A+	A+	A+
Moody's	A1	A1	A1

railways, highways, airports, water supply, electric power stations, Internet, big data centers, public infrastructures, urban renewal, and emerging industries. It implements the decisions and instructions of the State Council and the policies and plans of the Chinese Communist Party Central Committee. It became a joint stock corporation in 2008. Its mission encompasses management of risks of different types. The strategy is to balance between capital investment and future debt repayment in project financing to avoid causing financial risks and over-indebtedness of borrowers, and to accumulate experience for infrastructure financing. One of the sources of funding for CDB is the issuance of bonds to the market; currently, the main subscribers are local small and medium-sized banks, followed by large banks and funds, and some small number of individual investors. It is the largest policy lender by assets in the country: figures in Table 4.4 are expressed in billion yuan; the table shows as well CDB's regular profitability.

Its clients are SOEs, local governments (often through LGVF), and foreign governments. In China, major investments financed by CDB include the Three Gorges dam, the Xian–Chengdu railway, and Beijing Airport. Abroad, CDB lent more money to Venezuela than to any other country in the world. Venezuela has the world's largest proven oil reserves (greater than Saudi Arabia's). It has borrowed $50 billion from China since 2007. It was expected to reimburse by deliveries of oil. Yet, this was hampered by the fall in the price of oil and the political situation in the country. CDB also finances infrastructure projects in Southeast Asia, the Middle East, and Africa. It is now engaged in funding projects related to the Belt & Road Initiative. And, in 2021, CDB created a special lending program to issue loans to scientific and technological innovation and basic research, with a focus on basic and applied research and conversion of research outcomes.

China Exim Bank was created to implement the "Go Global" strategy of the Chinese government. It supports China's foreign trade investment and

Table 4.4.   Financial Highlights on CDB

In billion yuan	2021	2020	2019	2018	2017
Total assets	17,168	17,104	16,505	16,180	15,959
Loans	13,262	13,050	12,200	11,679	11,037
Equity	1,538	1,481	1,394	1,301	1,240
Profit	81	119	118	112	114

international economic cooperation. The bank's primary function is to facilitate exporting and importing Chinese machinery and products, and complete sets of new and state-of-the-art products. It lends money to domestic enterprises that need funding for exporting products, want to do some overseas investments, need to fund domestic projects based on foreign investment, etc. It looks very much like the US Exim Bank except for the fact that the US Exim Bank was created in 1934. China Exim Bank lends money to different countries not only located in Africa (e.g. Algeria, Ethiopia, Kenya), Central Asia (e.g. Kyrgyzstan), Southeast Asia (e.g. Thailand, Vietnam), and the Pacific but also to Russia, Iran, and Argentina. China Exim Bank offers $200 to 250 billion in loans to the foreign trade industry. Between 2000 and 2010, Exim Bank lent $67 billion to African countries. Yet, it carries the burden of loans to countries facing financial difficulties like Sri Lanka, Laos, Pakistan, Angola, Zambia, and Ukraine; this might come from an acceptance to invest in riskier projects than other international lenders.

Development projects financed by China Development Bank and the Export–Import Bank of China were criticized for paying very little attention to the societal impacts of those projects on the natural environment and indigenous communities, especially for energy projects. Another recurrent criticism is that China entraps poor developing countries in Africa (e.g. Angola), Latin America (e.g. Venezuela or Equator), and Asia (e.g. Sri Lanka or Laos) by loading them with vast amounts of debt that, most likely, will not be repaid.

The Agricultural Development Bank of China (ADBC) is the sole agricultural policy-oriented bank in China. It was created by transferring some assets from the ABC and the Industrial and Commercial Bank of China (ICBC). It is under the direct leadership of the State Council. Its core policy role is to safeguard national food security and to stabilize market prices for agricultural products. It supports the development of agriculture, rural areas, and farmers. It raises funds on markets. It has a network of branches all over China, lending money to agricultural enterprises.

4.3. The Asian Infrastructure Investment Bank: A Tool for Foreign Policy

China is entering a new phase. As substantial investments have been made inside the country, on the coast and also in the hinterland, the issue is no longer about building where you had nothing in the past. The challenge is now much more about maintaining and marginally improving the existing facilities. The implementation of the future 6G network to replace the 5G network is an example of what will be done in the future. That's why the Chinese authorities push for a geographical diversification of Chinese construction companies. The following is part of the rationale for the creation of the AIIB.

4.3.1. *A Chinese Initiative*

The Asian Infrastructure Investment Bank (AIIB) was created by the Chinese leadership in 2014 to finance the development needs of Asian countries for roads, bridges, energy production, and other infrastructure. This means, for example, building a deep-water port in Kyaukpyu (Burma) opening into the Bay of Bengal and the Indian Ocean, or a pipeline and a hydroelectric dam at Myitsone (north of Myanmar). The motto was clear: Develop Asian countries and regional integration while reducing the influence of the USA in the area. It is about developing the connectivity and economic integration of the countries of the region.

The headquarters of the AIIB are in Beijing. China pledged 50 billion US dollars in capital, and India is expected to contribute $8 billion; the total endowment should reach $100 billion. The AIIB, like other development banks, does not create money. It exclusively funds itself with the emission of bonds. It began operating in 2016. Its projects range from $20 million to $1 billion. China sees it as a support to the Belt & Road Initiative (see Chapter 8) and as a way to reinforce the internationalization of its currency.

4.3.2. *An "Anti-Bretton Woods" Project*

China challenges the international order established in 1945 under the aegis and for the benefit of the USA. The new bank arises as a potential alternative to the major multilateral banking institutions as illustrated in Table 4.5 – the World Bank and International Monetary Fund (created in 1945), the Asian Development Bank, the Islamic Development Bank, and the European Bank for Reconstruction and Development. All those banks are called "multilateral" because they were established by several countries.

Table 4.5. The Five Largest Development Banks

	World Bank	Asian Development Bank	Islamic Development Bank	European Bank for Reconstruction and Development	Asian Infrastructure Investment Bank
Creation	1945	1966	1973	1991	2014
Headquarter	Washington (USA)	Manila (Philippines)	Jeddah (Saudi Arabia)	London (UK)	Beijing (China)
Geographical focus	No	Asia-Pacific	Muslim countries	Central Europe and Central Asia	Asia
Number of members	189	68	57	71	105
Dominant shareholder(s)	USA	Japan	Saudi Arabia	France, Germany, Italy, and Japan	China (26.5% voting shares)
Employees	19,000	3,000	1,000	3,000	500
Capital ($ billion)	223	160	150	30	100
Moody's rating	AAA	AAA	AAA	AAA	AAA
Standard & Poor's rating	AAA	AAA	AAA	AAA	AAA
Fitch rating	AAA	AAA	AAA	AAA	AAA

China feels it does not have the representation it deserves in the World Bank (or the IMF). It only has 3.8% of the voting rights at the World Bank, dominated by the USA (16.75%), while it represents more than 15% of the world economy (for comparison, France and the United Kingdom each have 4.3% of the voting rights). China does not feel more comfortable in the Asian Development Bank (ADB). Founded in 1966 and based in Manila (Philippines), the ADB represents 68 members and $160 billion; it is largely under the control of Japan (which holds 16% of the voting rights, tied with the USA), and China has only 6.5%. China considers that it has no other option than to create its own institution with its own rules in order to become a credible regional political leader.

4.3.3. *A Successful Launch Establishing China in the World International Order*

The number of countries involved in the AIIB reached 89 in 2022. Beyond a series of expected countries (i.e. India, Singapore, Malaysia, Indonesia, the Philippines, Thailand, Saudi Arabia, and Qatar), China has managed to convince the United Kingdom, France, Italy, Germany, Sweden, South Korea, and Australia to become founding members. The decision by the United Kingdom, one of the closest allies of the USA, was particularly remarkable. And, Australia has also crossed the Rubicon by joining the AIIB, while Japan has not entered. This Chinese success is viewed as an embarrassment for Washington.

The bank will undoubtedly reduce the power of the USA in the region. Considering that the Americans and the Japanese have stayed away from it, the standards of the world economy are likely to be less American and more Chinese in the future. Jin Liqun, a former vice-president of the ADB, became the first president of the AIIB. In 2018, the AIIB entered into a partnership with the Islamic Development Bank to co-finance infrastructure projects in Africa. It could lend approximately $20 billion annually.

4.4. Conclusion

Investments in infrastructures have been a major engine of China's growth since 1978. Clear objectives set by leadership, the well-anchored Chinese practice of planning, the always gradual implementation (trial and error) of policies, and the reticular organization of the Chinese Communist Party have all helped the success of the infrastructure strategy. Specific institutional banks were created to support the financial side of those projects. As such, China probably concentrates the largest pool of expertise in infrastructure financing in the world. The AIIB was created in 2014 to finance infrastructure projects in Asia. Yet, for China, the AIIB is also a means to serve its political competitive position *vis-à-vis* the USA and Japan by reducing their impact in the region.

Looking at the future, several scenarios exist. As China's stock of infrastructure bypassed the global average and now reaches a level comparable to developed nations, the country will be able to ease domestic investments. Until now, the development of infrastructures has been almost totally under the responsibility of the government. Public–private partnerships might be one solution in the future.

Takeaway from Chapter 4

1. With several other incentives (including the huge Chinese market and the low cost of labor), the construction of infrastructure has been key for Chinese leadership to attract foreign direct investments (FDI). Foreign companies want to operate in a place where energy supply is uninterrupted, where roads, trains, airports, and ports are modern and well maintained, and where telecommunication equipment is reliable.
2. Infrastructure also means industrial parks offering relevant services, educational institutions playing their role, science and technology parks for technology creation, urban development for employees, etc. Compared to other developing countries like India or African countries, China has a solid competitive advantage in all these domains – which explains why the country was able to attract record levels of FDI.
3. Infrastructure development in China went along two parallel paths: modernization and geographical expansion. Modernization means a constant update of the means. This started in 1978 by closing the gap with industrialized nations. Since the 2000s, the challenge

became the reproduction of Western infrastructures. The next step is the outpacing of the West – investment in robots being the latest requirement. Geographical expansion also has two dimensions: one is the "Go west" policy, i.e. from the coast to the hinterland, and the other one is from large cities to smaller ones.

4. Without any surprise, the construction of infrastructure is dominated by Chinese state-owned companies. The system is again Sino-centric, and almost fully state-owned with regard to financing; 99.9% of the financing is done by Chinese banks. After a period where commercial banks provided financing for infrastructure, in 1994, Chinese leadership created three dedicated policy (or institutional) banks: the China Development Bank (CDB), the Export–Import Bank of China (Exim Bank), and the Agricultural Development Bank of China (ADBC).

5. CDB was founded to finance major infrastructure projects in mainland China; it has also started to lend money to foreign countries. Exim Bank was created to implement the "Go Global" strategy of the Chinese government; it lends to Chinese entrepreneurs and also to many foreign countries. ADBC is entirely focused on China so as to ensure the food supply of the Chinese population. All three banks are headquartered in Beijing (and they are not listed).

6. China has filled the gap for most of the transportation, power, and telecommunication infrastructures. The country entered a phase where the challenge is not to build infrastructure but to modernize what already exists. The country is looking at opportunities abroad to duplicate the infrastructure strategy which has served its development so well. This rationale was behind the creation of the Asian Infrastructure Investment Bank (AIIB) in 2014, a multilateral bank competing with the World Bank and the Asian Development Bank to finance infrastructure projects in Asian countries.

7. Not all investments are successful. China bears the burden of inefficient or oversized infrastructures, i.e. roads going nowhere, deserted highways, underperforming and highly polluting power stations, underutilized airports, unfinished buildings, vacant neighborhoods, empty stadium, and ghost cities. All these discrepancies come with major societal and financial consequences.

Bibliography

Agricultural Development Bank of China (ADBC), Annual Report 2021, 206 pages.

Atif Ansar, Bent Flyvbjerg, Alexander Budzier, and Daniel Lunn (2016), Does Infrastructure Investment Lead to Economic Growth or Economic Fragility? Evidence from China, *Oxford Review of Economic Policy*, Vol. 32, No. 3, pp. 360–390.

China Development Bank (CDB), Annual Report 2021, 193 pages.

China Export-Import Bank (EXIM), Annual Report 2021, 186 pages.

Dominique Jolly (2022), *The New Threat: China's Rapid Technological Transformation*, Palgrave Macmillan, Asian Business Series, 154 pages.

Global Infrastructure Hub (Sydney, Australia), Case Study on the China Development Bank, china-case-study.pdf (gihub.org).

McKinsey Global Institute (2017), *Bridging Infrastructure Group: Has the World Made Progress?* Discussion Paper, 12 pages.

McKinsey & Company (2022), Global Infrastructure Initiative.

Peyrefitte Alain (1973), *Quand la Chine s'éveillera*, Fayard, Paris, 544 pages.

Rodhium Reports, China Investment Monitor Rhodium (rhg.com).

Chapter 5

Investing Abroad: The Primacy of Geopolitics Over Business

This chapter is devoted to Foreign Direct Investments (FDI). FDI are "an investment involving a long-term relationship and reflecting a lasting interest and control by a resident entity in one economy (foreign direct investor or parent enterprise) in an enterprise resident in an economy other than that of the foreign direct investor (FDI enterprise or affiliate enterprise or foreign affiliate)" (UNCTAD, 2017, World Investment Report). As illustrated in Figure 5.1, FDI can be classified as *inward* or *outward* regarding a specific country. Inward FDI is when foreign companies invest in China and outward FDI occurs when Chinese companies invest outside China. All these investments can be carried by publicly owned or state-owned companies.

The first section of this chapter analyzes the evolution of FDI – both inward and outward since 1978. The second section lists the different types of objectives pursued by Chinese companies when investing abroad; three generic motivations are explained. Finally, the third section explains the role played by China Investment Corporation (CIC) – the sovereign fund created by the Chinese authorities.

This chapter will also show how investment decisions are driven by geopolitics. We argue that Deng Xiaoping, followed by Jiang Zemin, and then Hu Jintao framed Chinese geopolitics with a strong economic

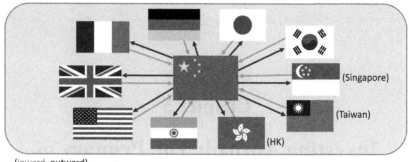

(inward, **outward**)

Figure 5.1.   Foreign Direct Investments: Inward and Outward of China

component; we can call it "geo-economics". However, since Xi Jinping came to power, we have returned to "realist" geopolitics.

The primacy of geopolitics over business is embodied in the new Silk Road. This major initiative was launched by President Xi Jinping in 2013 – his masterpiece foreign policy. It gave a strong impetus to outward FDI and created a significant stream of revenue for Chinese companies (state-owned as well as privately owned). The opportunities and the challenges related to the Belt & Road Initiative (BRI) will be examined in Chapter 8.

5.1. Evolution of Inward and Outward FDI

5.1.1. *The Story Started with Inward FDI*

The initial situation of the People's Republic of China (PRC) from 1949 to 1978 was one where China relied on its own strengths and was closed to the rest of the world. This was the self-sufficiency diktat of former President Mao Zedong. This means that, during this period, very few foreign companies made investments in China. The historical development of FDI in China genuinely began in 1978; four phases are identified in Figure 5.2.

The process was initiated when President Deng Xiaoping opened the country in 1978. After a decade of hesitation, during which a few foreign pioneer companies decided to jump into China, the country truly became a destination for foreign firms in the 1990s. FDI was essentially inward FDI, as shown by the statistics of investments (these are flows and not

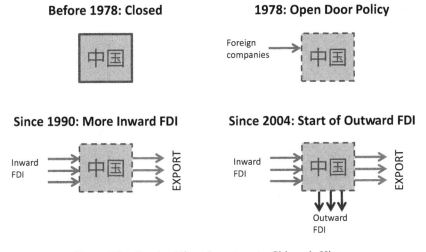

Figure 5.2. Foreign Direct Investments: Chinese's History

stocks) from the World Bank depicted in Figure 5.3. China's entry into the WTO in 2001 acted as a catalyst. With the exception of the drop in 2009 due to the 2008 financial crisis, inward FDI fluctuated in the range $250–300 billion yearly. Tensions between China and Japan, decoupling between China and the USA, and the second crash of the Chinese stock exchanges explain why inward FDI sharply decreased from 2014 to 2017. Then, in the period between 2018 and 2020, about $180 to 250 billion were invested by foreign companies yearly in China. The 300-billion bar was even crossed in 2021.

Inward FDI came mostly from OECD countries. The USA, Germany, France, the United Kingdom, Australia, the Netherlands, and Sweden were very active. Once again, geopolitics is the driver. The USA has been the leading investor by far in the past. Yet, the tensions between China and the USA significantly reduced US investments. On a smaller scale, Australia's investment followed a similar pattern with similar explanations.

Foreign multinational companies came to China with a large range of resources: industrial know-how, product and process technologies, research equipment, managerial skills, and brands. They set up exogamic partnerships with complementary resources brought in by their Chinese partners, i.e. the access to physical assets, labor market, local suppliers,

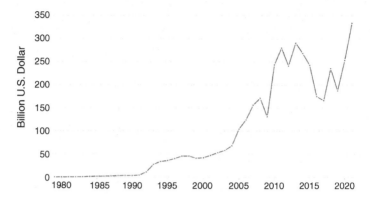

Figure 5.3.   Foreign Direct Investments: Net Inflows to China
Source: World Bank.

utilities, distribution networks, and *guanxi*. The synergistic combination of those differentiated resources associated with a low labor cost gave birth to a compelling manufacturing house.

China progressively became a very powerful export country exhibiting a positive commercial balance, which helped the country build the largest foreign currency reserve in the world (about the equivalent of $3,000 billion in 2022, mostly in US dollars). The next phase has been the use of the colossal reserves to make investments abroad by Chinese companies. The 10th five-year plan (2001–2005) officially launched the "Go Global" policy. This was the start of outward FDI, which effectively originated in 2004.

5.1.2. A Radical Takeoff of Outward FDI in Less Than a Decade

Before 2004, China's outward FDI was a few billion dollars per year – which was a ridiculous amount for such a big country. While in the early 2000s observers were focused on the inflows of investment entering China from foreign countries to build manufacturing units and establish distribution networks in China, the outflows to foreign countries took on an unprecedented scale in less than 10 years as the result of the specific industrial policies of the 10th five-year plan, as shown in Figure 5.4. These movements take shape mainly through buyouts and, to a lesser extent, greenfield investments (which potentially create more jobs at the

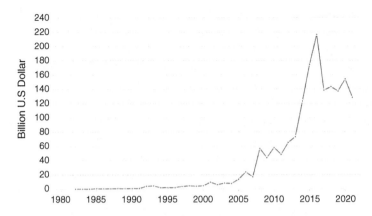

Figure 5.4.   Foreign Direct Investments: Net Outflows of China
Source: World Bank.

place where funds are invested compared to a simple buyout). This emanated mostly from coastal provinces and municipalities (Guangdong, Shanghai, Beijing, Zhejiang, Shandong, Jiangsu, and Tianjin).

At almost zero until 2004, outgoing FDI exceeded $50 billion in 2008 alone. In 2012, outward FDI reached $65 billion out of a total of $1,350 billion for the world (including 329 invested by the USA) according to the United Nations Conference on Trade and Development (UNCTAD). The conditions for approval of outward FDI were considerably relaxed by the Chinese authorities in 2013. Outward FDI rose to $108 billion – which was still three times less than that of the USA. In 2015, the figure rose to $175 billion. In 2016, outgoing investments reached a record figure of $220 billion. Indeed, Chinese companies now have financial capacities which contrast with the difficulties encountered by European or American firms. Rather than investing in the interior provinces of the country, some Chinese companies prefer to invest increasingly abroad.

Yet, unlikely moves financed with huge debt from some Chinese companies such as Anbang[1] or HNA (Hainan Airlines), came as an alarm that indebtedness of those companies went too far. Consequently, restrictions imposed by the authorities pushed outward investments down. The 13th five-year plan (2016–2020) highlighted the need for more quality in outward FDI: It called for less outward FDI, but more control over risks,

---

[1] The name of Anbang started to be known outside China in 2014 through the spectacular takeover of the Waldorf-Astoria in New York (see the vignette in this chapter).

less probability of failures, and more attention to quality of the investments. Once again, the political authorities had the final say.

Two factors impact the investments abroad of Chinese companies. First, outward FDI is possible because China controls the highest stock of foreign currencies[2] in the world; this stock of dollars, euros, yens, Swiss francs, etc. can be used to take positions abroad. Second, it is no surprise that the Chinese government acts as a powerful conductor. This fact explains the title chosen for this chapter: the primacy of geopolitics over business. This is the consecration of Beijing's "Go Global" policy: Investment abroad was promoted by the "Go Global" policy launched in 1999 to help Chinese companies exploit market opportunities abroad and by the successive five-year plans. The capital development of Chinese companies outside China was an objective of the 12th five-year plan (2011–2015). According to the latest five-year plan, for the period 2021–2025, China will accelerate the promotion of a new development model whereby domestic and foreign markets can strengthen each other, with the domestic market being the pillar. This plan implements the "dual circulation" strategy mentioned by Xi Jinping in May 2020, which aims to promote domestic demand ("internal circulation") in order to limit the Chinese economy's dependence on the dynamism of world demand, while preserving an efficient export system ("external circulation").

The spectrum is large. The USA, the United Kingdom, and Australia have been the main targets for mergers and acquisitions (they are also the top destination countries for FDI globally). Investments were also done in Canada, Brazil, Switzerland, Germany, and France. China invested as well in Kyrgyzstan, Tajikistan, Cambodia, Bangladesh, Sri Lanka, and Niger. The trend is nevertheless for recipient countries to be more cautious with Chinese investors. The most obvious pushback came from the USA with rejections made by CFIUS.[3]

---

[2]This stock of foreign currencies is made with inward FDI and exports. When a foreign company invests in China, it comes with its own currency which is converted by the Central bank to yuan – increasing the Chinese stock of the foreign currency. When a Chinese company (state-owned or privately owned) exports goods, it is paid with a foreign currency which is converted to yuan. The reserve of foreign currencies is reduced when a Chinese company wants to take a position abroad and needs to convert its yuan to pay for its acquisition.

[3]In the USA, the CFIUS (Committee on Foreign Investment in the USA) is in charge of rejecting foreign investment projects in American companies that could affect the security

Companies' motivations may be to reduce their dependence on the Chinese economy. But, it is unclear whether Chinese entrepreneurs are seeking to leave China or whether they are seeking to balance their holdings between China and abroad. Some of the disbursements are also made by individuals; for example, internet brokers are helping Chinese companies invest in overseas equity markets. A large part of outward FDI goes through financial entities in offshore financial centers and in particular tax havens such as the Virgin Islands, the Cayman Islands, and Bermuda. Remittances can be skewed by falsifying the price of imported or exported goods to circumvent the law. That's also why the Chinese government has decided to implement more stringent monitoring of capital outflows and some restrictions in 2016 and 2017.

5.1.3. State-Owned Enterprises Originally Led Overseas Investment

Chinese state-owned companies (such as Sinopec, China Three Gorges, China Investment Corporation, Chem China, State Grid, Bright Food, and Weichai Power) are investing more abroad than private companies (such as Dalian Wanda Group, Geely, Fosun, Lenovo, and Huawei). Some operations have symbolic value (let's not forget that the Chinese people love symbols). In the energy sector, the purchase, in 2013, of Canadian Nexen by CNOOC (China National Offshore Oil Corporation) for more than $15 billion (£12.5 billion) – 60% more than the value of the shares – was a landmark move. The name Nexen disappeared and was replaced by CNOOC Petroleum North America; unfortunately, the new entity went through multiple rounds of layoff due to tensions in the industry.

In transport and maritime logistics, there was also the concession in 2008 of two-third of the port of Piraeus (Greece) to Cosco (China Shipping Corporation) – the first Chinese shipowner – for 500 million euros for 35 years, to which Cosco added 230 million euros in renovations. The equipment should allow the distribution of Chinese products throughout the European market. Cosco has, in fact, significantly

---

of the nation: defense, critical technologies, technologies affecting infrastructure, etc. For example, it blocked the sale of American semiconductor companies to Chinese companies, including Lattice, because the products had military applications.

revitalized the port. The Chinese planners have won their bet: In 2019, Piraeus became the leading port in the Mediterranean Sea. Cosco could potentially buy the rest of the port that the Greek government intends to privatize. On the other hand, the Greeks will be dependent both economically and politically. This opening toward Central Europe is not the only move. The Shanghai International Port Group (SIPG) signed a 25-year contract with the city of Haifa in Israel to extend the port with the goal to reach the Middle East. These moves can be related to the so-called "string of pearls" strategy – a metaphor originating from the USA to describe the network of ports developed by China around India, on the east coast of Africa, in the Middle East, and in Europe to secure their maritime routes.

As for private companies, there is, in particular, the case of the takeover of Volvo by Geely (see the second vignette in this chapter) and the case of Wanda's takeover of American Multi-Cinema (AMC), the number two American multiplex. Private companies are increasingly active. In 2017, non-state-owned enterprises' investment overtook outward FDI of state-owned companies.

5.1.4. *Chinese FDI Stocks Abroad Remain Low*

The stock of Chinese investment abroad was multiplied by 15 between 2008 and 2017! But it still represents only 6% of the world total vs. 35% for the European Union, 21% for the USA, and 5% for Japan. Very concretely, in the USA, Chinese companies employed 140,000 people (in 2017) while American companies employ 1.7 million Chinese citizens in China. With the tensions between the two countries likely to increase, those figures will probably not rise in the near future. In Europe, over the period 2000–2014, Chinese investments were mainly made in the United Kingdom, Germany, and France. While the stock of Chinese investment in Europe was only six billion euros in 2010, it quadrupled to reach 27 billion euros in 2012. But, this stock only accounts for 3–4% of the total FDI in Europe in 2014. This means that China has the potential to make more investments in the future.

There have been less than favorable reactions to Chinese investments abroad: Chinese entrepreneurs love Bordeaux châteaux and the international media keeps reporting on acquisitions of famous domains, presenting those moves as a major threat. However, this threat is unsignificant.

Only a 100 vineyards have come under Chinese control on a total of the 7,000 or 8,000 vineyards in the Bordeaux region. The trend for Chinese investors is now to resell those properties. Similarly, the acquisition, by a Sino-Canadian consortium of a stake (49.9%) of the operating company of Toulouse-Blagnac airport in France in 2014 ultimately amounted to 300 million euros, excluding the offers of national competitors, Aéroports de Paris and Vinci. The buyer was put under pressure given that the runaway was contiguous to the Airbus assembly workshop and raised suspicions of commercial espionage. At the same time, the Chinese representative was accused of corruption and has since disappeared. In the end, the consortium sold its shares to Eiffage for 500 million euros in 2019.

5.1.5. *Headwinds for Growth of Outward FDI?*

Should we bet on the continued rise of Chinese outward FDI? Is this a repeat of the arrival of the USA in Europe in the early 1950s or of the Japanese in Europe in the early 1980s? Or will the trend of Chinese outward FDI subside? As mentioned previously, the margins for progress are certainly considerable. At the end of 2014, Xi Jinping predicted a total of $1,250 billion in outward FDI over the next decade. Data from the World Bank (see Figure 5.4) show that cumulative outward FDI is already close to $1,000 billion over the period 2015–2020. As such, Xi's prediction will probably come true despite COVID.

Chinese companies are following acquisition practices of the US, European, Japanese, or South Korean companies. This standardization of strategies is a factor of political stability in the sense that it multiplies interdependencies. Chinese outward FDI is normally carried out by a small number of large firms and can also attract smaller firms.

Yet, not all Chinese companies are prepared or willing to internationalize. For example, while ICBC bank is one of the top 500 companies in the world (simply due to the size of the Chinese market), the bank is not very internationalized. Investments of Chinese banks in the Western world have also been very limited.

Furthermore, the host country is not always willing to receive Chinese investments. For example, Sany (the Chinese Caterpillar), which had planned to invest in a wind farm in the USA (in Oregon), was prevented by the CFIUS on the grounds that this site was too close to a Navy training center. In 2017, the CFIUS also opposed the takeover of Lattice

Semiconductor on national security grounds.[4] This is one of the reasons why the Chinese companies often prefer Europe to the USA (¼ of outward FDI goes to Europe).

Chinese companies (public and private) have to follow the rules; when some companies go too far, the conductor, i.e. the Chinese authorities, can decide to eject the managers in charge of those companies out of the orchestra – as has been the case with HNA and Anbang (see the vignette).

Vignette: Authorities Taking Control of Anbang

Anbang was a private group based in Beijing. Its core business is insurance with state-owned competitors like China Life Insurance, China Pacific Insurance and private competitors such as Ping An. Anbang was developed by Wu Xiaohui, who is well connected politically since he married Zhuo Ran, the granddaughter of Deng Xiaoping, and was supported by Red Prince Chen Xiaolu (son of Chen Yi, a hero of the civil war). With capital of $76 million in 2004, the group experienced a vertiginous ascent: It was valued in 2017 for more than $150 billion (2,000 times more!).

Anbang became known outside China by the public at large through the takeover of the iconic New York Waldorf-Astoria building for nearly $2 billion in 2014. Between the takeover of the Waldorf in 2014 and 2017, the group went on an acquisition frenzy of more than $17 billion. Anbang had offered $14 billion in 2016 for the takeover of the American hotel group Starwood Hotels & Resorts (St. Regis, Westin, Sheraton, and W Hotel) before giving up. Anbang also ended its attempt to take over the American insurer Fidelity & Guaranty Life in 2016 after having failed to adequately explain the group's ownership structure.

Chinese authorities feared that daring financial deals pose challenges to the Chinese banking sector. They first asked the group to reduce their investment ardor outside of China since the group experienced very rapid and risky growth. The flamboyant Wu Xiaohui was then placed in detention in June 2017; the group was put under the control of the China Banking and Insurance Regulatory Commission (cf. Chapter 1). Hotel activities were sold to the South Korean Mirae Asset Management in

---

[4]Germans also have a law which makes it possible to block acquisitions carried out by companies outside the European community likely to harm national security or public order.

(Continued)

September 2019 for $5.8 billion. The company was then renamed "Dajia Insurance". The regulators plan a capital injection. Wu Xiaohui was sentenced to 18 years in prison in 2018 for embezzlement. Concerns remain regarding the future of the group – the State may consider its sale to the private sector.

Not all deals have been concluded. The Chinese company Zoomlion, for example, had sought to buy American Terex; but it was the merger with Finland's Kone that was preferred by shareholders. We are also starting to see Chinese companies reselling companies they had previously acquired. Thus, in 2019, Chinese companies sold more than 40 billion assets (according to Dealogic).

5.2. Motivations for Outward FDI

The previous section stressed that China's colossal foreign currency reserves (again, more than the equivalent of $3 trillion) gave Chinese companies the opportunity to invest outside the country. This move was also facilitated by decisions made by the Chinese authorities: driven by the conviction that it was time for Chinese companies to conquer the world, not only by exporting but also by investing in foreign economies by acquiring foreign companies. What were the expected benefits of such moves for Chinese companies? Beyond the willingness to counterbalance activities conducted in China, and the risks associated with China, three generic motives can explain why Chinese companies invested abroad as illustrated in Figure 5.5.

5.2.1. Facilitate the Access of the Acquired Firm to the Chinese Market

When a Chinese group acquires a company abroad, it often seeks to give the company access to the Chinese market. This has been the case with the takeover of Volvo (see the vignette), Club Med, Pirelli, and the Danish Bang & Olufsen.

Figure 5.5.   Model of the Incentives and Benefits of Outward FDI

Vignette: Volvo Acquisition by Geely Boosted Volvo's Sales in China

The Chinese carmaker Geely showed the way when it bought Sweden's Volvo from Ford in 2010 for $1.8 billion (£1.3 billion). This deal opened up China to Volvo with two new assembly plants and an engine plant. The attitude adopted by Geely toward Volvo contrasts with the choices made by the Chinese SAIC when acquiring the Korean SSangYong in 2004; SAIC did not understand the culture of South Korean workers and moreover tried to bring SSangYong's R&D to China which turned out to be a disaster, i.e. the bankruptcy of SSangYong in 2009. Geely has no doubt learned lessons from the SSangYong case and chose to give free rein, at least operationally, to Volvo.

Stefan Jacoby, the first CEO, was quickly expelled by Geely's founder, Li Shufu, in 2012 and replaced by Hakan Samuelsson – who joined the board in 2011. The year 2013 marked the return to profitability. A Volvo model (the S60L) produced in China in Chengdu was exported to the USA. A common Volvo–Geely platform was developed in Sweden, and design centers were shared. Geely also took control of Lotus and acquired 49% of Malaysian manufacturer Proton.

Volvo produced 534,000 vehicles in 2016 and 570,000 in 2017. In 2017, Volvo announced that it would no longer have 100% petrol cars in its 2019 catalog, paving the way for 100% electric and hybrid. The year 2017 marked a rebound in profits ($1.67 billion). Also in 2017, building on its success in the turnaround of Volvo Cars, Geely took 8% of Volvo Trucks for 3.5 billion euros. Volvo produced 662,000 cars in 2020. In 2021, production almost reached 700,000. In 2022, Hakan Samuelsson was

---

(Continued)

replaced by Jim Rowan, a former employee of Dyson, unknown to the automotive sector.

Geely became the first private Chinese car manufacturer in the world, relegating BYD to the position of second private car manufacturer. If the takeover of Volvo by Geely attracted much visibility, it was not a major acquisition, in the sense that Volvo is a relatively small car manufacturer in the world. There have not yet been Chinese players in the automobile industry who have concluded acquisitions as significant as those made, for example, by Mittal in the steel industry.

It is the same logic which guided what was a record at the beginning of 2016: the takeover of Syngenta by the state-owned group Chem China (led at the time by Ren Jianxin) for $43 billion (Chem China succeeded where Monsanto failed a year earlier). The Swiss agrochemical firm with 28,000 employees specializes in seeds and pesticides. It will find itself having to modernize Chinese agriculture, increase the productivity of Chinese farmers, and maybe also distribute its products in Africa. The agreement was approved by the USA (without any veto from the CFIUS) in August 2016 and by the Europeans in April 2017. The new owners have announced that they want to increase R&D in order to develop more efficient insecticides. After merging with the agricultural activities of Chem China, the new Syngenta Group totals approximately 48,000 employees.

5.2.2. *Catch-Up Strategy: Outward FDI as a Channel to Missing Assets*

Chinese acquisition of a foreign company can also be implemented to gain access to foreign technologies or methods unavailable in China (because they have not been transferred previously through Sino-foreign joint ventures or by foreigners in a wholly foreign-owned enterprise). Chinese companies have, for example, invested in Israeli information technology companies, medical technologies, food, and agro-tech precisely to gain access to their portfolio of technologies. The risk of transferring the corresponding activities to China seems limited; it would be necessary to recreate in China the same ecosystem adapted to their functioning, to reconfigure the current state of division of labor, and to be able to manage the political impact of the transfer.

Another type of missing asset sought through these acquisitions may concern image or reputation. Creating an esteemed brand from scratch is very costly and requires many years of patient investment. The cases of the takeover of New Zealand milk producer Synlait in 2010 by Bright Food, of the American Smithfield Foods (leader in pork) by Shuanghui – the first Chinese producer of pork – for $4.7 billion in 2013, or of the Australian infant formula producer Bellamy in 2019 by the dairy company Mengniu share the same logic. They aim at restoring the letters of nobility to a Chinese food industry shaken up since the scandal of the milk tainted with melamine (and without threatening the security of the USA).

5.2.3. *Pure and Simple Geographical Diversification*

Chinese groups that take over foreign companies may also seek to reduce dependence on the Chinese market. The objective then is geographical diversification. The Chinese company maintains its positions at home, but will seek to establish itself in a new geographic market. This is the case with the takeover of American AMC Entertainment by Wanda. This is also the case with the takeover of the largest private electricity distribution company in Brazil – CPFL Energia – by State Grid in 2016 for $12 billion or the takeover by State Grid of Oman Electricity in 2019.

Similarly, Haier's takeover of General Electric's household appliances division for $5.4 billion is a geographic diversification in a market where the Chinese had very little presence. The same idea of geographic diversification prevailed when Anta Sports Products (based in Fujian) bought the Finnish chain Amer Sports in 2018 for 5.6 billion euros. In maritime transport – an already highly concentrated sector (the top ten make up 70% of the fleet) – China Cosco Shipping strengthened its business by acquiring Orient Overseas International (from Hong Kong) in 2017 for $6.3 billion. Sometimes, companies can also diversify their product portfolio through these acquisitions.

However, Chinese companies do not always have a clear idea of why they are buying. Beyond the abovementioned three reasons, it could also be a question of prestige, history, or reputation. Thus, the takeover of Volvo enabled Geely's founder, Li Shufu, to become a national hero – the point is as important as access to technology. This success now makes it easier for him to obtain a license to, for example, start a new factory.

5.3. The Role of China Investment Corporation (CIC)

5.3.1. *The Financial Arm of the Chinese Government*

China Investment Corporation (CIC) is a sovereign fund created in 2007 by the Chinese authorities and is based in Beijing. Its mission is to diversify China's foreign exchange holdings, seeking maximum return with acceptable risk. The principle is, as with the Singaporean model of the Government Investment Corporation (GIC), to invest to prepare for the future of the country; countries like Norway, Kuwait, and the UAE have adopted the same model to manage the oil dividend. Table 5.1 depicts the top sovereign funds in the world. CIC appears, with the Russian National Wealth Fund, as the most recent fund; this shows again the immaturity of Chinese financial institutions.

The CIC has three subsidiaries: CIC International, CIC Capital Corporation, and Central Huijin Investment. It is placed under the authority of the Chinese Minister of Finance and, therefore, ultimately under the central political power. It follows the guidelines given by the Council of State Affairs and the Ministry of Finance. As its owner, it pays dividends to the State Council. As illustrated in Figure 5.6, initially endowed with $200 billion (67 + 67 + 67) taken from Chinese foreign exchange reserves, its capitalization has increased several times (in particular in 2009 with $100 billion). In 2014, it represented a market value of $650 billion. Total assets surpassed the $800 billion mark in 2017 to end at $941 billion by the end of the year. Assets in 2022 reached $1.2 trillion.

5.3.2. *An Increasingly International Investment Strategy*

As shown by Figure 5.6, the funds were invested in 2007 in Central Huijin Investments and the takeover of ABC and CDB. But the funds were also partly invested abroad through the CIC International subsidiary. Its first big investments were a 10% investment in Blackstone and 10% in Morgan Stanley (after the subprime crisis). A number of other commitments followed: 15% of Noble Group, 10% of Diageo, 30% of GDF-Suez Exploration production, 12% of Uralkali, etc. Its investments were more often equity holdings than takeovers.

The investment strategy appears to be curving. Indeed, the CIC has recently been dealing with larger movements; in 2017, it bought European

Table 5.1.   Top Sovereign Wealth Funds in the World

Fund	Country	Year of Creation	Strategy	Resources	Assets 2022 (US$ billion)
China Investment Corporation (CIC)	China	2007	Diversify revenue streams	Positive commercial balance	1,222
China National Social Security Fund (NSSF)	China	2000	Support future social security expenditures	Allocation from the government	447
Abu Dhabi Investment Authority (ADIA)	Abu Dhabi (United Arab Emirates)	1967	Invest in international markets	Excess oil reserves	698
Mubadala Investment Company	Abu Dhabi (United Arab Emirates)	2002	Diversify the economy of Abu Dhabi; invest locally and abroad	Abu Dhabi government	243
Investment Corporation of Dubai (ICD)	Dubai (United Arab Emirates)	2006	Invest inside and outside the country	Dubai government	305
Government Pension Fund Global (GPFG)	Norway	1990	Invest mostly in Europe, except in unethical businesses	Petrol revenue	1,338
Public Investment Fund (PIF)	Saudi Arabia	1971	Invest inside and outside the country	Saudi government	620
Kuwait Investment Authority (KIA)	Kuwait	1993	Diversify Kuwait's future revenues; invest inside and outside the country	Kuwait surplus from oil exports	738
Government Investment Corporation (GIC)	Singapore	1981	Invest only outside Singapore	Singaporean government	578
Temasek Holdings	Singapore	1974	Invest inside and outside the country	Initial endowment by Singapore government	484
Hong Kong Monetary Authority Investment Portfolio (HKMA)	Hong Kong	1935	Invest in private equity and private real estate	Hong Kong commercial surpluses	200
Qatar Investment Authority (QIA)	Qatar	2005	Invest mostly outside	Gas and oil reserves	450
Russian National Wealth Fund (NWF)	Russia	2008	Invest mostly inside the country	Taxes on oil and gas	175

Source: Sovereign Wealth Fund Institute (SWFI) and funds websites.

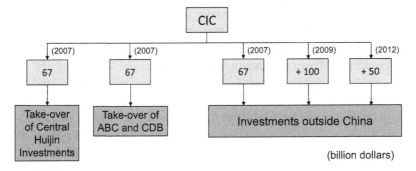

Figure 5.6. The China Investment Corporation (CIC)

warehouse manager Logicor from Blackstone for 12 billion euros. In 2018, CIC sold its very first investment in Blackstone. And, it has reduced its pace of investment. The CIC was started by Lou Jiwei, former deputy finance minister. He left this position in 2013 to become Minister of Finance. He was replaced by Ding Xuedong, who was also deputy finance minister. This shows how important the CIC is to China. CIC even opened a fund with BNP-Paribas and Eurazeo in 2019.

5.4. Conclusion

China's rapid economic development over the last 40 years originated from its proven capability to export massively. At the beginning, FDI was mostly inward when foreign companies were investing in China to start manufacturing activities and develop distribution networks in the country. More recently, in the last 20 years, China started a new chapter of its international development. The country started to invest abroad significantly not only through its state-owned enterprises but also thanks to its private companies. As such, Chinese companies aligned their practices with standard maneuvers employed in developed countries.

As usual in China, figures of outward FDI quickly reached very high levels. This outward FDI trend started as China was accumulating huge foreign currency reserves, mostly thanks to its positive commercial balance and inward FDI. Consequently, the expansion of Chinese companies outside China relied mostly on resources under their control – foreign debt is, by far, the main driver.

At the micro level, three rationales can motivate investments abroad: (a) the benefits the Chinese company gains by facilitating access to the Chinese market to the acquired firm, (b) the direct channel given to the Chinese buyer to specific intangible assets detained by the foreign company which Chinese companies need for their development and their catch-up strategies (e.g. technology, methods, and reputation), and (c) the benefits gained from geographical diversification in foreign markets.

As stressed throughout the chapter, geopolitics has primacy over business. All those capitalistic moves need to be strictly aligned with the Chinese government policies: Go Global policy, BRI policy (see Chapter 8), five-year plans, FDI approval policy, dual circulation, etc. Political authorities decide on geopolitics; they are the undisputed conductor of the orchestra. They control the state-owned companies, especially China Investment Corporation, as the main means for investing abroad. They also control privately owned companies since the internationalization plans proposed by those firms must comply with the mandate that they received from the government.

Takeaway from Chapter 5

1. Geopolitics defines the rules of the game. Geopolitics is blocking the way or, on the contrary, giving impetus to foreign direct investment (FDI), either inside or outside the country. Since 1978, the Chinese leadership has gradually opened the economy to inward FDI. Consequently, the country became a significant target for foreign companies during the 1990s, attracted by a huge market and low labor costs. Investment came mainly from OECD countries, the USA being on the top of the list. Foreign investments were initially concentrated in the coastal areas and came to the hinterland later.

2. Sino-foreign joint ventures served as the recipients for the assets brought in by foreign and Chinese companies. Inward FDI helped to transfer new know-how, new managerial practices, modern product and process technologies, and recent product models from industrialized countries to the Chinese economy. Thanks to the

learning accomplished by Chinese employees in those exogamic partnerships, transfers allowed them to upgrade outdated Chinese manufacturing facilities beyond the joint ventures.

3. Outward FDI was not the priority of the Chinese authorities during the 1990s. Outward FDI started to grow and became significant only after 2004 once the leadership pushed for it. Outward FDI originated mostly from the coastal provinces and municipalities. State-owned companies took the lead, but private companies quickly caught up. Outward FDI developed at a strong rate, and some Chinese companies (like Anbang) realized meteoric moves abroad which the Chinese authorities decided to curb, asking for less quantity, but more quality in outward FDI.

4. The stock of Chinese FDI outside China is still low compared with other developed economies like the USA or most European countries. Consequently, the margins for progress of outward FDI are still high. And, China retains colossal reserves of foreign exchange currencies (the highest in the world). Nevertheless, China must deal with unfavorable reactions when Chinese companies are investing abroad – especially from the USA, where the Committee on Foreign Investment in the USA (CFIUS) has rejected several Chinese projects.

5. Chinese companies are investing abroad at least for three reasons: (a) facilitating the access of the acquired firm to the Chinese market; (b) establishing channels to transfer missing assets (such as technologies, methods, reputation, etc.) from the acquired firm to China; and (c) diversifying purely and simply along a geographical dimension. Geely's acquisition of Volvo falls into the first category. The acquisition by Shuanghui (the first Chinese producer of pork) of the well-reputed US Smithfield Foods (also leader in pork) exemplifies the second category. And, Haier's takeover of General Electric's household appliances division illustrates the third case.

6. Inspired by the Singaporean model of the "Government Investment Corporation", Chinese authorities created the sovereign fund "China Investment Corporation" to channel State financial input to the capital of foreign companies. It is placed under the authority of the Chinese Minister of Finance.

Bibliography

Belloc Bernard & Jolly Dominique (2016), «Investissements chinois sortant de Chine: Quelles en sont les motivations?», *Gérer & Comprendre*, Juin, n° 124, pp. 5–13.

China Investment Research and Dezan Shira & Associates (2021), Real Value in Securing Chinese Investors as Minority Shareholders, *Asia Investment Research*, December issue.

Hale Galina and Long Cheryl (2012), *Foreign Direct Investment in China: Winners and Losers*, World Scientific, Singapore, 188 pages.

Ilan Alon and John R. McIntyre (2007), *Globalization of Chinese Enterprises*, Palgrave Macmillan, Basingstoke, 272 pages.

Jolly Dominique (2004), Bartering Technology for Local Resources in Exogamic Sino-Foreign Joint Ventures, *R & D Management*, Vol. 34, No. 4, pp. 389–407.

Jolly Dominique (2005), The Exogamic Nature of Sino-Foreign Joint Ventures, *Asia Pacific Journal of Management*, Vol. 22, No. 3, pp. 285–306.

Molnar Margit, Yan Ting, and Li Yusha (2021), China's Outward Direct Investment and Its Impact on the Domestic Economy, OECD Economics Department, Working Paper 1685, 51 pages.

Rhodium Group Statistics, https://rhg.com/.

Salidjanova Nargiza (2011), *Going Out: An Overview of China's Outward Foreign Direct Investment*, U.S.–China Economic & Security Review Commission, 30 pages.

Seaman John, Huotari Mikko, and Otero-Iglesias Miguel (2017), Chinese Investment in Europe – A Country Level Approach, European Think-tank Network on China (ENTC) Report, 169 pages.

Spigarelli Francesca, Alon Ilan, and Mucelli Attilio (2013), "Chinese Overseas M&A: Overcoming Cultural and Organizational Divides", *International Journal of Technological Learning, Innovation and Development*, Vol. 6, No. 1–2, pp. 190–208.

UNCTAD (2017), Methodological Note, World Investment Report on FDI.

Wang Bijun and Gao Kailin (2019), "Forty Years Development of China's Outward Foreign Direct Investment: Retrospect and the Challenges Ahead", *China and World Economy*, Vol. 27, No. 3, pp. 1–24.

World Bank statistics database, https://data.worldbank.org/.

Chapter 6

Technology in the Banking Industry

After spending 40 years borrowing and copying product models and technologies from the West, China has now adopted a techno-nationalist posture. China wants to become a technology creator; it wants to be on the world research and development (R&D) map. This appears in the successive five-year plans as well as in the "Made in China 2025" plan.

This means that the access of Chinese companies to technology, whether through internal development, i.e. in-house R&D, or acquisition, has to be financed. The first section of this chapter explains the booming market for financing technology development. The second section describes the most impressive, or visible, technological accomplishment which has been the efficient use of the smartphone network for digital payment purposes. The third section shows several strides accomplished by FinTech start-ups at the intersection between technology and finance. Since these start-ups collect large volumes of consumer data, it is evident that control of the Internet is becoming key even within the banking industry.

Previous chapters showed that banking is a sector which experiences a high degree of State activism and government interference. Interestingly, FinTech has generated some transformations emerging from the private sector with its own market mechanisms and forces. Yet, we will see that the government is willing to reaffirm its control over it.

6.1. Financing Access to Technology

China has set up the objective of steadily increasing the R&D spending continuously in public laboratories, in State-owned companies, and in private companies (large and small). In particular, the 14th five-year plan (2021–2025) aims to strengthen China's global competitiveness in areas such as robotics, new energy vehicles, aircraft development, and agricultural machinery, among others. Expenditures are expected to account for a higher percentage of GDP than that during the 13th five-year plan (2016–2020).

As depicted in Figure 6.1, to support internal technology development, or acquisition, China combines public and private money. Public money for financing technology creation includes direct subventions, fiscal and duties reduction, and taxation policies. Private money comes from banks and capital markets. The first source comes from governmental programs which are associated with sources of financing for technological innovation. This comes with tax advantages and includes exemption of import (and export) duties, reduction of the tax on benefit, and deductibility of R&D expenses. Public subsidies come at all levels: at the central level, and the provincial, the municipality, and the district levels. High-tech start-ups will be supported if they decide to settle in a science and technology park. The government will continue the policy of granting an extra tax deduction of 75% on enterprises' R&D costs and raising this to 100% for manufacturing enterprises.

Banks support technology companies through lending. Yet, the traditional dominance of the State-owned banks which favor State-owned

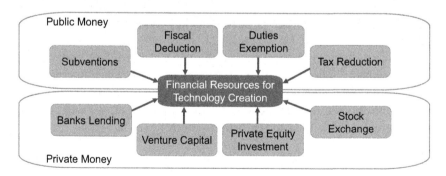

Figure 6.1.   Financial Resources for Technology Creation

companies is a handicap for private companies – large and small. On top of this, because of their administrative origin, banks do not take risks if they do not have solid guarantees.

Two other options are venture capital (VC) and private equity investment. This goes mostly for start-ups with risky projects. Chinese companies raise funding not only from Chinese investors but also from venture capital companies, numbering about 3,500 in China. They include foreign companies as well as Chinese companies. Among the largest ones, we have China Venture Capital, China Growth Capital, Shenzhen Capital Group, Qiming Venture Partners, Shunwei Capital, Suzhou Venture Group (SVG), Sinovation Ventures, UDG Capital, China Merchants Capital (subsidiary of China Merchants Group), Genesis Capital, GGV Capital, Mirae Assets China (South Korea), China Renaissance, Legend Capital, Sequoia Capital China, and Cowin Capital. These VCs cover the seed stage, middle stage, late stage, and growth investment. Yet, the preferred model is the pre-IPO. The amounts raised have considerably increased since 2005. China has created the world's second-largest VC market in terms of annual VC investment, after the United States (US). China's activities from 2016 to 2020 have doubled compared to the prior five years (2010–2015). China became the first place in Asia for venture capital, and its market is expected to grow further despite a sharp fall in 2022 due to the country's tech crackdown and the draconian zero-COVID regime.

Chinese technology companies also have access to financing through the stock exchange. The first place dedicated to technology companies was the ChiNext – launched on the Shenzhen Stock Exchange in 2009. More than 500 companies are listed on ChiNext. Two other options exist: the Star Market, launched in Shanghai in 2019 (see the vignette below), and the Beijing Stock Exchange, which reopened in 2021 (the Beijing Stock Exchange was closed in 1952). The Beijing Stock Exchange will be dedicated to innovative SMEs, thus reproducing in Beijing the "Star Market" model set up in Shanghai. It can accommodate 200 to 300 introductions per year.

Vignette: The Star Market – The Chinese Nasdaq?

Star Market was launched in 2019 as a board of the Shanghai Stock Exchange. It is also known as the "Science and Technology Innovation Board". It is dedicated to scientific and technological companies. The launch of Star Market followed the creation in 2009 of ChiNext (based in Shenzhen) and the New Third Board (NTB) compartment in 2013 – all three launched with the same objective of enabling Chinese technology companies to access public savings (NTB has since fallen into limbo). Star Market is the third Chinese attempt in 10 years. The rationale was for a more flexible regime. It is therefore, part of a long-term strategy. The creation of the Star Market is also linked to the "Made in China 2025" plan in the sense that the activities targeted by Star Market largely overlap with those of the plan.

More generally, this launch consolidates China's position as a new player in technology creation. Star Market started with 25 companies listed from fields such as bio-tech, semiconductors, information technologies, new materials, and new energies – not well known outside China; the bar of 300 companies listed was bypassed in summer 2021. Without surprise, the place is a Sino-centric one (i.e. reserved for Chinese companies only); Star Market is specifically for Chinese tech companies and Chinese investors. Foreigners who wanted to invest in the Shanghai Stock Exchange already had to obtain the status of Qualified Foreign Institutional Investor (QFII) in order to finally hold a total of less than 5% of the securities in the platform (cf. Chapter 2). They will still have to wait to be accepted at the Star Market club. While there are 200 Chinese companies listed in the USA – including the famous Alibaba and Baidu on the NYSE – there is no foreign company listed on Star Market.[1] Once again, the question of reciprocity, or rather the absence of reciprocity, arises. And interestingly, the Chinese government targets the hundred million Chinese stock marketers since they are asked to have a low minimum portfolio (the equivalent of $70,000) and two years of trading experience.

---

[1] Several private Chinese companies, like Didi, and some state-owned companies, like Petro China and Sinopec, decided to quit the New York Stock Exchange and switch to the Hong Kong Stock Exchange because of stricter regulations in the USA.

6.2. The Revolution of Mobile Payment

6.2.1. *Chinese Consumers Stopped Using Cash*

Everything is going fast in China. That's the fascinating side of the country when you come from a Western country.[2] Chinese consumers have skipped the computer stage at home: They immediately embraced the smartphone. China has surpassed one billion Internet users – 97% of who use mobile. Chinese consumers have a large number of options not only with Samsung and Apple but also with many Chinese brand competitors like Huawei, Xiaomi, Oppo, Vivo, Lenovo, Gionee, Meizu, and Honor (see Appendix 3). All of these companies have recently entered this field of activity, each producing tens of millions of units. Xiaomi (see Appendix 1), for example, was created in 2010 and bypassed 100 million smartphones sold over one year in 2018.

The smartphone has invaded the lives of Chinese citizens far more than it has invaded the lives of Westerners. In public transport, it is getting harder to find someone who is not looking at his/her smartphone. People don't look at each other anymore; they don't talk to each other – they're online. Younger people are on games – "Honor of Kings" has 200 million registered users in China. Adults are listening to their voicemail, or watching a movie or TV show. Others shop on Jingdong.com, others surf, others read, etc. On the street, the great days of hailing taxis are over; everything now happens through the Didi (see Appendix 1) reservation center – the "Chinese Uber". As always, China stuns us with its numbers. The value of Didi – a company founded in 2012 – went up to $80 billion in 2021, but went down to $10 billion in 2022.[3] And the company continues to build an ecosystem around the automobile. In Europe, Didi has invested in Bolt, the rival of Uber, expecting the same success. The difference for the users in Europe and in China is that users in China can use this type of service within the WeChat-built ecosystem without downloading the Didi application, while users in Europe must go through the necessary and time-consuming process of downloading the application. It is not a user-friendly scenario to keep the users within a closed-loop ecosystem.

---

[2]Conversely, one of my former Chinese Ph.D. students, who spent several years in France, enjoyed living in the country, except that she found it too slow.

[3]Didi's value fell due to competitive pressure from outsiders, driverless technological substitutions, fines from the Chinese government for breaking data security laws, and listing/delisting from the New York Stock Exchange.

Not so long ago – less than 10 years – everything in China was paid in cash. Now, at Carrefour, Walmart, or Lotus, the vast majority of customers – and not just young people – pay for their groceries in a second using their smartphone. Even in traditional wet markets, most vendors and/or small producers display a QR code to receive payments. Even beggars outside train stations have bypassed the traditional money collection method by just displaying a QR code in front of passengers as they know that no one will give small change anymore. Many Chinese citizens abandoned the use of cash several years ago – they no longer know where they leave their wallets in their apartments (or they do not remember the last time they took cash out of an ATM). What a journey in such a short time! Let's get it right: This is not about payment by credit card but about payment via electronic wallets. This is bad news for ATM manufacturers like Nixdorf, NCR, or Hitachi. Thus, the Chinese citizens have also skipped the stage of the bank card, the use of which has remained marginal. The practice of paying by smartphone has spread to university campuses where students pay their expenses using their smartphones – even for a single kuai (one yuan). The wave is so powerful that it spills over the country's borders. The 28 million Chinese citizens who visited Japan in 2018 convinced traders in the Land of the Rising Sun, whether in Ginza or elsewhere, to provide them with the means of payment they are accustomed to and therefore offer them Alipay. The same goes for Russia. The same thing happened in France at Printemps, Galeries Lafayette, and with most of the luxury brands belonging to LVMH or the Kering Group. In 2018, Tencent launched its WeChat payment platform in Malaysia, but India refused it.

6.2.2. *The Alibaba–Tencent (see Appendix) Duopoly*

China has witnessed the fastest-growing gold period for mobile payment. In everyday life, the use of smartphones has become widespread to pay bills and expenses with WeChat Pay or with Alipay. In 2018, around 83% of all payments were made via mobile payment modes as opposed to 3.5% in 2011. The WeChat application (Weixin in Chinese) was launched in 2011 by Tencent (see the vignette). While WeChat is a social network that offers the WeChat Pay payment method, Alipay is a payment platform that has been embedded into the young generation's daily e-commerce activities, notably with the top e-commerce platform Taobao, built by Alibaba group. It must be said that consumers do not pay any fee to use WeChat Pay or Alipay (whereas you have to pay to have a bank card).

Vignette: WeChat Pay by Tencent

Tencent launched WeChat in 2011 as a messaging application. It now offers a wide range of functionalities: photo, audio, video, localization, blogging, and mobile payment. It is a mix of Facebook, WhatsApp, Uber, Paypal, and Amazon. In 2018, WeChat exceeded one billion monthly active users and Tencent exceeded $500 billion in capitalization. It now has close to 1.2 billion active users. In China, you cannot avoid it! It has become the norm for communicating with friends and family, for paying for the metro, for ordering and paying at restaurants, for listening to music, for watching videos, for ordering taxis, for paying for groceries, for paying for coffee at Starbucks, for renting bikes, for paying rent, for sending a "red envelope" during the holidays etc. In fact, WeChat does everything to ensure that users do not leave the WeChat environment. There are of course limits: you cannot buy a Rolls Royce with your WeChat account. But, the limits in place are more than enough for the life of the middle class.

Without any surprise, Tencent looks carefully at the communications in the WeChat network to make sure they are aligned with the requirements of the Chinese government (nothing about Tibet, Xinjiang, etc.). The WeChat ecosystem is centered on China. Developing WeChat in Europe would require one to create an entirely new ecosystem. That's probably why the development of WeChat outside China is focused on Chinese communities abroad.

These two private technology companies carried out a real takeover of the means of payment in a very short time: Alipay took more than 50% and WeChat Pay nearly 40% of the $16 trillion of payments by mobile (according to Analysys). This is a concern for the Chinese government which sees this as a rise in power of private actors but at the same time as a means of controlling financial flows. It is perhaps to break this duopoly that the Chinese government in 2019 granted Paypal the license – the first to a foreign firm – to enter the payment market.

6.2.3. Differences with Europe and the USA

The paradigm is therefore very different depending on whether you are in Europe, the USA, or China. There is Apple Pay and Google Pay, but few people use them. People in the West use the bank card that the system wants to maintain. Contactless has long been in its infancy and is just starting to take off (with the exception of some advanced countries like

Sweden). Although there are wallets like Lyf Pay, Lydia, and Pumpkin as a complementary means of payment, the usage still remains marginal due to the lack of ecosystem such as that in WeChat Pay or Alipay in China. In addition, Europe and the USA have lived through "uberization" of established activities (taxis, hotels booking, etc.), which was about attacking distribution players head-on. The stakes are exactly the opposite in China: companies like Alibaba, Tencent, and Baidu are looking to offer new channels to distributors. These Internet players are also making life easier for users by offering them an ever wider range of services. In return, users implicitly agree to let Internet companies commercially exploit the data that describe their behavior (analysis of the content of their emails, posted messages, requests on a search engine, etc.). And the actors of this revolution are accumulating an impressive amount of data on the purchasing behavior of the consumers from China at an unprecedented scale.

This is tangible proof of the technological revolution underway in China. In fact, the Chinese citizens make 10 times more in mobile payment than the Americans: there are 450 million mobile payment users in China vs. 50 million in the USA (and 50 million in Europe). As China has now exceeded $10,000 in GDP per capita, we can see the weight of the movement. This example of the widespread use of smartphones shows how China can very quickly meet high standards. It is up to foreign FinTech companies to reproduce the Chinese model in their country. China is very advanced with digital payments. But surprisingly, Chinese retail banks are archaic regarding onsite administrative processes. For example, transferring money abroad requires one to assemble several paper documents and physically go to the bank.

6.3. The FinTech Landscape

6.3.1. *A Large Range of Applications*

What is FinTech and why it is important? Financial Technology, or FinTech, is the implementation of innovative technologies to bring about disruption in the financial sector. It consists of new forms of banking and a renewed financial system. FinTech covers a large range of applications. CB Insights identified 19 domains reported in Table 6.1.

There are many factors which could explain the boom. With the rapid growth of the economy during the last 40 years, China has witnessed the quick growth of the middle-class population, especially in the big cities in

Table 6.1.   FinTech Range of Applications

1. Accounting and finance
2. Asset management
3. Business lending and finance
4. Capital markets
5. Core banking and infrastructures
6. Credit score and analytics
7. Cryptocurrency
8. Digital banking
9. Financial services and automation
10. General lending and marketplaces
11. Insurance
12. Mobile wallets and remittances
13. Payments processing and networks
14. Payroll and benefits
15. Personal finance
16. Point of sale and consumer lending
17. Real estate and mortgage
18. Regulatory and compliance
19. Retail investing and secondary markets

Source: CB Insights.

the coastal areas. The Chinese tradition of putting aside enough savings for educational purposes, unexpected illnesses, accidents, retirement needs, etc., plays an important role. The Internet finance business immediately attracted large amounts of spare money from the young generation to the middle-aged population. Big data technology has been largely used to analyze consumer behaviors and thus could serve as an analytical tool to auto-propose the most adapted services and respond to consumer needs with complex calculation methodology. It largely helped Internet finance grow during the past few years.

6.3.2. *A New Industry Is Emerging*

The business model has been changed tremendously since the beginning of the millennium by giant e-commerce platforms such as Taobao,

JD.com, Yihaodian, and Dangdang.com. Alipay, as the sole payment method to support the Taobao e-commerce platform at the beginning, accumulated over one billion users while the social messenger platform WeChat accumulated over 1.1 billion users. The two giant FinTech companies have continuously invested into the ecosystem to create the stickiness of the user experience by incorporating daily expense-related services such as public service payment, mobile top-up, airplane and train ticket booking, taxi riding, hospital registration, etc. Clients are gradually using these platforms to repay their credit cards and even invest their personal savings due to the convenience of instant investment, withdrawal and visibility without using the traditional banking tokens or a time-consuming process.

Many companies offer different kinds of digital products for the financial services industry. There are various types of global FinTech companies in the payment industry, like Paypal or Alipay, or international money transfer industry, like the UK-based company Transferwise. FinTech companies in China grew over the last 10 years, especially those with a focus on finance-related services. Table 6.2 offers a picture of the top Chinese FinTech companies.

As illustrated in Table 6.2, there are many new FinTech companies which became successful in China. Some developed in the context of the X-border e-commerce boom a few years ago. The vignette on Ping Pong offers one example.

Table 6.2.   Top Chinese FinTech

Company	Equity	Creation	Headquarter	Number of Employees	Business
9F Group	Nasdaq	2006	Beijing	740	Financial services
Ant Financial	Alibaba	2014	Hangzhou	17,000	Mass financial services: Alipay, Yu'e Bao, MYBank, Cloud, etc.
Bitmain Technologies	IPO in 2018	2013	Beijing	400	Mining solutions for cryptocurrencies
CMC Capital Group (formerly China Media Capital)	Private	2010	Shanghai	7,900	Private equity investment

Table 6.2.   (*Continued*)

Company	Equity	Creation	Headquarter	Number of Employees	Business
Duxiaoman Financial (formerly Baidu Finance)	Baidu spin-off	2015	Beijing	350	Payment systems, wealth management, micro-lending services
Dianrong	Private equity	2012	Shanghai	3,500	P2P lending platform
JD Digits (formerly JD Finance)	JD.com	2013	Beijing	10,000	Connect financial and physical industries
Jiedaibao	Renrenxing technologies	2015	Beijing	n.a.	Lending among acquaintances
Lakala Payment	Shenzhen Stock Exchange	2005	Beijing	2,500	Consumer financial services
Lufax (Lujiazui International Financial Asset Exchange)	Shanghai municipal government and Ping An	2005	Shanghai	92,000	Wealth management and P2P lending
Ping An Technologies	Ping An	2008	Shenzhen	4,800	Financial technology solutions for small and medium-sized banks
Pingpong	Private investors	2015	Hangzhou	1,000	Payment facilitator
Suning Financial Services	Suning	2015	Nanjing	200	Online to offline payment platform
Tencent	Naspers (31%), Ma Huateng (8%), diffuse shareholding	1998	Shenzhen	116,000	WeChat, WeBank (digital bank)
Tiger Brokers	Xiaomi, Nasdaq, HKSE	2014	Guangdong	1,100	Online brokering stock market transactions
Yixin Group	HKSE	2014	Shanghai	4,300	Online automotive transaction platform

Source: Press and websites.

Vignette: Ping Pong

Ping Pong Financial Group was created in 2015 in Hangzhou (Zhejiang). It has been benefiting from the worldwide development of electronic commerce. It is a B2B company specializing in trans-border transactions. It serves Chinese companies using electronic platforms to sell outside China. Ping Pong is the first Payment Service Provider (PSP) to obtain an EU delivery payment license in Luxembourg in 2017, which demonstrates its determination to compete with US and Western peers such as Payoneer in the vast cross-border trade. Ping Pong offers a virtual account of money at any time that can be used across borders, changing from one currency to another. In December 2020, Ping Pong extended its license to an Electronic Money Institution (EMI) license, which will allow it to access the EU 27 countries in a broader way. Under the Luxembourg CSSF regulation, Ping Pong was one of very few FinTech companies to get the EMI license, which also shows that this leading FinTech company has set up top-tier company governance, a risk management framework, and respects market standards in this competitive market.

Ping Pong has a good understanding of the huge merchant base in China and its product design helps it to better respond to merchant requirements by taking into consideration the EU regulations. As one of the PSPs recognized by Amazon in 2021, Ping Pong will be among the limited PSP providers to work with Amazon to provide the merchant-based collection services via virtual accounts. It supports more than 10 currencies (US dollar, euro, British pound, Mexican peso, Japanese yen, Polish zloty, etc.), and claims to be transparent, secure, and fast, with a low fee. The company has been able to sign several license agreements in different countries and cities (including New York, San Francisco, Hong Kong, Japan, and Luxembourg). Since March 2020, the company value bypassed the bar of $1 billion, making it one of the Chinese unicorns.

6.3.3. *Leapfrogging to the New Technological Generation*

Contrary to Western countries where credit cards still play an important role as payment methods, credit card use per capita in China is very low (0.47 vs. 2.6 cards per person in the USA according to the statistics in 2018). The lack of legacy in traditional banking also brings the opportunity for FinTech companies to explore user-friendly wallets to meet the needs of the population. China had also witnessed the exponential growth of smartphone subscribers and in 2019, registered over 850 million people, which represents huge business opportunities for the FinTech companies, especially in the finance service industry. Additionally, the rapid growth benefits from the national policy of Internet finance inclusivity.

The emergence and development of digital financial inclusion pose new challenges to regulation systems. By extensive expansion of digital finance, some large Internet-based companies, such as Alibaba and Tencent, established financial service platforms with various products including lending, insurance, and wealth management. These all-inclusive platforms have largely shortened the financial service gap between the highly developed coastal cities and rural areas. The fast growth of these Internet finance companies also increased the difficulty of regulation on Internet-based mixed financial operations.

6.3.4. The Conductor Is Regaining Control

Alibaba is among the most fascinating cases in China. The astounding economic success of its founder and its group, the dominant design embodied by the company, and its multiple business units developed over time make it a reference as illustrated in Figure 6.2. Such a range of businesses comes with the most extended set of big data in China.

Yet, the China tech giants have now gained too much prestige and influence in the eyes of the authorities. The Chinese leadership discovered that Alibaba (see Appendix 1) had a better understanding of Chinese citizens than the Chinese Communist Party itself. The political elite foresee

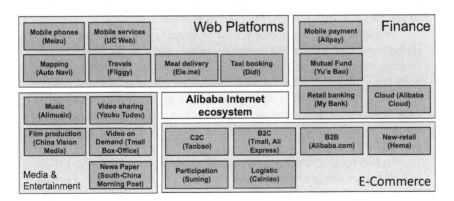

Figure 6.2.   The Core Business of Alibaba

those private companies as a threat to the party. As such, a strong clampdown has been undertaken. The vignette on Alibaba illustrates this case.

Vignette: Alibaba – Too Much Prestige and Influence

Alibaba was established in 1999 in Hangzhou in the wealthy coastal province of Zhejiang. The founder – Jack Ma (Ma Yun in Chinese) – has a very strong personality. He started from nothing: no lineage of Red Nobility, no inheritance, no computer studies abroad, no experience at Google. However, he built one of the most powerful private Chinese groups. His success in business has made him known to all Chinese citizens who have developed a very good image of him and see him as an iconic entrepreneur, a bit like Steve Jobs.

Alibaba, initially, was a B2B platform for Chinese companies that wanted to sell their products abroad to other companies. TaoBao was then added to this initial base – a C2C platform (like eBay). Then, Alibaba created a B2C e-commerce site called Tmall (like Amazon). At the same time, leading logistics tools, structures, and companies were put in place; the Cainiao freight subsidiary is probably the best known of these. Other activities were also launched such as taxi booking, in alliance with Tencent.

An important financial component was also developed over the years. Alibaba became known at first for its Alipay application, used by half of the Chinese citizens to pay for their purchases with their smartphones. The business evolved into online banking and wealth management. Alibaba also launched the Yu'e Bao Mutual Fund with great success. All these financial activities were housed in a specific company – Ant Financial – which has become Ant Group. Jack Ma owned up to 50% of Ant, but had to sell part of it under duress from the authorities.

While the initial development of the Alibaba Group was accomplished through internal growth, the company quickly grew through acquisition. Among the most significant takeovers were those of Weibo (a Chinese platform similar to Twitter), Youku Tudou (a Chinese platform similar to YouTube), Auto Navi (for mapping), and Ele.me, a site for the distribution of ready-made products. Though it unfortunately did not succeed in buying the American Money Gram, Alibaba has nearly a thousand affiliates at present.

To sum up its strategy, we can say that Alibaba has explored just about everything we can imagine doing on the Web. This has generated a portfolio of diverse but very synergistic activities. If we were to combine all the

(Continued)

behavioral databases made up of all the activities conducted by Alibaba, we would have the most complete information base imaginable on the profile of the 1.4 billion Chinese citizens.

While Alibaba has managed to win over roughly 1.4 billion Chinese citizens, its success outside of China hasn't gone much further than the Chinese diaspora. Attempts to grow in the United States failed. However, the group has built positions in Southeast Asia and India.

But at the shareholder level, powerful foreign shareholders are present in Alibaba. The company notably counts the Japanese SoftBank – which attained the status of shareholder very early – and the American Yahoo – since the transfer of its Chinese activities to Alibaba – as shareholders. The company entered the New York Stock Exchange with a record in terms of funds raised.

Jack Ma retired from his position as CEO in 2014 at the age of 48. He gave up his position as President in 2019 to devote himself to philanthropy and education. His public criticism of banks and financial supervision in October 2020 unleashed the wrath of the Chinese authorities who saw an opportunity to contain the power of the group and who notably prevented the IPO of Ant Group. Jack Ma faded from the media scene only to return to China in early 2023 when the announcement was made that the group would be split into six separate units. The political authorities thus ensured that the nightmare of an octopus knowing everything about the 1.4 billion Chinese went away.

6.4. Conclusion

The emphasis placed by the Chinese authorities on sciences and technology creation had two consequences: (a) the boom of the research and development (R&D) function in many different businesses, which induced those companies to find ways to finance their R&D activities, and consequently ask for loans from banks or look for financial resources on the stock exchange and (b) the emergence of a new segment of high-tech start-up companies dedicated to the disruptive use of technology in banking and financing.

Surprisingly, the banking business which was considered a low-tech business in the West, i.e. a business which allocated no money to R&D, generated a different perspective in China. This low-tech business might have been stimulated by its high-tech companies' clients. The need to finance a massive investment in technology creation served as a drive to reconsider banking activity and to transform it with the use of technology, generating an impressive number of FinTech start-ups and unicorns. Interestingly, this vibrant sector has been entrusted to the private sector – the exact opposite of the banking sector. One of the most visible phenomena is the disappearance of cash and its replacement by payment using smartphones. The creation of ChiNext in Shenzhen, Star Market in Shanghai, and the Beijing board offers dedicated compartments for technology companies on the stock exchange platforms.

As emphasized in this chapter, because of the new role of technology in the financial system, the goal is now not only to collect money but also to collect data. Banks and other financial institutions are now fighting to gather data on consumers' behaviors, practices, value for money, and propensity to spare money, i.e. all attitudes related to money. By attracting such data easier than traditional banks, the new digital companies are changing the balance of power in their favor.

Takeaway from Chapter 6

1. For many years, the Chinese leadership wanted to anchor the country on the world R&D map. The technological domains to target were defined by the authorities. Incentives to invest were developed. And, all the necessary ingredients for establishing a true "national system of innovation" were put in place over the years: public research centers, universities involved in fundamental research, infrastructures such as science and technology parks, incubators for start-ups, unicorns, public and private companies doing R&D, a regulatory framework to protect innovators, and sources for the financing of technology creation.
2. R&D spending has to be sustained over a long period of time. The Chinese financial system was entrusted the responsibility of offering options for the financing of technology creation. Financial resources come from bank lending and from the stock exchange platforms. Two other options are venture capital (VC) and private

equity investment, which strongly developed in China with not only local actors but also foreign actors.

3. Dedicated boards were created on the three stock exchange platforms. The first place devoted to technology companies was the ChiNext – launched on the Shenzhen Stock Exchange in 2009. Shanghai followed in 2019 with the "Star Market" and Beijing did as well in 2021. All three have the same objective of enabling Chinese technology start-ups to access public savings. Without any surprise, these places are Sino-centric ones.

4. Two private internet companies – Alibaba and Tencent – created what is almost a duopoly with Alipay and WeChat Pay, respectively. The apps are third-party digital payment services that use smartphones. They profited from the low use of the China Union Pay card, and a situation where the smartphone percolated throughout Chinese society. All Chinese citizens (in cities and the countryside) enthusiastically embraced those options. That is an impressive technological achievement in the finance domain considering the size of the country. Consequently, Chinese consumers stopped using cash.

5. An impressive development of the so-called "FinTech" applications took place in China. These are start-ups working at the interface between technology and finance. The sector encompasses start-ups, unicorn, and large companies. The "FinTech" sector covers a large range of applications, including, for example, credit score analysis, digital banking, mobile wallets, cryptocurrency, and assets management.

6. Interestingly, the Chinese leadership decided to let this transformation emerge from the private sector, and gave the mandate to private entrepreneurs. This sector has been entrusted to the private companies – the exact opposite of the banking sector – because of its newness. The vibrant Chinese FinTech industry has its own market mechanisms and market forces.

7. China internet giants have now gained too much prestige and influence in the eyes of the authorities. The government is willing to reaffirm its control over the giants. The actors of this revolution are accumulating an impressive amount of data on the behavior of the Chinese consumers on an unprecedented scale. This challenges the

Chinese Communist Party: Jack Ma, through the large portfolio of companies in his group, has a much better knowledge of Chinese citizens than the party itself does. This is a real danger for the party, much more than the discourteous presentation Jack Ma did in October 2020, which criticized banks and financial authorities.

Bibliography

CB Insights, https://www.cbinsights.com/research/report/top-fintech-startups-2022/.

Dominique Jolly (2021), "Is China Going to Run the Digital World?" In Francesca Spigarelli and John R. McIntyre (editors), *The New Chinese Dream: Industrial Transition in the Post-Pandemic Era*, Palgrave Macmillan, Cham, pp. 69–85.

Dominique Jolly (2022), *The New Threat: China's Rapid Technological Transformation*, Palgrave Macmillan, Cham, Asian Business Series, 154 pages.

Fu Xiaolan, Chen Jin, and McKern, Bruce, *Oxford Handbook of China Innovation*, Oxford University Press, New York, 832 pages.

George S. Yip and Bruce McKern (2016), *China's Next Strategic Advantage: From Imitation to Innovation*, The MIT Press, Cambridge, MA, 304 pages.

Georges Haour and Maximilian von Zedtwitz (2016), *Created in China: How China is Becoming a Global Innovator*, Bloomsbury, London, 200 pages.

Hurun Report, Hurun Rich List (www.hurun.net).

Lewis James A. (2018), *Technological Competition and China*, Center for Strategic & International Studies (CSIS), available in online, 8 pages.

Mei Ni Yang (2021), *China Private Equity and Venture Capital – Too Big to Ignore*, Mercer Report, 19 pages.

Chapter 7

The Financial Impact of Chinese Societal Challenges

It is the opinion of the author that a number of societal challenges will have serious financial impacts on the future of China, including the following:

- the cost of addressing the ecological damage that the manufacturing and transportation industries have had upon the natural environment (inferior water quality, heavily polluted air, soil damage, etc.);
- the foreseeable costs to the Chinese citizens for their sanitary loss resulting from inappropriate living and healthy conditions due to the last 40 years of unrestrained economic development;
- the reduction of discrepancies regarding non-equitable revenue distribution (worse than in the USA), geographical gaps between the coastal areas and inland areas, and infrastructure development and medical treatment available between cities and the countryside. Moreover, this has to be done in parallel with the reduction of external dependencies on exports and imports for food, energy, and semiconductors;
- the development of domestic consumption and the pursuit of domestic technology creation (two core objectives of the 14th five-year plan[1]).

---

[1] The 14th plan stated this challenge with the concept of "dual circulation". China needs to reduce its dependency on exports. It has to rebalance growth toward the domestic economy. The challenge will be to stir up internal demand. Industries like insurance, health, tourism, and leisure will need to be stimulated and the banking system will have to find its way in this new framework.

Figure 7.1.   Societal Challenges Creating Immediate Financial Turmoil

Dealing with these challenges will require a long-term perspective. From a short-term perspective, as depicted in Figure 7.1, this chapter focuses on three major effective changes: (1) the issue of the real estate industry and the potential debt crisis and bubble explosion which it may generate, (2) the need for financing retirement pensions because of the aging population, and (3) increasing debt, especially in the corporate world.

7.1. Real Estate: Toward a Debt Crunch?

7.1.1. *A New Industry Resulting from Massive Urbanization*

Real estate has been a pillar of the Chinese economy since 1998 when the market was liberalized. It benefited from the great migration of people from the countryside to the cities: The Chinese urban population went from 450 million in 1998 to 900 million in 2021. The world's biggest property boom has been a profound driver of growth. Despite its core position in the economy, it has predominantly been driven by private companies to which the authorities gave the mandate to develop housing. Those firms made significant profits. Fortunes were made in a short time. And China is now the country with the highest rate of ownership as shown in Figure 7.2 (from Rogoff and Yang, 2020). What an impressive move over 20 years!

But the development of the industry came with several well-known negative externalities: high speculation, increasing prices, and the risk of overcapacity. There are empty flats when, at the same time, there are

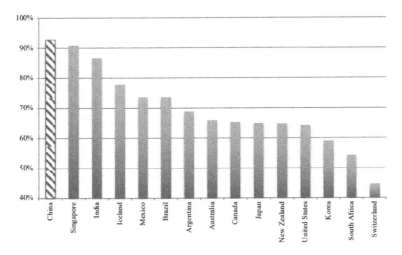

Figure 7.2.   Home Ownership by Country

Source: EMF Hypostat, IBGE: Instituto Brasileiro de Geografia e Estati, OECD Affordable Housing Database, Statistics Canada, Statistics of Japan, Statistics Singapore, Stats NZ, United States Census.

still Chinese people waiting for a decent place to live. The Chinese government decided to fight these problems by reinforcing rules for contracting debt (the so-called three red lines). The latter is what caused difficulties for several real estate companies – Evergrande being the first one.

7.1.2. *Social, Economic, and Financial Changes*

Real estate includes both residential and non-residential. The latter encompasses offices, commercial centers, hotels, stadiums, hospitals, and airports. Residential real estate is one of the areas where progress in terms of the quality of life of Chinese citizens is the most concrete and visible. In the recent past, Chinese families lived in overcrowded premises with bathrooms and kitchens shared by several families. Until the late 1990s, urban residents typically accessed an apartment through their work unit ("dan wei" in Chinese). The real estate market has been totally free only since the reform of 1998; privatization is therefore barely more than 25 years old! The migration of Chinese citizens from the countryside to the city, although limited by the internal passport, the "hukou", has created a strong demand for housing. This comes with renovation operations in downtown areas, where displaced residents usually receive subsidies to move to the suburbs.

China is a country that has poured millions of cubic meters of concrete in the recent decades; the European cement manufacturers Lafarge and Holcim were not mistaken in their commercial calculations and they have a big presence in China. As shown in Figure 7.3, these investments, without doubt, have driven some of China's recent growth.

Data reported in Table 7.1 show that the percentage of real estate in GDP went from 4% in 2000 to more than 7% in 2020. Real estate investment, combined with construction, accounts for over 15% of GDP. Some evaluations go even as high as 25%. Land sales have been an extraordinary source of income for local governments, which are the owners and have a monopoly on land sales. The two words "land sales" are used here as a shortcut but they might be misleading. The real contract term is not a sale, but the right to use the grounds for a period of 40 years. After this period, the local authorities will still be the owner of

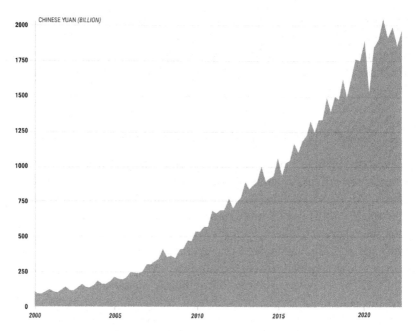

Figure 7.3.   Quarterly Real Estate Contribution to Chinese GDP

Source: National Bureau of Statistics.

Table 7.1. Real Estate to GDP

Year	China Real Estate (100 Million Yuan)	China GDP (100 Million Yuan)	China Real Estate/GDP (%)
2020	74,553	1,015,986	7.3
2019	69,632	990,865	7.0
2018	64,623	919,281	7.0
2017	57,086	832,036	6.9
2016	49,969	746,395	6.7
2015	42,574	688,858	6.2
2014	38,086	643,563	5.9
2013	35,340	592,963	6.0
2012	30,752	538,580	5.7
2011	27,781	487,940	5.7
2010	23,327	412,119	5.7
2009	18,761	348,518	5.4
2008	14,600	319,245	4.6
2007	13,714	270,092	5.1
2006	10,321	219,439	4.7
2005	8,483	187,319	4.5
2004	7,152	161,840	4.4
2003	6,157	137,422	4.5
2002	5,335	121,717	4.4
2001	4,706	110,863	4.2
2000	4,141	100,280	4.1

Source: National Bureau of Statistics.

the ground.[2] The real estate activity brings with it steelworks, cement producers, aluminum smelters, copper producers, glass-makers, furniture manufacturers, other producers of household goods, manufacturers of air conditioning systems, elevator operators, etc.

---

[2]Under those terms of contract, if the law is not modified, it means that this source of revenue is endless for local authorities.

7.1.3. The Emergence of Powerful Real Estate Developers

According to the rankings of the wealthiest Chinese people (cf. the Hurun List), it is in the real estate industry that some of the biggest Chinese fortunes have been made. Large private structures such as Wanda, Vanke, Evergrande, Country Garden, and China Resources Land have thus emerged. Table 7.2 depicts the profile of those five large companies.

Wanda is a private conglomerate, present in particular in real estate and in high-end shopping centers. For instance, the hundred Wanda Plazas are well known to the Chinese people and can be found in almost all major cities, as are high-end chains in cinemas and luxury hotels. Wanda is the largest company in this industry in China, and it is the world's leading real estate developer. Its founder, Wang Jianlin, is the son of a Chinese army officer who took part in Mao's Long March in the 1930s. After spending 17 years in the Chinese army, he started his business in the 1980s in Dalian (Liaoning). While in Dalian, Wang Jianlin met the red prince Bo Xilai who was mayor of the city. In 2009, Wang Jianlin transferred the headquarters to Beijing. Its clients, today, are local governments with development projects. Wang Jianlin aims to develop a division focused on entertainment and in particular, theme parks. After this, the group diversified abroad through acquisitions (American Multi-Cinema, Sunseeker, Infront Sports & Media, World Triathlon, and Legendary Entertainment).

China Vanke was founded in Shenzhen in 1984 by Wang Shi who remained in charge until 2017. He married the daughter of a former provincial governor and amassed political connections. The company became the first private developer in a state-controlled sector. Baoneng Insurance Group, also from Shenzhen, sought to take over Vanke in 2016, taking 25% of the capital. Vanke joined the public sphere in a reaction to a buyout of 29% of capital by Shenzhen Metro.

Founded by Xu Jiayin in 1996 in Guangzhou (Guangdong), Evergrande has become one of the largest real estate developers; Xu Jiayin gained fame through the acquisition of the Guangzhou Football Club. In 2009, Vanke turnover reached 60 billion yuan; Evergrande successfully fulfilled the IPO in Hong Kong and surpassed Vanke in 2016 in terms of total assets and turnover to become the leading company in the industry. Yet, since 2021, Evergrande (see Appendix 2) has been in complete turmoil due to repeated defaults of the company to reimburse its debt – which reached the colossal figure of $300 billion.

Table 7.2. Key Players in Real Estate

	Wanda	China Vanke	Evergrande (Hengda)	Country Garden	China Resources Land
Financial structure	Belongs to Wanda Group – a diversified conglomerate	Listed in Shenzhen (since 1991) and Hong Kong (since 2014), controlled (29%) by Shenzhen Metro Group	Listed in Hong Kong (since 2014)	Listed on HKSE (since 2007), Ping An (10%)	State-owned company, listed in HKSE (since 1996), subsidiary of China Resources Group
Founder	Wang Jianlin (1954–), member of the Chinese communist party, member of the Chinese People's Political Consultative Conference	Wang Shi (1951–), founder, chairman of the board (1988–2017), honorary chairman, passionate mountaineer	Xu Jiayin (1958–), member of the Chinese communist party, member of the Chinese People's Political Consultative Conference	Yang Guoqiang (1954–) transmitted his company to his daughter Yang Huiyuan (who is now one of the richest women in Asia)	Wu Bingqi (1972–), replaced Tang Yong, CEO from 1996 until August 2022 when he was excluded from the CCP for corruption
Position on Hurun list (2021)	32	na	172	47	na
Active in	Residential and non-residential projects (plaza, hotels, malls, …)	Started in residential, diversified in non-residential	Centered on residential		Mostly residential

(Continued)

Table 7.2.   (*Continued*)

	Wanda	China Vanke	Evergrande (Hengda)	Country Garden	China Resources Land
Headquarters	Beijing (originally headquartered in Dalian, Liaoning)	Shenzhen (Guangdong)	Guangzhou (Guangdong)	Foshan (Guangdong)	Shenzhen (Guangdong)
Founded	1988	1984	1996	1992	1994
Diversification outside China	USA, UK, and Australia	USA, UK, and Malaysia	No	Malaysia, Indonesia, and Australia	Centered on mainland China
Position in Fortune Global 500	380	160	122	147	69
Revenue 2021 (billion dollars)	50	66	72	73	28
Employees	156,000	140,000	123,000	102,000	38,000
Market capitalization (January 2020)	(went below $30 billion)	$54 billion	$38 billion	$37 billion	$37 billion
(January 2022)	NA	$39 billion	$3 billion	$21 billion	$33 billion

Source: Press and Value.today.

Country Garden suffered difficulties in 2021. In the summer of 2022, the Hong Kong Stock Market reacted poorly to the group's sale of new shares to raise funds – Yang Huiyan, daughter of the founder and majority shareholder of Country Garden, but also the richest woman in Asia ($23.7 billion in 2021), saw its fortune melt by half. In August, the company announced a fall in its half-year profits from 15 billion yuan ($2 billion) to 600 million ($88 million). Country Garden issued bonds as of September 2022 for five billion yuan guaranteed by China Bond Insurance (following a request from the Chinese regulator).

China Resources Land is a subsidiary of China Resources, a state-owned company known for its stake in the beer producer Snow (the company was created in Hong Kong in 1938, but is headquartered in Shenzhen). It is focused on residential properties in large cities. It is rated BBB+ by Fitch. In June 2022, China Resources Land had a debt of 270 billion yuan ($40 billion). The former CEO was fired in the summer of 2022 after being accused of corruption.

Beyond these five big players, there are thousands of real estate developers across China. Despite the high number of competitors, and thus the opportunity for a variety of styles and looks in group housing, apartment buildings are lacking in character; they are generally all the same from one city to another. This is in sharp contrast from the housing available in London, Paris, Rome, Berlin, Barcelona, and other major cities in the world. There are very limited numbers of masterful towers that identify Chinese cities.

7.1.4. *Easily Earned Money*

Since 2003, the Chinese government has officially promoted real estate as a pillar industry, and subsequently related industries have been developed. China's real estate industry experienced high growth until 2007. After the financial crisis in 2008, several leading real estate groups like Vanke and Evergrande experienced liquidity risk, leading to social uneasiness in some cities. In order to promote the economy, the Chinese government called for a series of economic measures to increase the investment of four trillion yuan in 10 strategic industries including steel, marine, automobile, and petrochemical areas, which indirectly stimulated the real estate market. From 2008 to 2017, domestic real estate investment grew to 11 trillion yuan and accumulated a total investment of 74 trillion yuan.

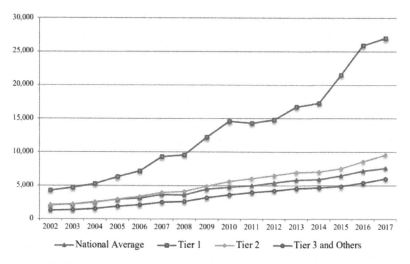

Figure 7.4.   Residential Housing Prices by City Tier

Source: National Bureau of Statistics.

Real estate is the quintessential speculation area whether it is the construction of apartment buildings, offices, and shopping centers or infrastructure. Between 2000 and 2011, prices of apartments increased 3.6-fold in Beijing, fourfold in Shanghai, and threefold in Guangzhou. Price increases differ according to the size of the city as shown in Figure 7.4. Tier 1 cities show impressive growth.

Many apartments remain empty. This is not because their owners fail to rent them out but because owners assume that there is much more to be gained from a capital gain than by renting the property: For a long time, the capital gain exceeded the expected rental income. In addition, the transfer costs do not exceed 0.5% in China and there is no tax on capital gains or property tax (despite this being tested in a few cities). These gains first served the generation that profited from privatization in the late 1990s. All that easily earned money could well guide these annuitants into idleness. Speculation, on the other hand, poses a problem for new generations who are struggling to finance the purchase of their homes.

7.1.5.   The Risk of Bubbles due to Irrational Hypertrophy

The days of easy money are over. Figure 7.5 shows the evolution of square meters sold from 2010 to 2021. In 2010, 1.05 billion square meters

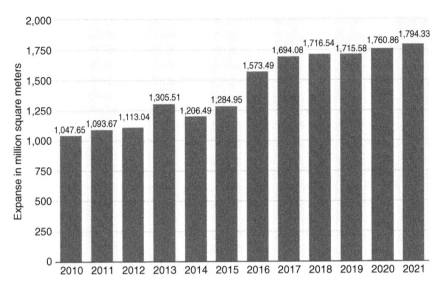

Figure 7.5.   Floor Space of Real Estate Sold in China (from 2010 to 2021)

Source: Statista, 2023.

were sold in China. In 2021, the figure reached 1.79 billion. If the urbanization movement continues, its pace will drop and this decline of growth rate will have an effect on the real estate market. With the exception of top-tier cities, real estate seems stabilized – the drop in transaction volume is noticeable and demand is slowing as supply continues to advance.

Chinese real estate is regularly cited as a sector with a bubble. A bubble is defined as an excessive increase in prices relative to the fundamental value of traded goods and incomes. Such an increase tends to worsen as a result of the speculative behavior it generates, i.e. purchase decisions made with the sole purpose of reselling the property for more money. The usual criterion to examine is the ratio of the average house prices to the average annual household income. The acceptable ratio is considered to be around 3 or 4. Beyond 4, the ratio is usually considered risky and an indicator of a bubble. As illustrated in Figure 7.6, in China, the ratio went up to 8 in Tier 3 cities, up to 10 in Tier 2 cities, and even much more in some coastal cities, i.e. Tier 1 cities. This is why home ownership is becoming increasingly difficult in large cities and also given the large increase of required down payment.

The authorities are thus engaged in a continuous fight against overheating. To calm the market, the government restrained the enthusiasm of

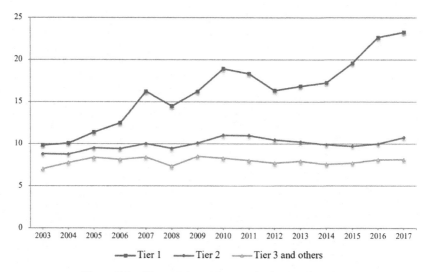

Figure 7.6.   Home Price-to-Income Ratios by City Tiers

multi-owners in the early 2010s. Concern over the real estate market stems from the skyrocketing of vacant flats waiting to be sold: They have gone from 150 million square meters vacant in 2007 to 500 million in 2013. Unsold housing went down to 450 billion in 2016. It went back to 250 billion at the end of 2020. The stock is still high; the crisis did not lead to de-stocking. Developers (like Vanke) have been forced into discounts to ensure de-stocking. Authorities in Meishan (Sichuan), for example, have gone so far as to team up with developers to provide subsidies to attract rural people to new housing developments. As of 2022, there were still more than 230 million square meters of unfinished housing developments.

The effect has even been felt on the side of material suppliers such as cement maker Anhui Conch, steel maker Baosteel, or construction equipment suppliers such as Sany (see Appendix 3), Zoomlion, and Hyundai. In turn, foreign countries which export natural resources to fuel Chinese construction (to take just one example, Australia makes 50% of its exports to China) are also feeling the consequences of a drop in Chinese real estate. The effect is also perceived in the banking industry. Banks which heavily lent to the real estate industry are facing difficulties as borrowers fail to reimburse their loans. One serious case is that of China Minsheng (see the vignette).

Vignette: China Minsheng

China Minsheng Bank Corp. (CMBC) was founded in 1996 by Jing Shuping (1918–2009) – a Chinese businessman connected enough with the authorities to obtain a banking license. It has long been an exception in the Chinese financial landscape. It is the largest private bank in the country in terms of assets. Yet, it remains weak in retail banking with assets of two trillion yuan (end of 2021) compared to three trillion yuan for Ping An Bank or 10 trillion yuan for China Merchants Bank. CMBC has been designated by the Chinese authorities as a national systemically important bank.

The issue is that CMBC is among the banks that could be the victim of the real estate debt crisis. The bank saw a 36% decline in profits in 2020. At the end of 2021, its shares in Shanghai closed at 3.9 yuan ($0.61), down 25% from the beginning of 2021 – one of the worst performances of the Bloomberg World Banks index. The bank has made it a priority to reduce its holdings of real estate debt for 2022. It is potentially more affected than state-owned giants like Agricultural Bank of China or ICBC. According to Citi Group, it might have $20 billion of exposure to high-risk developers, or 27% of its capital. The bank is one of Evergrande's biggest creditors. It has also lent to China Fortune Land Development, another struggling developer, and to Sichuan Languang Development, Tahoe Group, and Oceanwide Holdings – medium- to high-risk real estate companies. CMBC is likely to struggle to collect these debts as property company sales have plunged and their financial stress has increased. The entry of an outsider into the bank's capital has not been excluded. CMBC has been rated "BB+" by Fitch Ratings.

Minsheng intends to base its future growth with retail banking and lending on small and medium enterprises – areas that have the support of the Chinese authorities. The bank may find salvation in wealth management for which it obtained a license from the authorities in June 2022 to launch a unit; Minsheng Wealth Management will be based in Beijing.

The downturn in the real estate market could be accompanied by an overcapacity crisis. The question today is whether the correction in house prices will be gradual or sudden. The risk of dropping out exists considering the anxiety-provoking cases of Ordos (Inner Mongolia) or Zhengzhou New District (Henan), i.e. new towns where occupancy rates remain below 25%. Smaller towns such as Qinhuangdao (in Hebei, the province surrounding Beijing) are also facing an oversupply of housing and funding disruption. In Yuncheng (Shanxi), the closure of the Highsee Iron & Steel Group steelworks came with its procession of devastation: 10,000 employees left behind, empty apartments, deserted hotels, etc.

A real estate crash would be socially explosive – especially for those who plan to finance their retirement through the resale of apartments. Real estate could become the black hole in the Chinese economy; President Xi Jinping's "Chinese Dream" could turn into a nightmare. Yet, the government still has some slack: it can have cash by carrying out privatizations of state-owned companies. Incidentally, more and more lawyers are taking the place of government mediation in the settlement of disputes between buyers and developers and between developers and local authorities.

Evergrande announced that the industry was experiencing difficulties at the end of 2021 (see the vignette). The critical turning point was when stakeholders were waiting for the Chinese government to intervene. It is likely that the government will not let Evergrande go bankrupt as real estate is key from an economic perspective, but is also critical for societal concerns. The government asked big actors from the real estate sector to take over parts of Evergrande. The government can expect banks to support bad loans considering the very large scope of big Chinese banks (we heard a lot about Evergrande from September to December 2021; the fact that very little was said during 2022 might be due to the new lockdown in many large cities as many projects were stopped). Financial issues can be under control when the debt is domestic, i.e. in yuan; in that case, entrepreneurs might try to use their political power to benefit from new debt to cover their existing debt if they are aligned with the three red lines. The issue is mostly when those real estate companies borrowed in dollars. To maintain trust with foreign lenders, a solution has to be found for effective reimbursement of those loans. The other issue is to identify which new economic activity could replace real estate in the future; Chinese authorities must give a job to all those people currently working for the real estate value chain: land, material supply, construction, and commercialization.

7.1.6. *Chinese Real Estate Developers Have Diversified Outside of China*

Several developments have been carried out in Thailand, Malaysia, and South Korea. Some Chinese developers also found a niche in Kenya and

Vignette: Seven Lessons from the Fall of Evergrande (see Appendix 2)

1. The excesses of Chinese real estate – skyrocketing prices, runaway debt, dependence of municipalities on income from the sale of land, corruption, vacant properties for years, and even ghost towns – were already known. The ticking time bomb was in place.

2. The Evergrande case is one of the signs of the end of the Chinese economic miracle. We are at a pivotal moment. What has been the main engine of the Chinese economy has been frozen for at least a decade. And if real estate is to crash, what will be the future engine of China's economic growth?

3. The case illustrates the omnipotence of the Chinese regulator. The collapse of Evergrande is the consequence of the stricter rules wanted by the Chinese state. Real estate developers are mostly private companies in a competitive situation. But it is the government that holds the reins.

4. The problem is systemic. Multiple interactions generate chain reactions, at least in the Chinese real estate sector on the side of shareholders, creditors, suppliers, and employees. In the expected reactions, the difficulties of Evergrande could lead to a mistrust of the middle class and clients of the promoters and could be the basis of social uprisings. And by extension, it is also the authority of the Chinese Communist Party that could be challenged in the context of destabilization of the economy.

5. Chinese real estate is making a lot of people nervous, but the problem shouldn't go far beyond China's borders even if future off-shore bond issuers will reduce their confidence in Chinese borrowers. The activity is Chinese, with land under the control of Chinese local authorities, developments made by Chinese promoters, Chinese customers, constructions built by Chinese construction companies, and financing coming largely from Chinese banks. The activity therefore cannot be compared to the threats hanging over the Taiwanese production of semiconductors, which is a global product requiring suppliers throughout the world, which finds customers throughout the planet.

6. In these moments of tension, the cards are redistributed. Under pressure, assets are sold off and acquired at low prices by economic agents. There are therefore players in the sector who will disappear but also others who are more capable, will be able to hold their own in the context of this debacle, and who could be strengthened in a few years.

> *(Continued)*
>
> 7. The fortune amassed in record time by the founding boss collides with the public mission of its interlocutors, whether they are local governments for the purchase of land and for obtaining construction permits, or state-owned banks which finance the projects. This large gap is often at the origin of operations tainted by corruption.

South Africa. One of the most significant overseas operations was conducted by Greenland (a Chinese state-owned company) in New York in association with Forest City, a US partner. Private developer China Vanke also has a project in San Francisco.

Beijing needs to find an alternative to housing and infrastructure to sustain its future economic development. The Chinese leadership is willing to base future development on domestic consumption, technology creation (as stressed in Chapter 6), and advanced manufacturing, yet there is no guarantee this will work.

7.2. Aging Population: How to Finance Retirement Pensions?

The economic equation of retirement pensions is complicated. Many economic trends do not go in the right direction: The growth rate of the economy is going down, the working force is declining, China's population is aging rapidly, and is beginning to shrink.

7.2.1. *The Negative Consequences of the One-Child Policy*

The one-child policy came at the end of the 1970s. It made it possible to bring down population growth very sharply. The proven change helped China transform itself because there were millions of fewer mouths to feed. The one-child policy, although it has been rather well accepted by a resigned Chinese population, was not only an obstacle to individual freedoms but has also induced several major negative externalities over time.

The first externality is that the country must now deal with a drop in the proportion of young people in the population – which leads to a drop in the active population and therefore a loss of the economic advantage associated with this pool of labor. The second consequence is that the proportion of elderly Chinese people is growing to alarming proportions. China may soon have the highest proportion of elderly people in the world. This is also a problem for young people because, in a Confucian culture, children have to take care of their parents when they get older. This drop in the ratio of the number of working people to the number of retirees casts doubt on the country's ability to provide seniors with a serene retirement.

Since the Plenum of the 18th Congress (in 2013), a second child is allowed for couples in which one of the two members was born as the only child (previously both partners had to be the only children). Since 2015, all couples have been allowed to have two children. These relaxations of the one-child policy came too late, and have not had any effect on demography so far. Chinese couples have to want a second child, and this is no more the case. When countries get richer, which is the case with China, people have fewer children. The trend has been initiated. In 2017, the number of births decreased (17.23 million vs. 17.86 in 2016). It fell again by two million in 2018 (15.23 million). It stood at 14.65 in 2019, fell to 12.02 million in 2020, and fell further to 10.62 million in 2021. Beyond the costs (education, real estate, health, etc.), this drop in the birth rate is also due to a reduction in the number of women of childbearing age and a drop in fertility. The Political Bureau of the CCP has again relaxed the constraint, and since 2021 couples are allowed to have three children!

7.2.2. *China with White Hair*

The Middle Empire is showing a noticeable aging population. A society is considered to be aging when the proportion of people over 60 years exceeds 10%. At the end of 2014, China had 212.4 million people aged 60 or over, or 15.5% of its total population. At the end of 2016, the figure rose to 231 million, or 16.7% of the population. In 2018, 249 million Chinese were over 60 years of age, or 17% of the population. Figure 7.7 shows this long-term and overwhelming pattern. By 2030, the figure could reach 330 million, or 24% of the population.

The trend remains the same even if we change the threshold to 65 years as the beginning of the aging population. Thus, the number of people over 65 represents 137.6 million, or 10.1% of the total population; this proportion could reach 18% in 2030 while it was 9% in 2011.

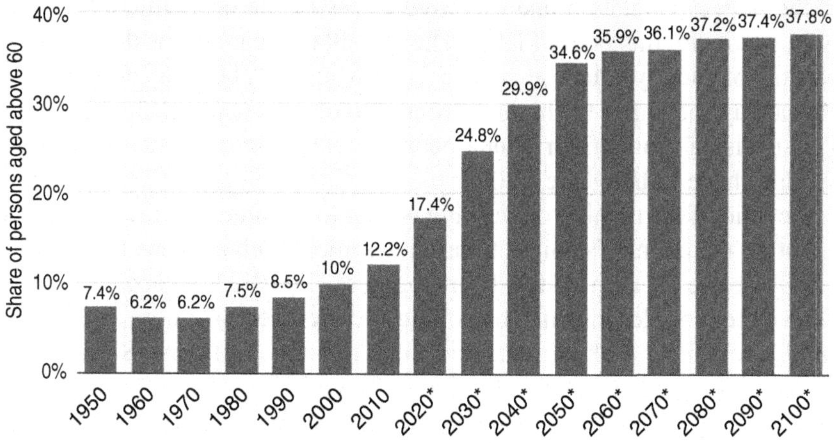

Figure 7.7.   Share of Population Above 60 Years of Age in China from 1951 to 2020 (and Forecast until 2100)

Source: Statista, 2022.

7.2.3. The Financing of Pensions

The general mechanism is a tax of 28% on salary with 20% paid by the employer, and the other 8% by the employee. The current resources are sufficient to cover pensions today – however, this will not last. There will be more and more pensioners. In addition, there are fewer and fewer contributors as China is experiencing a shortage of young people entering the labor market. As shown in Figure 7.8, the labor force in China has stabilized and is now shrinking. Many observers question the country's ability to double the related health budget.

The Chinese Academy of Social Sciences (CASS) has calculated that under current conditions, pension funds will be empty in 2035 due to the drying up of the workforce. As a result, China will be old before being rich.

7.2.4. Raise the Retirement Age

Chinese citizens retire on average much earlier than Westerners, i.e. around 50 for blue-collar women, 55 for white-collar women, and 60 for men. That's a legacy from a period when life expectancy was much lower than it is today. Lifespan is still lengthening: Expectancy has increased from 72 years in 2000 to 76 in 2016. For comparison, it is 69 years in India, 79 in the USA, and 82 in France.

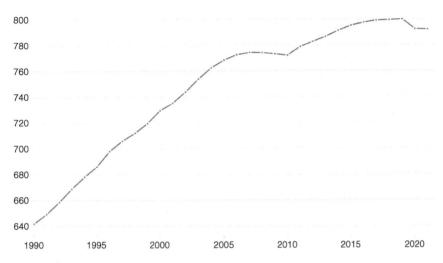

Figure 7.8. Chinese Labor Force (in Million, from 1990 to 2021)
Source: World Bank, 2022.

To solve the problem of having sufficient funds to cover the pensions of the elderly in China in the future, it will be enough to ask seniors to work additional years (this will also reduce skills losses). In fact, the government plans to gradually postpone the end of working life by five years through a gradual increase in the legal retirement age. The retirement age has now been moved from 60 to 63 for men. Will this be enough to absorb the increase in life expectancy? Raising the retirement age is likely to meet opposition from grassroots workers in factories and may slow down the entry of new generations into the labor market.

7.2.5. *Senior Citizens Also Offer an Economic Opportunity*

Senior citizens are also a huge market. As foreign companies are allowed to establish themselves freely in this market, the English company Starcastle and the American firm Cascade have come to push their pawns. With their recognized know-how, the French companies Orpea, Domus Vi, and Colisée Patrimoine are also present and are finding a way to develop in the face of a stagnant French market. Orpea opened a wholly owned subsidiary (Baoting Xianlin). Domus Vi has established a branch in Shanghai. Colisée Patrimoine signed a cooperative agreement with China Merchants Group. Chinese companies have sought access to know-how through acquisition; this, for example, explains Zhonghong's acquisition of Brookdale Senior Living for $4 billion in 2017. The impact is not just on nursing homes. The development of the senior market will also affect areas of activity such as pharmacy and tourism. The unprecedented development that retirement homes (for the rich) are experiencing clashes somewhat with Confucian values. As previously mentioned, in Confucian culture, it is assumed that children will take care of their parents when they get older.

7.3. Increasing Debt

Before 2000, there was no debt issue in China; the question arose only recently. Other Asian countries such as Japan, Thailand, or Malaysia also significantly increased their debt-to-GDP ratio in the recent past. This can be explained by the Asian financial crisis in 1997. The USA is also heavily indebted.

This rise in Chinese debt coincides with the launch of the recovery plan sought by China in response to the 2008 crisis. Following the worldwide financial crisis, the Chinese government decided to put emphasis on maintaining economic growth. To do so, the State Council launched a huge stimulus plan. No less than 4,000 billion yuan ($600 billion) was made available to local governments and state-owned enterprises willing to invest in infrastructures (roads, railroads, airports, etc.). Chinese banks lent more in the first semester of 2009 than over the years 2007 and 2008.

7.3.1. *Is the Chinese Economy Developing an Addiction to Debt?*

As a percentage of Chinese GDP (which declined to 6–7% per year before COVID), the total debt (government, companies, and individuals) has increased from 160% to 300% of the GDP from 2008 to 2018. Figure 7.9 shows how debt has inflated by categories.

There is a convergence between several different sources on the accumulation of private and public debt: In March 2014, Standard Chartered Bank placed the figure at 230% – the figure would even reach 250% of the GDP in June. Another source, the International Monetary Fund, gives a ratio of 200% of the GDP in April 2014 and 240% in August 2016. The total debt flirted with 300% of the GDP in 2018. All the commentators were unanimous in stating the danger. In comparison, the USA was at 260%, the UK at 277%, and Japan at 415% – but these are not emerging economies (having a large proportion of poor people and numerous empty apartments).

Debt cannot grow faster than the economy indefinitely. If there is a financial crisis, investment will shrink and the economy will shrink accordingly.

7.3.2. *Public Debt Has Grown*

According to the Chinese Court of Auditors, the public debt amounted to 56% of the GDP by the end of 2013. This percentage includes the debt of the central government and that of the local governments (provinces, prefectures, and districts) – 12.4 trillion CNY for the central government (1.64 trillion euros) and 17.9 trillion for local governments (2.37 trillion euros), or 30.3 trillion in total (4.01 trillion euros). The percentage approached 100% in recent years.

Debt alarms, especially of local governments, regularly come to the forefront. The debt that provinces, cities, districts, counties, and villages have encountered, in fact, increased since the launch of the 2008 stimulus plan, raising concerns about the stability of the financial system. In this context, it is the country that concentrates a high proportion of public expenditure for education, health, social protection, and environmental protection (in any case, much more than the countries of the OECD with federal systems). All local communities have taken on debt to invest heavily in infrastructure.

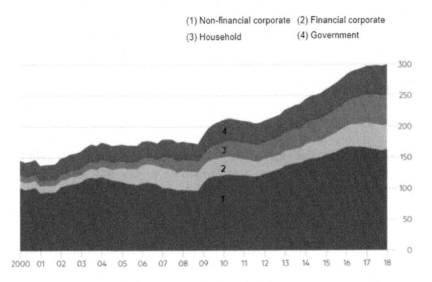

Figure 7.9.   Chinese Debt by Sector (% of GDP)

Source: IIF ©*FT*.

The central power wants local governments to better control their financial risks. Beijing, for example, asked the city of Baotou (Inner Mongolia) to stop its metro project – doubting its ability to repay. The pace of the projects in Hohhot (Inner Mongolia) and Wuhan (Hubei) were slowed down. On the other hand, the projects of Suzhou (Jiangsu), Nanjing (Jiangsu), and Changchun (Jilin) were approved by the central government (yet, the terminal of the last line (#2) of Suzhou remains mostly deserted). The Chinese government is, however, less indebted than European governments.

7.3.3. Corporate Debt Is Exploding

The growth of the debt in China is mainly due to companies' borrowing. Companies' debt is roughly twice the GDP while the debt of the government and of the households equals the GDP. This debt had fueled GDP growth. It could be dangerous as the GDP growth rate goes down: It might be difficult for companies to reimburse – especially when debt was contracted to finance infrastructures in remote rural areas which will not generate enough revenue to pay it back as people migrate. Overdevelopment might turn into a nightmare.

In this context, Chinese companies (and Chinese households) are increasingly in debt. It is the corporate debt that makes the difference: It represented 98% of the GDP in 2008 and it was 160% in 2015. These figures are in line with the estimates of Macquarie Securities, which assesses the debt of public companies at 88% of GDP, private companies at 55%, local governments at 41%, and central government at only 14%. In Asia, Chinese companies have the highest debt-to-capital ratio (around 85%). This is easily understood: China Railways, for example, was not able to build the world's largest high-speed train network in little more than a decade without going into debt. These signals come from the International Monetary Fund, rating agencies, and investment banks. Moody's, for example, downgraded its rating of China. The expected restrictions on credit will undoubtedly affect businesses first (which have been less supported than state companies have been by banks which are themselves state-owned).

Household debt has also grown: From around 20% of GDP in 2008, it represented 50% of GDP 10 years later. This is a real change in behavior in a society accustomed to savings.[3] Consumer loans have been on the rise

---

[3] Surveys regularly show that Chinese citizens save much more of their household disposable income (30–40%) than British and North American (10–20%), European, and even Japanese and South Korean households.

since 2011, notably through private loan platforms (P2P) such as Lufax, Dianrong, or Madai Finance (cf. Chapter 6). But these represent only a few percent of China's total household debt.

7.3.4. *Internal Debt*

As in Japan, the debt in China is domestic. It is mostly held by Chinese actors, and dominated by state-owned entities. State-owned banks owned and controlled by SASAC (see Appendix 3) lend money to state-owned companies owned and controlled by SASAC (it's the dad who lends money to mom). And private companies contracted loans with Chinese banks. A small portion of this debt is detained by foreign entities. Based on this situation came the idea that because this debt is internal, risk is mostly supported by local actors, and consequently it would be a limited issue for foreign banks. However, this may not be the case as there might be some externalities: The collapse of the Chinese financial system will have some repercussions abroad as the world economy has become dependent on China and some Western companies, especially in Germany, have created a strong dependence on the Chinese market.

Chinese debt is internal (it is financed by Chinese savings) – unlike, for example, debt from Turkey or the USA which borrow abroad (the USA with Treasury Bonds). Two-thirds of corporate debt comes from state-owned enterprises that have taken on debt with state banks. Everything is therefore under the control of the government. Of course, China does not depend on foreign capital. Chinese debt abroad is less than $1.5 trillion – a modest 13% of GDP by the end of 2016. It was only since May 2016 that the country had opened up its debt market to foreigners.

7.4. Conclusion

China is facing several situations in the economy which are leading to stress on its financial resources: (a) the real estate market, after being a strong engine of growth and the origin of many private fortunes, now faces severe tensions, (b) increasing pressures for finding ways to pay for retirement pensions of the elderly as the labor force is shrinking, and (c) increasing debt especially with companies, while the growth rate of the economy is declining.

The Chinese government has been able to avoid an explosion of the real estate bubble until now and is working on an extension of the retirement age. Unfortunately, all the issues covered in this chapter can potentially have a systemic impact far beyond the sector considered. And, alas, these demands come as the economy has been slowing structurally for more than 10 years – beyond the negative impacts of COVID. China will also have to respond to hidden costs such as addressing the destruction of some of its natural environment in the past 40 years.

Two different scenarios can be expected. On the one hand, Chinese citizens are not afraid. They trust the authorities. It is fascinating that each time there is a problem in China, the government is perceived as the Messiah who will deal with those issues. On the other hand, protests against the zero-COVID strategy have shown that there is a potential for social upheaval in Chinese society. A strong reaction can be expected from the proletariat when they understand that this is the end of the story for the working class, and that they are going to be stuck in their current situation as few changes will emerge.

Takeaway from Chapter 7

1. On a long-term basis, China will have to face the cost of several societal challenges, namely, the cost of repairing ecological damage, the cost of restoring the bad sanitary situation, and the cost of filling geographical discrepancies. Other societal challenges are more pressing and must be dealt with on an immediate basis. These are the potential crises of real estate, the financing of retirement pensions, and the increasing debt burden.

2. The liberalization of the real estate sector in 1998 restored Chinese private property (after having been erased in 1949). The government entrusted private companies with the responsibility to develop this activity in a competitive environment. The entire value chain of the industry benefited from a massive urbanization movement, and took a predominant share of the Chinese economy. The sector became another fringed oligopoly, with some major private companies and thousands of small real estate developers across China.

3. After being a hotbed for financial speculation, the real estate market is moving toward maturity. The days of making easy money are

over, and overcapacity is threatening the system. Chinese real estate is regularly cited as a sector in a financial bubble. This is why Chinese authorities decided to fight overheating and enacted new rules to reduce the indebtedness of developers; once again, it is the government who holds the reins.

4. The overreliance on debt led to financial pressures which are threatening the future of many real estate companies, Evergrande being the principal case. The issue is that this debt problem is systemic. All the participants in the entire real estate value chain might be impacted: customers, shareholders, suppliers, and employees – including banks like China Minsheng Bank. And the social risk is real.

5. The demographic challenge of China is well known: The proportion of elderly people is increasing, while the proportion of young people is decreasing, including the active population. On top of this, the overall population has started to decline, the number of births is dropping, and will not rebound in the near future. The issue is the financing of retirement pensions.

6. The growth rate of the economy is declining, and China may soon have the highest proportion of elderly people in the world. This situation is another illustration of the sad side of size effects: China will have to deal with hundreds of millions of people over 60 years of age. The government plans to gradually postpone the end of working life by five years through a gradual increase of the legal retirement age.

7. Public and private debt has constantly increased since the 2000s, especially since the 2009 stimulus government plan. This is the case for the central government, local governments (provinces, cities, districts, and counties), state-owned companies, private companies, and households. And, corporate debt has exploded while the growth rate of the economy is declining. The risk of failure is high. Fortunately, this debt is internal.

Bibliography

Hurun Report, Hurun Rich List, www.hurun.net.
National Bureau of Statistics, www.stats.gov.cn/english/.

Rogoff Kenneth S. and Yang Yuanchen (2020), "Peak China Housing", Working Paper 27697, National Bureau of Economic Research (NBER), Cambridge, MA, USA, http://www.nber.org/papers/w27697.

Zhao Litao (2017), *China's Development: Social Investment and Challenges*, World Scientific, Singapore, 176 pages.

Chapter 8

New Perspectives

The Chinese financial landscape is changing rapidly. Three aspects will be considered in this chapter: (1) the opportunities and the challenges attached to the Belt & Road Initiative (BRI), (2) the opening to foreign banking, and (3) the future of the Chinese currency.

8.1. The Belt & Road Initiative: A New Bet on Infrastructures

China proactively put in place a major initiative that will impact the 21st century: The Belt & Road Initiative aims at connecting China and Central Asia with Europe and Africa through investments in infrastructures for a total of $1 trillion. The rationale is to reproduce abroad the Chinese infrastructure strategy which served the economic development of the country so well (as explained in Chapter 4).

8.1.1. *The Most Significant Chinese Geopolitical Initiative in Decades*

Everyone remembers the "Silk Road" from their history lessons at school – and retains positive memories of it. The original Silk Road developed as a major trading network due to the infatuation of the West for silk, a refined fabric that only China then knew how to produce. More broadly, it was a bridge between East and West, which also served to transfer ideas and know-how.

The concept of the "New Silk Road" was skillfully developed by President Xi Jinping in 2013 (one year after taking office) in Astana during a visit to Kazakhstan (China's biggest neighbor after Russia and India, and also a former Soviet republic). Rail and pipelines replace caravans and camels. HP computers and inflatable beach buoys replace silk fabrics and spices. The road is not only land but also maritime and digital. The key word is "connectivity", not only between East and West, but also at the level of all intermediate segments like the China–Pakistan Economic Corridor (see the vignette) at the regional level. Although the announcement went almost unnoticed in 2013, the theme has since become the centerpiece of President Xi's foreign policy and international economic strategy. The geopolitical message is strong: It is about connecting China and Central Asia to Europe and Africa, i.e. facilitating economic cooperation with other regions and countries.

The operation was later renamed "One Belt, One Road" – "belt" for the new land route and "road" for the sea route.[1] As shown in Figure 8.1, the major axis starts from Chongqing, crosses Sichuan, Qinghai, and Xinjiang, and joins Europe via Kazakhstan, Russia, Iran, and then Turkey. China also wants to develop and secure sea routes to the Middle East and Europe: from the South China Sea to the Indian Ocean, East Africa, the Red Sea, and the Mediterranean Sea (sea transport is much less expensive than land transport). The land corridors between Xinjiang and Pakistan, and through Burma and Laos, complement the existing networks from the eastern Chinese ports for both export and import flows (energy, agri-food products, etc.).

The latest semantic development occurred because the Chinese authorities have been talking about the "Belt & Road Initiative" since 2018. This label is less restrictive. This initiative covers multiple objectives: economic, financial, geopolitical, military, cultural, and also image. Many projects have been branded with the BRI logo. Some Chinese companies have nevertheless labeled some real estate developments as "BRI" despite the fact that they were in fact casinos; tricksters were very common.

---

[1] The acronym OBOR was transformed by some writers into "Our Bulldozers, Our Rules", which is cynical, but not meaningless.

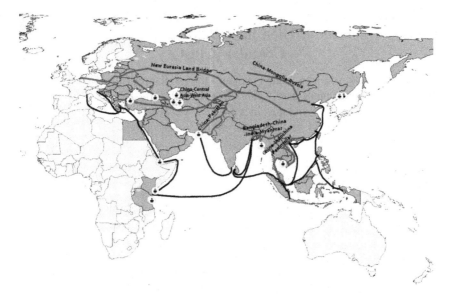

Figure 8.1. The Map of the "Belt & Road Initiative"
Source: World Bank 2019.

8.1.2. *A Trillion Euro Initiative to Spread Chinese Geopolitical Influence*

This is a colossal project, unparalleled in the history of mankind. This initiative takes shape through trade agreements, investments in transport networks (roads, railways, ports, etc.), energy production and transportation (dams, power stations, nuclear power stations, oil pipelines, gas pipelines, etc.), and financial support structures – all means of investing the extraordinary Chinese foreign exchange reserves (over three trillion euros) abroad rather than in US Treasury bills. One of the components is also the construction of a communication network with its batch of optical fibers, international submarine cables, satellites, and other related equipment. The China–Pakistan Economic Corridor (CPEC), announced in 2015, is a good illustration (see the vignette).

These are incredible bets considering that a pipeline is built for a few tens of years, but at the same time, the tap can be turned off overnight (as illustrated by what happened to the Nord Stream oil pipeline since the

Vignette: The China–Pakistan Economic Corridor (CPEC)

The project aims at upgrading Pakistan's infrastructure. The plan is to build a railway line of more than 1,800 km between Kachgar in the west of the province of Xinjiang and the cities on the south coast of Pakistan, Karachi (province of Sindh) and Gwadar (Baluchistan province). This Sino-Pakistani corridor also has a highway link, numerous (coal) power generators, power lines, an oil pipeline, a gas pipeline, and the deep-water port of Gwadar. This equipment will also have to compete with the renewal of the Iranian Chabahar port undertaken by India. It represents an initial investment of more than $46 billion, which increased to $62 billion as of 2020. Loans are provided by the Exim Bank of China, the China Development Bank, and the ICBC (cf. Chapter 4).

This is the price for China avoiding the Strait of Malacca and the South China Sea. It is also a key link to foster the development of Xinjiang. There are still some worries in Islamabad about the dependence created on China, making Pakistan equivalent to one of its provinces. In addition, the Chinese contractors face opposition from the supporters of independence for Baluchistan; several attacks have been perpetrated against Chinese contractors' interests.

Russian attack of Ukraine in February 2022). A 3,000-km high-speed train line has also been planned between Kunming (Yunnan) and Singapore; construction has been completed between Kunming and Laos (an investment of $6.7 billion). The construction of 30 nuclear power plants is in the pipeline in the countries concerned. China is using the BRI to penetrate as far as the Balkans (Albania, Bosnia and Herzegovina, Macedonia, Montenegro, and Serbia) – notably with infrastructure projects.

8.1.3. *All Good for China, Maybe for Recipients*

The BRI is the answer to a real infrastructure need in the targeted countries. But, on a short-term basis, it would primarily benefit Chinese companies that manufacture oil pipelines, high-speed trains, port cranes, telephone equipment, etc. And Chinese-made trucks and excavators will be used for the construction of this infrastructure. These are opportunities to deal with Chinese overcapacity in the production of steel, cement, and other construction materials, except that transportation of cement or steel is not economically efficient. It is up to European companies to conquer a part of these future infrastructure markets.

And it is Chinese banks that will finance the projects (cf. Chapter 4): China Development Bank, ICBC, China Exim Bank, Bank of China, China Construction Bank, and the New Development Bank. The new Asian Infrastructure Investment Bank (AIIB) which was created in 2014 and started operations in 2016 with an endowment of a hundred billion initial could be specifically responsible for financing these projects (cf. Section 4.3). The Silk Road Fund is also a new vehicle formed to help with the financing. It must be said that the Chinese banks often make getting loan approval conditional to the selection of Chinese contractors.

The benefits for the foreign countries depend on their abilities to foster economic growth on the basis of those infrastructure projects. Local entrepreneurs will gain access to good transportation links, to stabilized electricity supply, etc. But, they also need to bundle all the other resources needed to launch a new venture. And finally, in order to be beneficial to countries, the recipient needs to demonstrate its ability to sustain the diverse risks and to reimburse the loans.

8.1.4. *A New Wave with the Potential to Change the World Order*

The Belt & Road Initiative is not only economic-driven but is also a political opportunity for China to increase its international influence and to consolidate its position as a global superpower. Russian domination of the economy of Central Asia is challenged and the USA finds itself in the background. From the projected flows, it is striking to see that nothing is going to North America or South America. The conception is that of a Eurasian vision of the world. The new Silk Road is likely to help the development of the countries concerned – much like the Marshall Plan was central to the regeneration of Europe after World War II. The consequences were highlighted by the World Bank in a 2019 report.

The operation could well resemble a second opening policy for China after that of 1978. However, if like President Deng Xiaoping's open door policy, the project can carry the future growth of China, the similarities stop there. It is no longer a question, as in 1978, of using external forces to develop the interior of the country, but of using Chinese resources to develop countries outside China. And China cannot exert the political control it exercises over its provinces over these countries. Unlike its internal development, China has to accept the reality of the opposition that the implementation of its program provokes. It needs to gain the confidence of countries as it grows stronger, is more assertive, and strengthens its military forces.

China is seeking to extend its area of influence and to prepare a long-term rent, both economic (with the development of activity) and financial (due to the repayment of loans granted). The BRI is a strategy to shift the rules of world trade, just like the Pacific and Atlantic oceans were dominated by the USA in a recent history. With the idea of linking three continents together, it could allow China to extend its soft power both in culture and in the economy. The Chinese authorities argue that more business means more jobs and more stability. Chinese investments in infrastructure appear to adapt to foreign local cultures. This is the case in Pakistan where the China–Pakistan economic corridor (CPEC) has been created, the financing tools for which will partly come from Islamic finance. It is estimated that the CPEC would create over 700,000 jobs and add 2.5 points to Pakistan's GDP growth.

But it is also more debt which is already a problem for some of the countries concerned. Thus, the targeted countries are mainly financially risky countries such as Pakistan, Cambodia, and Sri Lanka. Will each country that goes into debt be able to support its debt? Or will it fall into a debt trap? The question was asked in particular by the IMF. In fact, if these countries fail to repay, it does not matter, as the Chinese government will end up owning the infrastructure concerned.

8.1.5. *Security in Question*

More than 70 rather disparate countries are involved – mainly developing countries. Kazakhstan, Turkmenistan, Tajikistan, Uzbekistan, Kyrgyzstan, Afghanistan, Pakistan, India, Iran, and Turkey are primarily affected. The commonalities with these neighbors and China are however limited. To take just one example, what do China and Pakistan have in common – apart from 500 km of frontiers? The culture? The religion? The history? The vitality of the economy? The political regime? If there is one thing in common between these countries, it is the political insecurity that reigns there. Any transport network (goods by rail, by road, oil, gas by pipelines, etc.) that crosses those countries must ensure a minimum of security for the sponsors of these physical flows.

Afghanistan is precisely on the route of this new Silk Road. China has only a common border of less than 100 km between Xinjiang and Afghanistan. But Uighur Islamist fighters have been established in Afghanistan for two decades with the Afghan Talibans. China wants to prevent terrorist contamination and to protect its interests in the Aynak copper mine (south of Kabul), an investment of $3.5 billion, and in oil exploitation. China has bent its traditional policy of non-interference. It is now involved in the political process, as evidenced by the frequent visits of Chinese officials, to try to restore calm in the country from which NATO has withdrawn since 2014. Faced with the comeback of the Talibans, China has taken a stand in Afghanistan by providing military aid since 2016 – however, very limited (less than $100 million). To complicate the situation, Japan is trying to position itself against the Chinese offensive.

8.1.6. *The Oppositions to the BRI*

The opposition comes from Western countries – especially Europeans – which believe that China is not sufficiently opening its door to tenders and that it is mainly Chinese companies that are the beneficiaries. In fact, a study by the Center for Strategic and International Studies (CSIS) published in 2018 revealed that 89% of contracts go to Chinese companies. As a result, countries like the UK are dragging their feet in joining the Belt & Road Initiative.

The opposition also comes from countries closer geographically which do not positively view the rise of China's power. Malaysia, for example, suspended several Chinese projects (a rail link and two pipelines) after Prime Minister Mahathir returned to power (2018–2020); the price of the high-speed train has finally been lowered. The Pakistani government also expressed a wish in 2018 to revise the past contracts. While investment in infrastructure (ports, pipelines, railways, power stations, etc.) must support economic development, some countries find it difficult to make their investments profitable and are therefore struggling to repay their loans. Sri Lanka failed to amortize the port of Hambantota, to the point that control of it has been granted to the Chinese contractor for 99 years. The Maldives also fall into the debt trap and are asking for the debt to be postponed. The same question is asked by many other countries: Mongolia, Montenegro, Laos, Djibouti, Kyrgyzstan, and Tajikistan. China's debt policy becomes an instrument of political influence. This is the return of the "unequal treaties", except that, this time, it is China that initiated them (and not the Western countries). The Belt & Road Initiative also entails a risk of asymmetry if these roads are just one way.

Beyond these competitive aspects, the ecological impact of the Belt & Road Initiative has so far produced little opposition. Yet, the new Silk Road is a frontal attack on the Paris Agreement (COP 21). This logistical development is a societal misunderstanding at a time when the common mantra is the relocation of industrial sites close to places of consumption. The ecological damage is immediate when it comes to the construction of transportation infrastructure, and it will be lasting.

8.2. Opening the Door to Foreign Investments in Banking

As stressed in Chapters 1 to 4, the financial system in China is strongly under the control of the Chinese authorities. Banks are massively controlled either by the State, or by provinces, municipalities, districts, or rural cooperatives. Chinese authorities consider banking as a "core" activity. They consider that the local industry made significant accomplishments since the revitalization of the top five (ICBC, CCB, ABC, BoC, and Bocom) during the eighties, and the creation of city banks, rural banks, and cooperative banks. There is less need to open the industry to foreign banks.

In this context, the role of foreign banks is almost nonexistent. The world of foreign finance has long been kept apart in China. Since the admission of China to the WTO in 2001, the country was expected to open the door to foreign banks. It did so in 2005. But, few foreign banks such as HSBC or Standard Chartered received "true" admission to local banking markets due to the complexity and non-transparency of regulation.

8.2.1. *A Meager Role for Foreign Banks*

After China was admitted to the World Trade Organization (WTO) in 2001, foreign financial institutions expected an opening of the banking industry in China. More than 20 years after, the influence of non-Chinese banks in China is still very low. Their market share is very low: foreign banks held only 2% of the total Chinese market in 2015. Some observers suggest that China did not comply with WTO regulations, and put some hurdles which make it difficult for foreign banks to operate in China. This opening has been limited not only because of the regulations but also because Chinese banks have developed to become powerful competitors. As Chinese banks, which are much bigger than foreign banks, are growing faster than foreign banks, the market of the latter has gone down to 1.5%. Their market share might even go down to 1% as Chinese banks continue to grow. Local banks will represent 99% of the market! Banking in China is Sino-centric.

Chinese banks are not very internationalized, either in terms of their shareholding or in terms of their operations abroad. Yet, big players like BoC and ICBC are actively opening new branches in many countries around the world. Their strategy is first to serve Chinese clients abroad (retail and corporate); they might finance local companies as well as a second phase of development.

The Chinese government has not felt the necessity to open the banking business to foreign banks more than what was expected since the admission of China to the WTO. This behavior is not aligned with what Chinese authorities did with the car industry or more recently with the electric car industry – all of which were largely opened to foreign car makers. The external stimulus needed in the car industry or the electric car industry was not needed for the banking industry as the Chinese banking system achieved acceptable performance without such an external stimulus.

The strong control of the Chinese State has proved beneficial because it generated some stability. Yet, there are pressures for reciprocity and consequently for opening. Given that China is in many industries the first or the second worldwide market, the Chinese government cannot close the door to foreign banks. The entry of foreign establishments has been extremely constrained.

8.2.2. *The Timid Entry of Few Pioneers*

As expected, the Chinese authorities opened the door of the Chinese market to foreign banks. A first step was accomplished when foreign banks were allowed to acquire up to 20% of a Chinese bank. For example, in 2005, Bank of America (BoA) was approved by PBoC to buy 9% of state-owned China Construction Bank (one of the five biggest Chinese banks), which stimulated the fast growth of this domestic bank. BoA even went to 10.75% before reselling these interests in 2011 and 2015. Another example, BNP Paribas, also in 2005, took 18% of Bank of Nanjing, a city commercial bank; it still maintains its participation. Similarly, Deutsche Bank acquired 19.99% of Huaxia Bank, a publicly traded commercial bank, founded in 1992, and headquartered in Beijing. The banking system must also be opened and the remuneration of savings gradually released. The ceiling on the remuneration of personal bank deposits was effectively removed in 2015.

A second step occurred since foreign banks were allowed by Chinese authorities to detain up to 51% of one joint venture with a Chinese partner or start a wholly owned subsidiary by themselves (this could have been done as a response to pressure from President Trump). This paved the way in 2017 for takeovers of Chinese financial institutions by foreign financial groups. Yet, those operations are bounded to local banks (the so-called city banks) and cannot be extended to large Chinese banks. Having ICBC or ABC under the control of a foreign institution is unthinkable. As a matter of fact, a limited number of operations have been effectively implemented. In 2018, the Swiss bank UBS was the first foreign bank to take majority control of a Sino-foreign finance joint venture. In 2019, JP Morgan Chase bank was authorized by the Chinese authorities (the CSRC) to take a majority of its activity in securities in China (brokerage, investment advice, underwriting, etc.) of which it previously held only 49%. In 2019, Japanese banking group Nomura was licensed to operate brokerage, investment consulting, proprietary trading, and assets management in its securities majority-owned joint venture in China. US Goldman Sachs is also in line. In 2020, Credit Suisse was authorized by the CSRC to increase from 33.3% to 51% in its joint venture Credit Suisse Founder Securities (CSFS).

In the financial industry, the Chinese government has also gradually opened the market. Most of the world's largest banks have entered China as illustrated in Table 8.1. The restrictions on the shareholding ratio for foreign investors in the financial industry were also removed generally. In 2020, foreign investors were allowed to hold 100% share in securities, funds, futures, insurance, and other types of financial institutions, or to acquire 100% interest in domestic financial institutions. Moreover, conditions for foreign investment to access the Chinese market were substantially relaxed. Paypal, which is the largest payment institution in the USA,

Table 8.1.   Foreign Banks in China

Europe	USA	Asia
BNP (France)	City Bank	ANZ (Australia)
Crédit Agricole (France)	Goldman Sachs	Development Bank of Singapore
Crédit Suisse (Suisse)	JP Morgan	Bank of Tokyo-Mitsubishi (Japan)
Deutche Bank (Germany)	Morgan Stanley	Sumitomo Mitsui Bank (Japan)
HSBC (UK)		Mizuho Bank (Japan)
Natexis (France)		
Santander (Spain)		
SEB (Sweden)		
Société Générale (France)		
Standard Chartered (UK)		
UBS (Suisse)		

having over 377 million users in the world, was approved in early 2021 to become the first foreign-invested payment institution to operate in China. American Express was approved to establish a payment and clearing institution, targeting the issuing of debit cards in the Chinese market. Citibank plans to set up a 100% shareholding Futures company as well as a wholly owned securities company.

The limit set at 51% of the capital is expected to rise to 100% somewhere in the future. Nevertheless, the geopolitical tensions with the USA, the COVID crisis, and the focus of Xi Jinping on domestic resources give a signal that is not positive: there is overall a trend toward less opening. Will the Chinese government pursue the opening of the banking sector to foreign banks? No, we are still far from a situation where foreign banks will be allowed to acquire 100% equity of a large Chinese bank. Because the Chinese authorities rarely fully open the door – rather, they prefer that the door be half-open, maybe even less than that – the actual picture is not going to change in the near future.

8.2.3. *Possible Options for Foreign Banks*

In practice, a foreign bank has to submit files to the regulators which will decide whether to give a license; decision criteria include the size of the bank, its specific abilities and expertise, and potential political issues. As a matter of fact, attributions are not particularly forthcoming. As such, foreign banks will or will not take advantage of the existing diplomatic ties between their country of origin and China.[2] Which domain are foreign banks going to target? Retail? Private? Or corporate?

8.2.3.1. *Foreign banks cannot enter Chinese retail*

Retail banking could be attractive because of the propensity of Chinese citizens to save money; money collected by banks would help to expand their lending capabilities. Some foreign banks like Société Générale have tried to do so, but it did not work. Retail is probably not the target for foreign banks for strategic reasons. With the exception of HSBC and Standard Chartered, which are targeting upscale clients in large cities and delivering a high level of service, foreign banks do not have retail activities in China. The reason is that it would be too costly to build a network from scratch and to displace the mastodon Chinese banks (ICBC, CCB, ABC, BoC, and Bocom) from their commercial positions due to their control over a large network of retail capabilities all over the country – Chinese retail banks even have branches in some small municipalities. And takeover of a Chinese bank would mean paying a high price as valuations are frequently at high levels.

8.2.3.2. *Corporate banking is to serve foreign MNCs in China*

Foreign banks prefer to enter China with inbound corporate banking activities.[3] They deliver banking services to non-Chinese companies operating in China, such as deposits, cash management, funding, hedging (currency and rates), advisory for mergers and acquisitions, and issue of bonds. This could be offered to large listed foreign multinational companies or to smaller companies. If small foreign banks are not able to serve Chinese companies, large foreign banks will work with Chinese companies having international development projects outside China. And they work as well with Chinese corporate clients in China.

---

[2] It has been more complicated for US banks since the Trump years.

[3] Similarly, Chinese banks have implemented branches outside China to support importation and exportation activities of Chinese companies. For example, the Bank of China operates one corporate branch in Paris for clients who are mostly companies.

8.2.3.3. *Toward exogamic[4] joint ventures in private banking*

Two levels of fortune have to be distinguished: average and high. Holders of average wealth can find appropriate services in China; the Bank of China, for example, has a dedicated division. They help clients invest in the stock exchange, in mutual funds, to transfer legacies, etc. Holders of high wealth might not receive appropriate services. As can be seen in Australia, Portugal, or Canada, rich Chinese people have bought real estate. It can be hypothesized that those people might have also transferred part of their assets outside China and used the services of private banks. Some foreign banks like HSBC with HSBC premier are operating in this segment.

Alternatively, foreign banks can also start private banking activities. Their knowledge about asset management is considered a strength in China. Yet, the big issue will be to build a portfolio of wealthy Chinese clients. One way to bypass this entry barrier is to establish a joint venture with an established Chinese bank. The benefit of such an exogamic partnership is to bundle complementary assets: the client base of the Chinese bank and the asset management capabilities of the foreign bank.

The strategy of foreign banks in China mainly depends on their strategic group. Large foreign banks, like BNP, HSBC, and Citibank, consider the whole Chinese market. Smaller banks, like SEB,[5] are more focused on specific client sections. SEB is in China to serve its European home market corporate clients who are doing business in China. SEB's clients in China include Swedish companies, and SEB's home market of Finland, Norway, United Kingdom, Germany, Austria, Switzerland, and more recently the Netherlands. Yet, SEB does not serve any Chinese company in China.

8.3. The Future of the Chinese Currency

Chinese authorities would like to decouple the yuan from the dollar to eliminate a strategic vulnerability (especially if China decides to invade Taiwan). China doesn't want the USA to use the dollar against them as a

---

[4]Exogamic means that partners come from unrelated environments and/or contribute to the joint venture with differentiated types of resources.
[5]SEB was founded in Sweden by the Wallenberg family to serve the Nordic market. Its first activity is corporate banking. But, SEB also has retail and private banking activities in Sweden.

weapon. And, China would like to make the yuan a regionally anchored currency. Schematically, we have to distinguish between the onshore Chinese yuan (CNY) used in the country and the offshore yuan (CNH).

8.3.1. *The Challenge of the Internationalization of the Yuan*

China is the world's biggest trading nation and the world's second-largest economy, but the yuan is not yet a true international currency. The US dollar remains the most widely used currency internationally for measuring prices, storing the value of savings, settling trade, and borrowing. The US dollar makes 41% of the global payments currency, the euro 36%, the GB pound 6%, the yen 3%, and the yuan only a bit more than 2%. Beijing would like to reduce the country's reliance on the US dollar. Figure 8.2 describes policies already in place.

The internationalization of the yuan is recent: It has been possible to transact in yuan overseas (CNH) only since 2009. For a long time, China has been wanting to decouple from the US dollar for its global trading operations. China wants to purchase what it needs from other countries using its own currency or the currency of the trading partner, and its own payment systems. To make the yuan a global reserve currency, foreigners have to find good reasons to use it.

Efforts to internationalize its currency include developing the trading of commodities, fostering activity in BRI partner countries, fostering its consumer role in Asia, and introducing new technologies to increase the use of the yuan. China is also trying to increase inflows of yuan through China's financial markets by removing restrictions on foreign investment

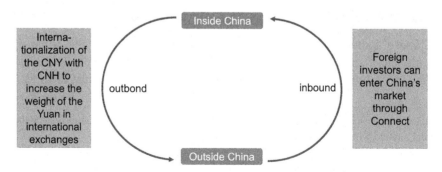

Figure 8.2.   Internationalization of the Financial Market

and providing more opportunities. Beijing has also launched its digital currency – the e-CNY for cross-border payments – and developed, since 2015, an alternative to SWIFT, i.e. China's cross-border trade settlement and communications platform known as China International Payment System (CIPS).

8.3.2. *The E-yuan: The Digital Currency as a Cash Substitute*

The project officially started in 2014. The e-yuan is an answer to the rise of cryptocurrencies (such as Bitcoin) and their underlying principle of decentralization. Yet, it is not a cryptocurrency, but a digital currency electronic payment (DCEP). The e-yuan was developed by the People's Bank of China (PBoC) which owns most of the technology – it issued 130 patent applications related to cryptocurrency ranging across issuance, circulation, and applications to support its development. The e-yuan requires users to download an electronic wallet application authorized by the PBoC and to link it to their bank accounts. Users can then pay their bills, get some cash, or execute money transfers. Chinese commercial banks will convert some of their central bank deposits into this digital currency. The money from the linked bank account would be converted into digital cash on a one-to-one basis.

China launched the e-yuan in September 2020 as a test in different cities (including Xiong'an, Chengdu, Shenzhen,[6] and Suzhou). In February 2021, Beijing hosted a small-scale test of near-field communication (NFC) wearables that support payments in digital yuan, while plans to expand pilot testing of the digital yuan in both Beijing and Shanghai emerged later that same month. The test was also conducted during the Winter Olympic games (in February 2022). At the end of 2022, there were pilot areas in 15 provinces. It should be expanded step by step to cover all of China. The challenge is high as it is hard to change payment habits and to challenge existing third-party payment platforms. PBoC needs to develop new expertise and to devote a high level of resources to promote the digital yuan.

China has taken the so-called "two-tier" approach, making sure their commercial banks are key in the ecosystem (as banks also invest in the infrastructure). The e-yuan currency is a substitute to cash in China; it

---

[6]Shenzhen is a growing hotbed for Chinese innovation.

should not replace cash but be a complement. One of the key differences from the private wallets (Alipay, WeChat Pay) is that the e-yuan can be used in offline mode (without Internet connections) and it does not require electricity. The main arguments in favor are its cost-effectiveness, efficiency, and risk control. In comparison to paper cash and coins, the digital yuan reduces transaction, operational, and maintenance costs. The Chinese government will be able to trace all cash flows, seize accounts, and shut down accounts if necessary, and the control will be strictly limited to the Central bank. As such, it should help anti-money laundering policies and reduce illicit uses. China wants to accumulate the experience as a forerunner. PBoC wants to include cross-border payments within e-commerce with other countries. This could be closely related to the commercial war with USA and the global currency competition.

In January 2021, a PBoC clearing center, CIPS, and Digital Currency Research Institute collaborated with SWIFT to form a joint venture called "Finance Gateway Information Services Co", in order to better incorporate the CNY X-border payment message into the global system and ensure the full compliance of standards into the process. This gives a strong indication to the world that China Central Bank is seeking to internationalize the digital currency in the X-border payment context to strengthen the position of CNY in the international arena. The timing of the digital currency electronic payment (DCEP) for cross-border payments may be uncertain as this would require coordination with central banks or payment supervisory authorities in foreign countries. China may seek to develop its DCEP with countries on the map of the Belt & Road Initiative to better support the trade development and infrastructural investment.

8.4. Conclusion

Chinese authorities proactively launched several initiatives to foster economic development – the first one being the BRI with $1 trillion investment. It interestingly aims to reproduce abroad the infrastructure scenario which has been so good in China. After 10 years, 70 countries are involved, and some significant achievements were made, such as, for example, the high-speed train between Kunming (Yunnan) and Vientiane (Laos), the port of Hambantota (Sri Lanka), railway projects in East Africa, and several industrial parks and economic zones. Yet, protests emerged from countries not accepted in the tenders and from developing countries caught in the debt trap.

Foreign banks are not in a good position in China because, contrary to markets like the car industry where foreign car makers were much better than locals, the Chinese banking industry was already benefiting from some advantages. The first advantage was its size due to existing dense commercial networks all over the country. On the top of this, the Chinese regulator enacted many rules which foreign banks find hard to comply with.

And this is not the end of the story. China took the lead with the current implementation of the e-yuan. As a golden rule, the implementation has been done step by step.

Takeaway from Chapter 8

1. The Belt & Road Initiative (BRI) is a bridge between East and West. Its aim is to connect China and Central Asia to Europe and Africa through a succession of regional segments and perpendicular land corridors. It involves land infrastructure (roads, railways, pipelines, power stations, etc.), maritime routes (ports), and digital telecommunication networks. It is a duplication of the Chinese infrastructure strategy beyond the frontiers of China in countries which have a need for those infrastructures. With an investment plan of $1 trillion, it is the most significant Chinese geopolitical initiative in decades.

2. The BRI is Sino-centric. The project emanates from China. The financing part of the initiative is entrusted to Chinese banks: Exim Bank of China, China Development Bank, the Bank of China, China Construction Bank, New Development Bank, the Asian Infrastructure Investment Bank (AIIB), ICBC, and the Silk Road Fund. The construction part of the initiative is mostly done by Chinese companies and the equipment is delivered by Chinese companies.

3. The rationale of the BRI is to use Chinese resources to develop countries outside China. China is seeking to extend its area of influence and prepare a long-term rent, both economic (with the development of activity) and financial (due to the repayment of loans granted).

4. The downside of the BRI is that the financial risk incurred by the target countries has already caused economic hardship in countries like Sri Lanka, Cambodia, and Pakistan due to their difficulty in reimbursing the loans they contracted with China. Another issue to deal with is the political insecurity of many countries on the route (e.g. Afghanistan). Finally, the ecological impact of the BRI undermines the legitimacy of the project.

5. Banking in China is sino-centric. Contrary to sectors like the automotive industry, the Chinese authorities considered that there was no need to open the industry to foreign banks. Yet, when China joined the WTO in 2001, the country was supposed to open to foreign banks. Changes in regulation have been progressive, starting from the authorization given to foreign banks to acquire up to 20% of the capital of a Chinese bank. The ceiling was then pushed to 51%. Since 2020, foreign investors were allowed to hold 100% share in securities, funds, futures, insurance, and other types of financial institutions, or to acquire 100% interest in domestic financial institutions.

6. As a matter of fact, these initiatives have not been enough to attract many foreign banks. With very few exceptions, foreigners are not involved in retail. Foreign banks offer corporate banking services to non-Chinese companies operating in China. And, some exogamic partnerships could emerge in private banking.

7. China is pushing to make the yuan a more respectable and a more internationally used currency. Progress has been made. Unfortunately, the yuan is still marginal in world commerce.

Bibliography

Center for Strategic & International Studies (CSIS), www.csis.org.

Diana Choyleva and Dinny McMahon (2022), *China's Quest for Financial Self-Reliance: How Beijing Plans to Decouple from the Dollar-Based Global Trading and Financial System*, Enodo Economics/Woodrow Wilson Center, Washington (USA), 203 pages.

International Bank for Reconstruction and Development, World Bank (2019), *Belt and Road Economics – Opportunities and Risks of Transport Corridors*, 159 pages.

Maliszewska Maryla and van der Mensbrugghe Dominique (2019), *The Belt & Road Initiative: Economic, Poverty and Environmental Impacts*, World Bank, Policy Research Working Paper 8814, 67 pages.

OECD Business and Finance Outlook (2018), *China's Belt and Road Initiative in the Global Trade, Investment and Finance Landscape*, 46 pages.

Xiao Gang (2021), *Financing China's Belt and Road Initiative: Investments and Infrastructure*, Routledge, London and New York, 118 pages.

Yu-Wai Vic Li (2019), *China's Financial Opening: Coalition Politics and Policy Changes*, Routledge, London and New York, 212 pages.

Conclusion

With the open door policy, which President Deng Xiaoping started to implement in 1978, the general rule has been to invite foreign companies to start manufacturing activities in China in designated geographical areas. The deal was clear: Foreign companies had to establish a joint venture with a Chinese partner (usually chosen by the government) and bring their knowledge and their technologies to the joint venture to gain access to the Chinese low-cost workforce and the Chinese market. This now seems to be an old story. Yet, this has been the key means for Chinese manufacturing companies to learn and update their facilities in industries like the car industry, the mass-retailing industry, the production of circuit breakers, or the construction of high-speed trains and airplanes. And all those inward foreign direct investments, and their spillovers, supported the expansion of China's exportation.

The big difference with the financial industry is that this activity was not opened to foreign companies in 1978. It is a Sino-centric activity. This has not been the only sector with no or with limited foreign entry. The foreign presence has been limited in the energy sector where there are very few foreign competitors which were allowed to enter China; energy production and transportation are governed in China by a limited number of giant state-owned enterprises (as is frequently the case around the world). The situation is also exclusively Chinese when it comes to the incredibly concentrated telecommunication services or domestic air transportation. The closed door in finance is because Chinese authorities view banking as a sovereign activity, with limited export potential. Opening of the financial industry started only after China joined the WTO in 2001.

And, the result of this opening has been a minor foreign market share in a well-established and well-performing Chinese banking industry. This does not mean that the Chinese financial industry has not learned from its counterparts in foreign countries; but the knowledge came mostly through returnees and business trips organized to Japan, Europe, and the USA.

The weak foreign presence is also clear in Chinese mainland stock exchange platforms – Shanghai, Shenzhen, and Beijing – and their different boards. Of course, there exist mechanisms allowing some selected foreign institutional investors (QFII) to buy local shares. But, their presence is very limited and there isn't any single foreign company listed on the different Chinese mainland stock exchange platforms.

Another specific feature of the Chinese banking industry is the massive control of the Chinese State. I used the metaphor of the conductor and his orchestra to explain who is the boss and who are the performers. We saw the power of the China Banking and Insurance Regulatory Commission (CBIRC) and of the China Securities Regulatory Commission (CSRC). And we saw that the main actors which are the banks are publicly owned – either through the State, the province, the municipality, or the district; very few banks are privately owned – we saw that China Minsheng is the only significant one. We saw that the infrastructure strategy of the country, which has been key to the country's development, has been exclusively financed by state entities. This situation is totally different from the choice made by the Chinese leadership with the Internet economy. In this domain, the drive was given almost only to private companies – especially the largest ones, Alibaba, Tencent, Baidu, ByteDance, and Jingdong. At the same time, all those privately owned companies benefited from the barriers erected by Chinese regulators to prevent the entry of foreign competitors. Chinese authorities entrusted to private entities the development of the Chinese real estate industry and also entrusted to a private company, Huawei, a central role in the development of telecommunication equipment. Yet, when it comes to financial resources, Chinese authorities are not prepared to give up the reins.

When the country is investing abroad, the most powerful Chinese investor is the China Investment Corporation (CIC), which is under State control. We saw that outward foreign direct investment came 20 years after inward foreign direct investment, showing the challenge of immaturity which Chinese companies had to overcome. Chinese companies, publicly owned but also privately owned, have learned a lot since they started to "Go Global" in 2004. I stressed how important geopolitical issues and decisions are as they impact companies' investment policies as shown, for example, by the sharp decline of Chinese investment in the USA in the recent years.

China is full of contrasts: (a) There exist many plans and policies written by the authorities to give guidelines to the economic activity – five-year plans, the Belt and Road Initiative, "Made in China 2025" plan, "Go Global" policy, FDI policy, etc. But at the same time, adaptability and opacity can also be the rule at the implementation stage. (b) The country claims a multi-millennial history. But, at the same time, we saw the newness of the financial industry – and even sometimes the immaturity of some structures such as the supervision authorities and regulation bodies. (c) The financial industry is a fringed oligopoly with some mastodons which do not seem to be very agile. But at the same time, the whole country switched to mobile payment in record time. (d) The banking sector is massively under State control, but the authorities gave the mandate to private companies in some specific financial segments like FinTech. The country demonstrates an astonishing vitality when it comes to FinTech, and this industry is almost fully privately owned. This investment in technology comes with a profound move of the country toward technology creation. The growth of R&D expenditures follows an exponential curve; and, it is not a surprise that some start-ups decided to explore applications in the finance industry.

There will not be any major change regarding foreign presence in the financial industry in the coming years. China might increase its opening to foreign banks. But, Chinese banks are so well anchored that it is going to be difficult to displace them. And the scenario for the future where the role of the State will be reduced is not likely! The challenges of the Chinese financial industry will first be endogenous. I stressed the need to deal with the real estate sector that is under strong pressure, the need to finance retirement pensions, and the need to deal with growing debt. The challenge is that all of this has to be done while the growth rate has considerably decreased and will not go back to the high levels of good times. Challenges will also take place outside China, like the internationalization of the yuan.

Appendices

Appendix 1: Value Creation from Some Major Chinese Private Companies

The case studies reported in Appendix 1 are cases used in the text. The sample uses eight large private Chinese companies, all developed from scratch in different industries (see following table) including B2C and B2B activities. These companies reached large market capitalization.

For each case study, the analysis was conducted on the basis of press reviews, published reports, company visits, books on the company, websites, etc. The description offered is not repeated along the same traditional items (like history, shareholders, R&D, product portfolio). It highlights some key points which are idiosyncratic to each company and allow one to briefly describe the company. Those key points help one understand the business strategy of the company, the sources of its financing, the reasons why it was successful, i.e. how it created value, or the reasons why it failed, i.e. how it destroyed value. We will see that some companies are still strongly dependent on the Chinese market (like Alibaba, Baidu, and Tencent) while others have been able to successfully develop outside China in foreign countries (like BYD, Huawei, or Xiaomi).

Company	Core Business	Creation, Place of Creation	Market Value (Billion US Dollars, 2023)	Place Where the Company is Listed	Revenue (Billion Yuan, 2022)
Alibaba	e-Commerce	1999, Hangzhou (Zhejiang)	225	New York, Hong Kong (but not in Shanghai)	853
Baidu	Search engine	2000, Beijing	49	Nasdaq, Hong Kong	124
BYD	Batteries and cars manufacturer	1995, Shenzhen (Guangdong)	99	Hong Kong	211
Didi	Taxi reservation	2015, Beijing	20	De-listed from New York (in 2022), moved to Hong Kong	170
Fosun	Conglomerate	1992, Shanghai	47	Hong Kong	83
Huawei	Telecommunication	1987, Shenzhen (Guangdong)	150	Privately owned by company's employees	637
Tencent	Online games and messaging	1998, Shenzhen (Guangdong)	563	Hong Kong	482
Xiaomi	Smartphone	2010, Beijing	40	Hong Kong	300

Alibaba

(1) In less than 25 years, Alibaba became the Chinese standard of e-commerce under the leadership of the iconic Jack Ma. It is a private business created in 1999 (five years after Amazon) in Hangzhou in the rich province of Zhejiang. Alibaba grew alongside China's Internet. Founder Jack Ma (Chinese name Ma Yun) became a popular personality in China. In 2019, he owned 4.8% of Alibaba and nearly 33% of Ant Financial (the financial arm of the group) – which makes him one of the richest people in China. The fairytale epic story of the hero winning against all odds fascinates people. Jack Ma is an idol of the Chinese citizens like Steve Jobs was the idol of the American people. The hero started from nothing. The story began when Jack Ma, working for the Chinese Ministry of Foreign Trade and Economic Cooperation (after having been an English teacher), found himself accompanying Jerry Yang (then boss of Yahoo) on a visit to the Great Wall. It was shortly after this event that Jack Ma started his B2B site (Alibaba.com) where he offered Chinese companies access to global markets. In 2014, Jack Ma decided at the age of 48 to retire from the position of Managing Director, and in 2018, he made public his succession plan – wishing to step down as President to focus on education and philanthropy. He handed over the reins to Daniel Zhang in 2019 on the occasion of the company's 20th anniversary. While his contemporaries, more or less all made copies of foreign models (a Chinese Google, a Chinese Amazon, a Chinese Twitter, etc.), Jack Ma developed an original model. The group employed 20,000–22,000 people around 2012–2014. The 50,000 employee bar was exceeded in 2017, which grew to 100,000 is in 2019 and to 250,000 people in 2021.

(2) Alibaba is the largest and the most diversified virtual bazaar in the world. It is a Chinese e-commerce giant. Alibaba covers 80% of Chinese e-commerce according to iResearch (Beijing). That's more than Amazon and eBay combined. The revenue of Alibaba Group was about 100 billion yuan in 2016, which increased exponentially to reach 850 billion yuan in 2022. The group has grown through a diversification strategy. At the very beginning, with Alibaba.com, it was a market place (B2B) which allowed Chinese companies to present their products to foreign companies; in fact, it attracted the most remote SMEs in China (this Alibaba.com subsidiary was listed in Hong Kong from 2007 to 2012).

Taobao.com (literally, the "treasure hunt"), established in 2003, is an e-commerce site between individuals (C2C) – like eBay (the American company closed its Chinese branch in 2006). However, Taobao sells many counterfeits and only one-third of the products are original (according to the State Administration for Industry and Commerce). This criticism comes as much from the brands sold on the site as from internal media. Alibaba has declared itself ready to act against the fakes, but the controversy continues. Tmall.com is an online commerce place (B2C) – like Amazon. There are more than 4,000 foreign brands selling their products on Tmall, including Zara, Esprit, Gap, Uniqlo, Cache-cache, and Mango. Since 2015, Tmall has even offered Japanese products to Chinese consumers. Alibaba is also an online search engine – like Google. Undoubtedly inspired by the American Black Friday, Alibaba is, among other things, the promoter in China of Singles' Day (on the numerologically auspicious date of 11/11), having taken over a party created in the 1990s by students for singles – who are more and more numerous in China, especially in large cities. Singles' Day results each year in an orgy of clicks and a one-time explosion of electronic commerce.

(3) Alibaba framed a ubiquitous diversification strategy which engendered an authentic and synergistic ecosystem. Alibaba built a portfolio of activities guided by the search for synergies. E-commerce became the cash cow that made it possible to invest in a large number of start-ups. Alibaba has nearly a thousand subsidiaries, of which more than 400 are outside China. In 2013, Alibaba acquired Xiami – a music streaming site. Alibaba also bought a stake in Weibo (the Chinese Twitter), owned 18% of Youku Tudou (the Chinese YouTube) before buying it entirely for $4.3 billion, and committed $800 million in 2014 to buying 60% of China Vision Media – a Hong Kong-based film and TV series production company. The company took control of Auto Navi (mapping) for $1.6 billion with the idea of locating merchants on its Taobao retail sales site and also using this application to book taxis. Alibaba also launched the Tmall Box Office service inspired by the Netflix model. Also in 2013, Alibaba launched Yu'e Bao (which can be translated to "treasury remnants"), a mutual fund offering better remuneration than depository banks, i.e. 4–6% returns compared to 3% offered by the big retail banks. Alibaba has also been imitated by Tencent with Licaitong and by Xiaomi with Huoqi Bao. Formally a mutual fund, Yu'e Bao is not subject to the remuneration caps applicable to Chinese banks. Alibaba raised 600 billion yuan ($87 billion) in two years under Yu'e Bao! Funds under management passed the 1,500 billion yuan ($220 billion) mark at the start of 2018. In 2015, after convincing the Chinese government to grant it a license (like five other companies), Alibaba opened MYBank, an online retail bank. Alibaba also made great efforts to switch to e-commerce from mobile devices (smartphones and tablets); in particular, in 2014 it acquired UCWeb (3,000 employees), the most popular smartphone browser in the country. Alibaba even took a $590 million minority stake in Chinese cell-phone maker Meizu in 2015. Also in 2015, Alibaba took a stake in Suning for $4.3 billion, a Chinese physical distributor with 1,600 stores. With Ali Cloud, Alibaba has also been in the cloud computing industry since 2010 – an activity that is not yet profitable despite its potential. Alibaba is also investing in artificial intelligence through a global network of R&D and in 2017 announced $15 billion of investments over three years. With Hema stores, Alibaba blurs the line between virtual stores and brick-and-mortar stores: At Hema, customers scan products, without putting them in their shopping cart, and have them delivered to their homes. In 2018, Alibaba acquired Ele.me, an online food delivery service. In 2023, Alibaba has planned to launch its own conversational software powered by artificial intelligence – like ChatGPT, the conversational robot developed by the Californian company OpenAI (of which Microsoft is the largest shareholder); Baidu promises to follow with its own Wenxin (Ernie Bot) chatbot. In short, Alibaba has developed its own ecosystem.

(4) Ant Financial Services Group is the financial arm of the Alibaba group. Ant Financial Services Group was established as a spin-off from Alibaba in 2011. It is the company that drives Alipay, which was launched in 2004 as a secure online payment method. Alipay announced 520 million users in 2018 and the figure reached 1.3 billion in 2020. Alipay claims an annual online payment volume of $17 trillion. Ant Financial is not just an online payment platform but has evolved into online banking and wealth management. It even tried in 2018 to buy the American Money Gram; the maneuver was prevented by CFIUS because it was not possible for American authorities to give Ant Financial access to sensitive information on American consumers. Ant Financial was valued at $150 billion in 2018, but went down to $64 billion in 2023 after Ant's IPO was halted in November 2020.

(5) Alibaba has powerful backup from foreign shareholders. The Japanese technology group Softbank (the third mobile phone operator in Japan, founded by Masayoshi Son, a Japanese billionaire) had contributed $20 million dollars to the creation of Alibaba and it was still a 34% shareholder until 2023 when it sold most of its shares. Yahoo had taken 40% of Alibaba in 2005 in exchange for the contribution of its activities in China which the American company was struggling to develop – Alibaba was then valued at $2.5 billion. Yahoo has since reduced to 15% shares (realizing a significant capital gain at the same time). It was precisely the presence of foreigners in its capital that led Jack Ma to create Ant Financial from Alibaba, on the grounds that, at that time, Chinese law did not allow foreigners to own financial activities.

(6) The 2014 stock market introduction did not happen in Hong Kong, but in New York. Since 1999, more than 150 Chinese companies have been listed in the US. In September 2014, Alibaba raised $25 billion on the New York Stock Exchange (alongside Walmart and Home Depot). It was the operation of the year and a historic turning point. Alibaba surpassed the $22 billion raised by the Agricultural Bank of China in 2010 in Hong Kong, the $16 billion raised by Facebook in 2012, and it also broke Visa's 2008 record. The managers of Alibaba initially wanted to run this introduction in Hong Kong. But they abandoned the idea on the grounds that there was no preferential regime in Hong Kong that would have allowed them to retain control of the company, i.e. where the shares of the founders have more voting rights (the so-called "dual-class shares"). The management authority of the Hong Kong financial center missed the opportunity by refusing to derogate from this rule. The value of Alibaba's share in New York, which peaked at $119 in November 2014, fell back to less than $60 in September 2015 to return to $80–100 in the second half of 2016. The company was valued at more than $200 billion and then $400 billion as of 2017. The share rose steadily to the $175–205 range in 2018. Market capitalization went up to $650 billion in 2020. This was a miraculous jackpot for Japanese Softbank and American Yahoo. Softbank partly realized its capital gain in 2016 by selling $8 billion worth of shares; it still holds the equivalent of $60 billion. After going public in New York in 2014, Alibaba also went public in Hong Kong in 2019. Alibaba become so powerful that the company could afford to take a stake in all Chinese start-ups. Such power can one day be challenged if public opinion thinks there is an abuse of a dominant position.

(7) While revenue is over 90% Chinese, can Alibaba develop out of China? Alibaba's activities remain 90% concentrated in China. The company is aiming for two billion customers – enough to make it a "data company". The Chinese market alone still has room for improvement. Ali Express is the structure in charge of the globalization of Alibaba's B2C activities. The group has built positions in Southeast Asia. But it is eyeing the US, India, and Russia. The firm launched 11Main in 2014 in the US – a B2C site comparable to T-Mall – but had to resell the site in 2015 after failing to develop it. Alibaba has also taken a position in India by investing in start-ups – 40% in PayTM (a payment system on smartphones) and a stake in Snapdeal, all for $680 million. The group is looking to leverage the growing mass of Chinese tourists to convince foreign merchants to accept Alipay. In 2016, it launched a global e-commerce platform. As a result, Jack Ma was increasingly on the political scene, meeting the greats of this world in Australia, Canada, Italy, and even the then President of the US, Donald Trump.

(8) The call to order from the authorities: Jack Ma, one of the most powerful business persons in the country, fell from grace. At the end of October 2020, Jack Ma suddenly and mysteriously disappeared. He had to slip away from the media scene for almost three months. This was because Ma dared to openly criticize financial authorities: He accused banks of having "a pawn shop mentality" and financial regulators "of stifling innovation", remarks deemed insolent in a Chinese cultural context. The Chinese authorities made the decision in November 2020 to block the listing of Ant Finance, of which Jack Ma controlled 50%, on the Hong Kong Stock Exchange – more than $30 billion was to be raised. Xi Jinping did not hesitate to target a firm admired around the world. This ban showed who is boss! Alibaba had acquired too much prestige and influence in the eyes of the Chinese authorities to the point of becoming a threat to the Party. The empire became too powerful and the authorities sought to better control it. Xi Jinping reformed Alipay so that the state had a majority there. The star of Chinese capitalism, Jack Ma, reappeared at the end of January 2021 in a short recorded video conference for the purpose of supporting teachers in rural areas. At the beginning of 2021, Alibaba was sentenced by the Chinese authorities (the State Administration for Market Regulation) to pay a fine of 18 billion yuan ($2.6 billion – or 4% of the turnover of 2019) for abuse of a dominant position. Jack Ma, taken by a surge of generosity, offered $14 billion to charities. His net assets, however, shrunk by 36% to $39.6 billion (according to Hurun) after the introduction of Ant Financial was blocked. Jack Ma's public appearances are now rare. He was seen in the Netherlands and Spain in October 2021. He reappeared publicly in January 2022 during a ceremony at a primary school in Changhao on the island of Hainan. And in the summer of 2022, he announced that he wanted to cede control of Ant Financial and reduce his share to less than 10%. It was also at the beginning of the summer that Ma moved to Tokyo with his family. He then traveled several times to the US and Israel. He was also seen in early 2023 in Thailand with the leader of Charoen Pokphand (a group founded by a member of the Chinese diaspora). He was then seen in Melbourne (Australia) in February.

(9) Alibaba is facing strong headwinds. Alibaba is only progressing at the margins, and the slowdown in the Chinese economy induced by the "zero-COVID" policy is weighing heavily on its ability to recover. No less than 10,000 jobs were lost between April and June 2022. Alibaba, like its rival Tencent, is switching to a cost-cutting strategy. Alibaba's shares, which had approached 300 US dollars in October 2020, fell below 70 US dollars in November 2022. Market capitalization went from 650 billion US dollars in 2020 to 225 billion US dollars at the beginning of 2023. In March 2023, the group announced that it would be split into six independent companies (with separate managing directors and boards of directors) headed by a holding company and will explore possible separate IPOs. The dismantling of the Alibaba Empire has begun!

Baidu

(1) Baidu is the Chinese search engine. With 56% market share, it overwhelms all the other competitors in China. This market share was even higher (around 80%) in the near past. Bing and Sogu gained market shares since 2021. Baidu dominates because it has responded better than its competitors to the expectations of a population of younger Internet users with lower incomes who are more motivated by entertainment than by the search for information. Baidu did not have to rub shoulders with Google as it was blocked in 2010 by Beijing on the mainland. Conversely, such a market share induces users' frustration in the absence of a credible alternative and opens the way to public criticism. In fact, the Chinese people are not immune to social media platforms like ByteDance (see Appendix 3) or WeChat. Baidu is headquartered in Beijing. The company was created in 2000 by Li Yanhong (Li Robin) with a small team of 20 people. Its workforce grew sharply until 2014 and then stabilized around 42,000 employees. Its turnover exceeded 124 billion yuan ($18 billion) in 2021. Baidu is listed on Nasdaq (BIDU) – Draper Fisher Jurvetson (DJF), an American venture capital firm, owns one-third of the capital. After reaching a peak in 2018 with capitalization exceeding $90 billion, it fell back below $50 billion. The company was ranked by the Boston Consulting Group as being among the 10 most value-creating companies over the period 2006–2010.

(2) **Google has been knocked out, but is not dead.** Baidu does not challenge Chinese political orthodoxy; in the eyes of the political authorities, the Chinese search engine is much more popular than Google. The American search engine left mainland China territory with a lot of noise in 2010 to take refuge in Hong Kong after having decided to no longer apply the rules of self-censorship requested by the Chinese political power. Google thus finds itself in a marginal position in China – even more so since 2014 when access to Google was prohibited from China. In 2015, however, Google negotiated with the government to return to China with the Google Play application store. Also in 2015, a stake taken by Google in the Chinese artificial intelligence start-up Mobvoi (Chumen Wenwen) could be seen as a sign in the same direction. In 2017, the organization of tournaments between the AlphaGo software and the Chinese champion Ke Jie also made it possible to maintain a link with China. And in 2018, Google spent half a billion dollars for a percent stake in retailer JD.com. There was even talk of making a comeback with its search engine and meeting Beijing's censorship demands!

(3) **Baidu has a strategy of diversification in the Internet in China.** It is one of the well-established Chinese brands in China. In 2012, Baidu launched its own smartphone, a low-cost model equipped with a Baidu Cloud system. In 2013, Baidu acquired "91 Wireless", a subsidiary of Net Dragon Websoft, specializing in mobile internet, for nearly $1.6 billion – a record at that time in the world of technology in China. The company had success in the distribution of applications (through App Stores) for smartphones on the Internet. Baidu also has its own blogging platform, Baijiahao, and its own video-sharing platform, iQiyi (the Chinese

equivalent of Netflix, competitor to Alibaba's Youku Tudou). In 2014, Baidu invested $600 million in Uber. In 2015, after Tencent (with WeBank) and then Alibaba (with MyBank), Baidu went into online banking with the help of China Citic Bank (from the state conglomerate Citic Group). The company's strategy increasingly lies in the collection of data. Li Yanhong is reported to have said, "Baidu knows you better than you know yourself." In fact, Baidu has accumulated an incredible amount of data through the queries posed by eight out of 10 Chinese people with its search engine. If Baidu is a dominant player in China, it is – unlike Google – absent from the rest of the world. Baidu makes less than 5% of its revenue outside of China.

(4) Baidu has made strong investments in R&D. The percentage of the revenue devoted to R&D has increased from 10% in 2010 to nearly 20% today. Baidu is engaged in R&D – particularly in artificial intelligence – with no less than 1,300 researchers in this field, and nearly 3,000 granted patents. Chinese leaders believe that artificial intelligence is an area where China has a chance to position itself. The company has stood out for its capabilities in voice recognition, deep learning, and other big data. Baidu is also betting on smart speakers for home use.

(5) Baidu is also a new competitor in the car business. Baidu entered the autonomous car industry with a subsidiary started in 2014 in California under the leadership of a Stanford professor with the objective of producing autonomous cars in series in the long term. Tests on the Californian public network began in 2016. Real-life tests were conducted in 2017 in China in the Beijing region. Baidu cooperates with Chinese manufacturers like BYD, Geely, Chery, and BAIC and also with foreign OEMs like Bosch and Continental (yet, the collaboration launched with BMW came to an end). In 2017, Baidu unveiled the Apollo Project – with open-source software for autopilot – looking to make it a dominant design (like Google did with Android in smartphones); it remains to be seen whether this standard potential could go beyond the borders of China. In June 2021, Baidu introduced the Apollo Moon robot-taxi designed in partnership with BAIC with the plan is to deploy a thousand such vehicles in China. In early 2022, Baidu presented its Jidu concept car developed with Geely. Baidu brought a concentrate of technologies with more than 30 sensors and equipped with its Apollo autonomous driving system (using an Nvidia chip). The car was accredited with level 3 autonomous driving. Mass production was announced for 2023. In September 2022, Baidu unveiled the prototype of an autonomous taxi, a large minivan, labeled Apollo RT6, with level 4 autonomous driving technology. Baidu is also present in auto insurance. Meanwhile, Waymo, the self-driving car subsidiary of Google founded in 2009, opened a dedicated subsidiary in China in 2018. Cruise, the subsidiary of General Motors, remained in the US.

BYD

(1) The adventure of BYD started with the production of cell phone batteries. The journey began in 1995 with the production of nickel cadmium batteries and electronic components in Shenzhen (Guangdong) under the leadership of Wang Chuanfu – a hybrid of Thomas Edison and Jack Welch. The company surfed on the development of the mobile phone and in 2002 became the second world producer of rechargeable batteries; BYD notably equips Motorola, Nokia, and Samsung mobile phones. The acronym "BYD" is said to stand for "Build your dream" – it may not be true, but it is definitely possible. BYD entered the Honk Kong Stock Exchange in 2002.

(2) BYD then entered the automotive sector by acquiring a marginal Chinese car manufacturer. In 2003, BYD acquired Qinchuan Automobile Company, a second-tier automaker. With widely publicized investments in the electric car, supported by the Chinese government, electric car manufacturers aimed for the technological leap. The Chinese entrepreneurs understood that their probability of achieving progress in the combustion engine was close to zero because the combustion engine technique is rooted in ecosystems that have been developed for more than a hundred years in industrialized countries. On the other hand, electric engines (because they are based on new technologies) are more open to competition and China has every chance of being successful. Interestingly, Warren Buffet entered in 2008 the capital of BYD at the level of 10% for $232 million. The stock had remained in the range of HK$40–80 between 2012 and 2019, then rose to between 200 and 300 between 2019 and 2022. That's why Buffet divested partially in 2023.

(3) BYD invested in R&D to innovate car batteries. BYD is betting on batteries to stock electricity, while others like Toyota are betting on the hydrogen engine. The bet relates in particular to lithium ion batteries, a component that is more abundant and consequently less controversial than cobalt or nickel (used by other battery types). BYD has been developing an innovative technology of more compact and reliable batteries called "blade" (Lithium Iron Phosphate) since 2020. In this field, its first competitor is the Chinese CATL – the world's leading battery manufacturer.

(4) The automotive branch, however, experienced a disturbed scale-up. In 2009, BYD put on the market the first Chinese car with a hybrid engine, the "F3DM". The manufacturer then had in its files an all-electric car, the "e6", which it aimed to eventually manufacture on a large scale and even sell in the US. Meanwhile, in 2009, BYD sold 450,000 small gas cars – including 290,000 of the popular F3 sedan. However, the year 2010 was marred by a collapse in profitability and the year 2011 by a sharp drop in sales (from 800,000 to 600,000), due in part to reduced investment in conventional cars (consequence of massive investments in electric vehicles). The end of government subsidies in 2017 also had a negative impact on sales. Yet, BYD was able to maintain its position of leading manufacturer of electric vehicles by number of units sold, in particular, because it equips a number of taxi fleets and also has electric buses (K9) in its catalog.

(5) In 2022 came the end of the combustion engine as well as the overtaking of Tesla. The manufacturer announced in 2019 that it wanted to increase its production capacity for electric vehicles by five. At the beginning of 2022, it completely stopped its production of vehicles equipped with combustion engines and focused on 100% electric and rechargeable hybrids. It exceeded Tesla in terms of cars sold in the first half (640,000 cars against 564,000) and sold 1.85 million vehicles over that year. BYD developed its exports strongly (Brazil, Australia, Singapore, and Norway) and planned to build its first factory outside China in Thailand (with an annual production capacity of 150,000 vehicles). A joint subsidiary with the Uzbek manufacturer Uz Auto for the production of electric vehicles was also planned in Uzbekistan. In 2022, BYD took over most of Mercedes' shares in Denza, the joint company that the two had created in 2010 in the electric car market. BYD even signed a contract with the German rental company Sixt. It even made its presence felt at the Paris Motor Show in 2022 with three high-end electric models. BYD also plans to launch the Yangwang brand focused on high-end automobiles and has plans to produce in Europe.

(6) BYD has not confined itself to the automobile industry and has undertaken diversification around electric mobility. BYD also produces buses (single and even double decks), trucks, and electric forklifts. Buses have even been delivered to Singapore. BYD has also diversified into the aerial monorail with its first project launched in 2017 in Yinchuan (capital of the small Hui Autonomous Region of Ningxia) which also hosts ZTE's smart-city project.

Didi

(1) To counter Uber in China, the two leading taxi booking applications, Tencent and Alibaba, decided to merge. In February 2015, the two Chinese Internet giants Tencent and Alibaba agreed to merge their two smartphone reservation applications for taxis or passenger cars with private drivers. Didi Dache (literally "beep-beep call a taxi") and Kuaidi Dache (literally "fast taxi") combined to form the Goliath Didi Kuaidi. It represents 100% of the taxi market and 80% of the private driver market (private taxis remained technically illegal in China until 2016 when the government legalized the activity). The merger aimed to counter Uber in China. After entering Shanghai in August 2013, the Californian company gradually spread over the major cities. Faced with a competitor as well established as Uber was in its territory, the battle of Uber against Didi was bitter. Each competitor used passenger discounts to build a customer base. Uber's key asset was its December 2014 agreement with Baidu, which aimed to help it penetrate the field. It was doing 100,000 daily trips in June 2015. Uber was then at loggerheads with Didi Kuaidi. By mid-2016, it claimed to have 150 million monthly users, which would have captured 10% of the market. Also in 2016, Apple invested a billion dollars in Didi Chuxing – the new name of Didi Kuaidi – no doubt to make a mark in Beijing (and also to invest in the automotive field). China Merchants Bank committed $2.5 billion. A dramatic change took place in July 2016: Uber transferred its Chinese activities to Didi Chuxing and found itself with 20% of the Chinese capital (decreased to 12.8 in 2021). This was the end of the competition between the two giants. The Uber–Baidu alliance was not enough to win the game. Didi was valued at $56 billion at the beginning of 2019. But it was much less profitable than Uber (3% vs. 20%). In 2021, Didi had 377 million users and 13 million drivers. The figure went up to 550 million users. The market value of Didi went down to 20 billion US dollars at the beginning of 2023.

(2) The race continues outside of China. Since 2017, Didi has no longer been satisfied with the Chinese territory alone, where it still had to face 200 competitors (admittedly much smaller) and where a possible diversification in the distribution of meals was hardly conceivable in view of the two Chinese giants (Ele.me and Meituan) already engaged in this activity. Didi then started rubbing shoulders with Uber to take positions outside of China. Didi took a series of stakes in the biggest markets: USA, India, Southeast Asia, Middle East, and even Eastern Europe. Didi also acquired "99" in Brazil. Didi aimed to launch its own self-driving car (so it doesn't have to pay drivers anymore) and rallied a whole group of automotive companies in this spin off activity (as Uber also did). With the plan of better exploiting its base of 550 million active users of its services, Didi launched its robot-taxi (driverless) service in Shanghai in 2019 in the Jiading district (SAIC and BMW have also received licenses). Uber, on the other hand, exited the self-driving car business in 2020. The company went public in New York (the largest capital market in the world) in June 2021 and raised $4.4 billion there (Alibaba, when it entered New York in 2014, had raised $25 billion).

(3) Could the tide be turning for Didi? In 2018, murders of passengers by its drivers cast doubt on Didi's control over its drivers. Additionally, the China Cyberspace Administration questioned Didi's handling of personal information and ordered its removal from app stores in China – preventing it from recruiting new customers. In 2020, Didi lost $1.6 billion. In 2021, China launched a corporate cybersecurity survey. In December 2021, Didi announced a drop in its turnover and a loss of $4.3 billion in the third quarter. In May 2022, a few months after going public in New York in 2021, Didi chose to exit Wall Street to move to be listed on Hong Kong Stock Exchange. In July 2022, the company was fined eight billion yuan ($1.3 billion) – or 4% of its turnover – by the Chinese Cyberspace Administration for having improperly used data on its drivers and passengers. The founding CEO, Cheng Wei, however, appeared in February 2023 at the Big Tech forum organized by the Internet Society of China.

Fosun (复星)

(1) Fosun is a private company which built a highly diversified business portfolio taking advantage of privatizations. The Fosun group was founded in 1992 in Shanghai by four former students of Fudan University. Its first activities were centered on advising foreigners willing to invest in China. Then, in the early 2000s, its founders decided to take advantage of the wave of privatizations. Fosun became an assemblage of very different activities. The group is now present in insurance, finance, pharmaceuticals, real estate, mining, steel, and tourism. Fosun is China's largest private conglomerate. It has been listed since 2007 in Hong Kong. Its market cap went up to 20 billion US dollars, but went down below 10 billion US dollars since the end of 2022. Its president Guo Guangchang (56 years old as of 2023) is one of the emblematic stars of Chinese capitalism. He and his three partners hold 70% of the group. He is the main shareholder and one of the richest men in China (his fortune is counted in billions of dollars). He made Berkshire Hathaway, Warren Buffett's fund, his model.

(2) Fosun has an offensive policy of foreign acquisition. Fosun is among the most active private Chinese groups with regard to foreign acquisitions and equity investments. According to Dealogic, the group spent $38 billion in 130 mergers and acquisitions between 2010 and 2016. It is known for having invested in the Greek luxury group Folli Follie in 2011. It also bought 85% of the Portuguese insurer Fidelidade (for 1.7 billion euros), 20% of Cirque du Soleil (for 200 million euros), the French Club Méditerranée (for 828 million euros), the American insurers Meadowbrook and Ironshore (for 314 million euros in 2014 and for 1.483 billion euros in 2015, respectively), the German private bank Hauck & Aufhäuser (for 173 million euros), and the building of the former headquarters of Uni Credit in Italy (for 284 million euros). The weakness of Chinese brands partly explains why Fosun acquired Club Méditerranée (although it has been making a loss for years). The takeover of Club Méditerranée (in which Fosun had been a 7% shareholder since 2010) was an event in 2014. In 2015, Fosun and Anbang Insurance took control for four billion euros of Novo Banco – the third Portuguese bank in terms of assets. Fosun, for its part, took a 10% stake in the capital of the English tour operator Thomas Cook (a little-known brand in China) before buying it in its entirety in 2019. In 2016, Fosun acquired the Indian Gland Pharma for $1.3 billion. The group also acquired British football club Wolverhampton Wanderers. In 2017, Fosun invested $900 million in Polyus, a Russian gold mine.

(3) Fosun makes no exception to the Chinese rule of connections between the business world and the political world. Guo Guangchang has a connection with the city of Shanghai. He is also a member of the Chinese People's Political Consultative Commission. At the end of 2015, he strangely disappeared for almost a week without anyone knowing exactly why. He might have collaborated in a police investigation related to the fight against corruption. Another hypothesis is that the founder of Fosun ended up in detention because he had refused entry to a representative of the Chinese government on the Fosun board. The disappearance of high-level leaders is not uncommon in China. A similar fate also befell Mike Poon, who invested in Toulouse airport in France, as well as Zhou Chengjian, the billionaire founding boss of the Metersbonwe clothing chain, and Bao Fan, the CEO of China Renaissance (Huaxing in Chinese), at the beginning of 2023.

(4) Doubts are emerging about the financial health of the Fosun conglomerate. In 2017, Fosun was among four Chinese companies closely scrutinized by the Chinese government for their investments abroad – but Fosun did not come under pressure like Wanda, HNA, and especially Anbang, whose boss was sent to prison. To counterbalance its investments abroad, Fosun bought 18% of Tsingtao. In 2018, Fosun took control of the Lanvin fashion house for 120 million euros. Fosun has now moved into another sphere; it will have to show its ability to generate value from these disparate investments. In 2022, a new charge was made, this time by the Chinese banking regulator. The group is in debt to the tune of 260 billion yuan ($38 billion). The Chinese financial institutions concerned would have started examining their exposure to the Chinese group.

Huawei

(1) Starting from scratch, Huawei became a global telecommunications giant in 40 years. It is undoubtedly, alongside Alibaba, the most famous Chinese company outside China. It is one of the few truly globalized Chinese firms, commercially present in more than 170 countries. It has been in the Fortune 500 rankings since 2010. The firm is known to the general public for its smartphones. But its historic business is telephone equipment (like Ericsson and Nokia), i.e. routers, switches, base stations, associated software, and submarine cables. Huawei employs 195,000 people – including 97,000 Chinese employees, who hold more than 90% of the capital of the company via a trade union committee since Huawei is a workers' cooperative (this status, established in 1980 in Shenzhen, disappeared shortly after). The company's internal governance procedures are not well known. However, given the power of trade unions in China, the company has a public character. No less than 7% of its employees are members of the Chinese Communist Party. The founder Ren Zhengfei, born in the poor province of Guizhou in 1944 (79 years old as of 2023), holds 1% of the company. The company has experienced strong growth. While the turnover was less than 10 billion yuan in 1997, it grew to 604 billion yuan ($92 billion) in 2017 and 721 billion yuan ($105 billion) in 2018 (with a profit of $8.7 billion). In 2019, the turnover went up to 859 billion yuan ($122 billion). However, under the effect of US sanctions, revenue declined to 637 billion yuan ($86 billion) in 2022.

(2) Huawei has made an impressive journey from a low-price strategy to a genuine innovation strategy. Huawei started in Shenzhen in 1987 as a supplier of telephone equipment in China. The strategy at the beginning was to target small towns and rural areas that foreign manufacturers had neglected. Once established in China, from 1997 the firm had an international strategy targeting territories where Westerners did not want to go. Huawei most likely benefited from official support in its international development – even though the company is deemed private. In 2004, with a turnover of $3.8 billion, Huawei represented only 1/6 of the then worldwide leader Ericsson in the telecommunications market. By targeting easily accessible countries, Huawei built a market base. Once this base was achieved, the company gradually entered developed countries. It now supplies first-tier operators such as SFR, Orange, Vodafone, British Telecom, Deutsche Telecoms, and Telefonica. In 2010, Huawei became ranked as number two in telephone equipment behind Ericsson. As of 2017, Huawei has the largest share of the global infrastructure market – 28%. Ericsson owns 27%, Nokia 23%, ZTE 13%, and several smaller players own the remaining 9%, including Samsung. Vietnam, which made the atypical choice of a national supplier, the Viettel company, finds itself sixth in the race. Huawei invests considerable sums in R&D with more than 50,000 people working for R&D. The company is mainly located in China, but is also present abroad (Sweden, USA, India, Indonesia, Russia, Ireland, United Kingdom, Italy, and France). R&D expenditures amounted to nearly $14 billion in 2017, or 15% of sales. This reached $22 billion in 2020, or 16% of the turnover. Huawei is said to hold no less than 87,000 patents; the company filed 5,400 international applications in 2018 and 4,400 in 2019.

(3) Huawei's second key strategic choice has been downstream integration into smartphones. The business was launched in 2003. In 2011, Huawei sold only one million cell phones. The figure rose to 75 million phones in 2014. The 100-millionth sale bar was crossed in 2015. The figure jumped to 139 million in 2016 and to 200 million in 2018. Smartphones were half of Huawei's turnover. The Chinese company was in direct competition with Apple and Samsung (which are losing ground in China). Huawei offered a wide range of smartphones that met the needs of the different segments present in China. The Ascend smartphone made Huawei known to the general public. Although it became the world's third-largest smartphone maker, the gap with Samsung remained noticeable. Huawei's strategy in smartphones is clear: move upmarket. Huawei thus developed its own processors and sourced optics from Leica. The manufacturer brought a 5G smartphone to market in 2019 – the Mate X – with a fold-out screen at $2,600.

(4) Huawei has also been conducting a product diversification strategy in parallel. Since 2015, Huawei has offered its own payment system developed with China Union Pay in a market dominated by Alibaba and Tencent. The company also offers cloud services (again in competition with Alibaba and Tencent). An agreement has been made with Microsoft which will provide applications on Huawei's cloud. The group is also engaged in research on 5G-based telecommunications systems enabling assisted driving. It also entered the business of connected watches. It has also invested in artificial intelligence and voice recognition. An irony of the trade war between China and the US is that since Huawei is absent from the American territory, it does not have to suffer the impact of the taxes that American iPhone buyers have to pay.

(5) The rise of the Shenzhen technological flagship caused a strong reaction in the US. Huawei remains absent from the US and Australia. In fact, the company concentrates everything that scares American citizens. US officials have had many doubts about the company. Americans were suspicious because Ren Zhengfei, the founding boss, is both a member of the Chinese Communist Party and a former cadre of the Chinese army (from which he came out in 1982); they suspected him of being the armed wing of the Chinese economic intelligence. They refused to entrust even a small part of their mobile telecommunications system (and in particular the routers which constitute its core) to a company potentially linked to the Chinese authorities. Huawei was therefore excluded from tenders for national security reasons. It was also prevented from acquiring American firms. In China, on the contrary, Ren Zhengfei has become a living legend; he is the embodiment of Chinese economic and technological success.

(6) The US has notably refused to open its territory to Chinese 5G fearing that it has backdoors. Huawei started researching 5G in 2009. The three Chinese operators – China Mobile (see Appendix 3), China Unicom, and China Telecom – started implementing 5G as early as 2019. China Mobile reached 614 million 5G subscribers, China Telecom reached 268 million, and China Unicom 213 million (Europe lags behind in rollout). In this Chinese market, Huawei captured the essentials, while foreigners only received a few crumbs. Outside of China, Huawei is seeking to license its 5G technology to telecommunications companies. But Americans do not view it that way. Investing in 5G networks developed by Huawei would be a nightmare for them. They fear that the Chinese government will use Huawei to spy on client countries or launch covert cyberattacks: This is the fear of a Chinese backdoor in Western networks. What Huawei will do with the colossal datasets collected is nevertheless a legitimate question. Chinese law allows the government to order a Chinese company to provide its data on customers. How can one ensure that the data collected will not be exploited by the Chinese government for geopolitical purposes? In view of the investments made by Beijing in the internal security of the country, one can imagine that the Chinese political leadership would have the same level of intelligence service for external security. And given the opacity and the porosity between public and private, the population surveillance practices, and the treatment of human rights that prevails in China, one can have doubts! Americans are probably not wrong to be wary of Huawei. The horizons of power opened up by 5G – communication between billions of connected objects (liable to be attacked) – mean that all countries will want to be perfectly sure of their suppliers. No one wants the content of their telecommunications to be intercepted. No ruler wants any outsider to interfere with their critical infrastructure networks: water, electricity, Internet, hospitals, traffic routes, etc. Ren Zhengfei's denials didn't change anything. Australia, New

Zealand, and Japan are opposed to a deployment of 5G by Huawei, like the US. India has threatened to ban Huawei. In Europe, the UK imposed restrictions on Huawei by allowing Vodafone and its competitors to buy peripheral hardware (like antennas and base stations) but not core hardware. The British have also capped Huawei's share at 35% of their market. In Sweden, Ericsson's homeland, Huawei and ZTE have been banned by the government from bidding. In France, since the so-called 5G law of August 2019, an operator who wants to install a 5G antenna from Huawei must obtain the approval of the National Agency for the Security of Information Systems (Anssi). Sensitive areas, such as Toulouse, the headquarters of Airbus and the capital of aeronautics, are *de facto* inaccessible to Huawei. Other European countries, such as the Czech Republic and Slovenia, have also banned Huawei.

(7) **The Americans have lost the 5G battle, but they intend to catch up on the next generation.** Industry players have started networking on 6G. This should make it possible to further reduce latency and provide increased power for the benefit of health, driverless cars, artificial intelligence, and financial markets. It will open up perspectives in the Internet of the senses and the Internet of behaviors. It should be effective before 2030. Chinese companies like Huawei and Unicom have also been active in 6G since 2018, and China announced that it has made progress in terms of speed.

(8) **The founder's daughter was suspected, as the group's financial director, of covering up exports of products containing American components to Iran, and was placed under house arrest in Canada for three years.** Meng Wanzhou, Ren Zhengfei's daughter, who is the group's financial director, was arrested in Vancouver in December 2018 on a request from the US, which suspects the Huawei group of selling products incorporating US components to Iran. Meng Wanzhou ended up under house arrest, with the threat of extradition to the US at any time. Her lawyers were busy opposing the extradition. After the arrest, diplomatic relations between Beijing and Ottawa became frosty. In May 2020, Canada confirmed its lawsuit. Chinese retaliation, i.e. the accusation of espionage brought about by Beijing against two Canadian citizens and the embargo on several agricultural products imported from Canada (such as canola), was not enough to break the *status quo*. In September 2021, the US Department of Justice gave the green light for the prosecution to be

deferred. It therefore took almost three years for Meng Wanzhou's house arrest to end and for her to be allowed to return to China. The two Canadians detained in China were also released. The tension between the two countries remains high as evidenced by the tense exchanges between Justin Trudeau and Xi Jinping on the sidelines of the G20 summit in Bali in 2022. Meng Wanzhou succeeded Eric Xu Zhijun as rotating president in 2023, and seems set to potentially succeed her father.

(9) US supply sanctions have cut off access to the most advanced chips and this may well change the face of the telecommunications industry in the future. Huawei bought $11 billion worth of components and services from more than a thousand American companies in 2018. Specifically, for 5G, Huawei sourced semiconductors from Broadcom, Xilinx, Texas Instrument, and Analog Devices. Just as the US was able to cause problems for ZTE by refusing to deliver processors to it, the US finally decided in 2020 to reduce Huawei's access to US semiconductors, which hurt the company's smartphone business – where access to the latest generation of components is key. The challenge also lies in the operating system as Huawei uses Google's Android operating system. But the threat of an American refusal to continue to supply Huawei looms. Losing access to Android could become a major handicap for Huawei outside of China. In the short term, Huawei has in fact suffered the repercussions of the American attacks by accruing a 29% drop in its turnover in 2021, which fell to $99 billion. The news for 2022 was no better and over the summer Ren Zhengfei publicly declared his pessimism for the future of the global economy.

(10) In response, Huawei wanted to reduce its dependence on foreign countries. Facing pressure, "de-Americanization" becomes imperative. Huawei has had its own semiconductor design center, HiSilicon, since 2004. This semiconductor design center, with 10,000 people, is notably where the Kirin chips originated. It outsources manufacturing to the Taiwanese TSMC and American Micron; 5G is a real opportunity for these two providers. But the tightening of US sanctions has prevented Huawei from sourcing 5G chips from them as TSMC uses American technology. The US's refusal to sell to Huawei might have galvanized the company's R&D capabilities; the American threat was also used by Ren Zhengfei to convince his teams that the solution required in-house component development. In fact, under the effect of the American embargo,

HiSilicon saw its turnover melt by 90% in 2021. In the event of a break with the Americans, Huawei could always solicit the Korean Samsung Electronics or SK Hynix, world champions of memory chips. In terms of software, the company has an internal substitute for Android with the Hongmeng platform and an evolution of Android with Harmony. Knowing that Huawei makes 50% of its turnover from telephones, tablets, and laptops, launching its own operating system (an idea that Nokia, BlackBerry, Microsoft, Intel, Palm, Firefox, Samsung, and Jolla have all failed to implement) would be a major handicap outside of China. It is indeed difficult for consumers to leave the Google ecosystem to which they are accustomed.

Tencent

(1) Tencent is the "T" of the famous "2BAT" quartet. Tencent is along with Alibaba, Baidu, and ByteDance (see Appendix 3) one of the four pillars of the Chinese Internet. The company was founded in 1998 by Pony Ma (52 years old as of 2023). It is a private company based in Shenzhen. It employs more than 112,000 people. It has experienced an exponential increase of its turnover since its creation: $3 billion in 2010, $10 billion in 2013, $16 billion in 2015, $23 billion in 2016, $47 billion in 2018, and $70 billion in 2020. In the year 2021, it reached a peak of $87 billion. But, for the first time, revenue declined in 2022. The company performs the checks expected from the Chinese government. A user's account may be suspended if the said user spreads "malicious rumors or other illegal content"; it should be noted that, at Tencent, censorship also affects accounts created abroad (including those of the diaspora).

(2) The company started with online games. Tencent makes 50% of its turnover from online games. The number of players can be counted in the tens or even in the hundreds of millions. The number of games in its portfolio is in the thousands – of which only a few are blockbusters. These games were developed not only internally but also purchased from American, Korean, and even Finnish companies. In 2016, Tencent took control of Supercell for $8.6 billion, the Finnish start-up behind the game "Clash of clans". Tencent also bought a stake in the French video game publisher Ubisoft in 2022. The game "Honor of Kings" was so successful (more than 200 million registered users in China) that Tencent had to, under pressure from Beijing, limit the number of hours young people could play it. The Chinese authorities see the video game in a rather bad light. First, they consider video game a threat to the public health of young people, who are likely to develop addictions. Second, video games are associated with the West and therefore seen as a threat to Chinese values. The authorities therefore froze authorizations to launch new games in 2018 (from March to December). Video games thus had to suffer from tougher access conditions to the Chinese market since 2019. And again, from July 2021, Beijing decided to reduce the number of approvals.

(3) Weixin (WeChat) can be considered the "Swiss Army Knife" application. Tencent's second business is messaging. Tencent launched the online instant messaging service QQ in 1999 and mobile phone messaging application Weixin (known as WeChat outside China) in 2011. Many users agree that while WeChat was inspired by an American product, its designers have been able to go further. WeChat is not just for contacting friends. The platform is now used to order meals and pay bills with Weixin Wallet (WeChat Pay), and even invest in financial products. The goal is accumulate all the time the consumer spends online; he must be able to do everything and above all pay for everything with his mobile phone. Since 2018, WeChat exceeded one billion active accounts per month worldwide (knowing that a user can have several active accounts). Advertising also accounts for a growing share of Tencent's revenue.

(4) There is also a powerful South African shareholder. Tencent has been listed in Hong Kong since 2004. The market value of the company was first counted in billions, then in the tens of billions, and now in hundreds of billions. At the end of 2017, the $500 billion bar was exceeded (a capitalization comparable to that of Facebook). But capitalization lost $200 billion in 2018 after the announcement of poor results (and the temporary ban on launching games). The bosses of the South African publisher Naspers are the happiest in the financial history of Tencent as they brought $34 million to Tencent in 2001 to help the development of the start-up. The initial investment was certainly diluted, going from 46.5% to 34% of the capital. But it is valued at more than $150 billion, making Naspers the biggest South African company by market value.

(5) Like Alibaba, Tencent diversified by function. Tencent's strategy is comparable to that of Alibaba. It is a question of constantly expanding the range of functions offered: music, portals, search engines, clouds, taxi reservations (in the Didi joint venture with Alibaba), meal deliveries, and above all online payments with Weixin Wallet. Launched on different bases, the two companies Tencent and Alibaba have converging portfolios of offers; it is a Chinese remake of the Coca-Cola–Pepsi war. In 2013, Tencent took 36% of Sogou, the country's third-largest search engine (a subsidiary of Sohu). Tencent is also engaged in the fight for online video dominance (streaming); an agreement with HBO (Time Warner) gave the Chinese company a legal gateway to American programs (provided they were approved by the Bureau of Censorship). In 2014, Tencent took 15% of JD.com. In 2017, Tencent Music & Entertainment (TME) and Sweden's Spotify (160 million users) exchanged cross-shareholdings. In 2018, TME was valued at $30 billion. In 2019, Tencent took 10% of Universal Music. Tencent is also a majority shareholder of Meituan – a leading food delivery firm. Tencent has also moved into the consumer lending business with Webank – a joint venture formed after Tencent obtained a banking license from the government. Tencent thus serves as a spur to large public banks. In the automotive sector, Tencent took 5% of the capital of Tesla (for $1.78 billion). Tencent also partnered with the Guangzhou Automobile Group in 2017 for the development of connected cars.

(6) Like Alibaba, Tencent's business is concentrated in China. Tencent tried to internationalize its base, but failed to exceed 100 million users outside of China; the Chinese company will undoubtedly have to go through the acquisition of foreign companies. In the US, Tencent took $2 billion of the equity of Snap (the parent company of Snapchat) in 2017. Tencent went so far as to attack African territory with the support of its largest shareholder Naspers (as mentioned, a South African company). In total, at the end of 2017, Tencent had invested $4.3 billion in 15 foreign companies (according to Dealogie). Tencent is said to have interests in more than 700 targets. It also has seats on the boards of 400 companies. Its investments abroad have even increased in 2021 – particularly in Europe in the gaming sector.

(7) Technological innovation is the engine of the company. About 50% of its employees are programmers (software engineers) recruited out of college, while 25% have a master's degree. The company owns a total of 5,600 patents filed in 20 different countries on instant messaging, e-business, online payment, search engines, and online games (for comparison, Microsoft holds more than 60,000). Tencent even ranked 18th in the "2013 World Most Innovative Companies" by Forbes magazine! And the company was the 12th in BCG's Top 50 "Most Innovative Companies 2015".

(8) Is the tide turning? Faced with Beijing's crackdown on big tech companies, renewed constraints on video games, and a recovering Chinese economy, Tencent suffered its first drop in revenue in the second quarter of 2022. Profits fell more than 50% and the company sold stakes and laid off 5,000 people. However, Tencent's story continues.

Xiaomi

(1) The founder, Lei Jun, is a serial entrepreneur. Xiaomi is a private company. It was created in 2010 in Beijing by the charismatic Lei Jun (54 years old in 2023), an Internet pioneer in China, who is widely said to be a clone of Steve Jobs. Xiaomi was not his first attempt. He first worked for Kingsoft, a software company, when he left university in 1992. He then ran Shunwei Capital, a venture capital fund, and launched multiple companies. He made his first move in 2004 when he sold the online bookstore Joyo.com, which he had founded four years earlier, to Amazon for $75 million. When Xiaomi was created, Lei Jun gathered around him an experienced team, many of whom had spent time in the US working for the majors (Microsoft, Oracle, Google, Motorola, etc.).

(2) The company experienced a meteoric rise. Xiaomi put a wide range of smartphones on the Chinese market using Google's Android operating system, thereby creating a dependence on the American while Apple controlled its software and hardware. Seven million units were sold in 2012 and almost 19 million in 2013. The figure reached 60 million in 2014 (the turnover reached $12 billion). It rose to 80 million units in 2015 – including 65 million in China. The 100 million bar was bypassed in 2018. 190 million units were sold in 2021. Xiaomi snatched the crown from Samsung in China in 2014, overtaking established Chinese players like Huawei, Lenovo (see Appendix 3), and ZTE and crushing other lesser known Chinese producers like Coolpad or Gionee. In 2015, Xiaomi took 15% of the Chinese market ahead of Huawei and Apple even as the Chinese smartphone market was heading straight for saturation. The start-up was valued at $4 billion three years after its creation, and $40 billion, four years after its creation. At the end of 2014, its workforce reached 7,000 people. It exceeded 14,000 employees in 2017. In 2019, nine years after its creation, Xiaomi enters the Fortune Global 500 ranking. It exceeded 20,000 employees in 2020 and 33,000 employees at the beginning of 2022 (before the pandemic).

(3) The founder cooperates with the Chinese Communist Party. Xiaomi is a nascent champion whose boss has established strong ties with the Chinese State. Lei Jun is a member of the Communist Party of China, a member of the 12th Chinese People's Political Consultative Conference (an assembly without decision-making power), and one of Beijing's representatives to the National People's Congress. He is also vice-president of the All-China Federation of Industry and Commerce, an entity responsible for linking the business world with the Chinese Communist Party. Lei Jun's personal fortune exceeds $10 billion.

(4) Xiaomi adopted a disruptive strategy by offering a half-priced iPhone for entry-level segments. Part of Xiaomi's success was the opportunity for Chinese consumers to express their nationalism while making a good financial deal. But that's not all. Xiaomi built its success on the trivialization of the smartphone in the largest market in the world (nearly 800 million users in China against 260 million in India, and 250 million in the US). The company is driven by the unrestrained use of the smartphone, surpassing the use of the PCs: Since 2014, there have been more Internet users in China via mobile than Internet users connected via desktop computer. Xiaomi tackles the lower and middle levels of the income pyramid. So, these are low-cost products. Apple claims that these are clones of its products. Foxconn is in charge of production. Xiaomi's smartphones are rated as good quality. At its inception, all products were sold on the Web, via Weibo, WeChat, Baidu Tiebo, and Xiaomi mall, i.e. where the young people are. It has no sales force and has very little advertising expenditure. Efficient use of social networks ensures that Xiaomi has good publicity and notably saves on the distribution activity. Recently, its products have also been available in stores (which accounts for at least 30% of sales). Moreover, the company continuously updates its products based on feedback received from customers. The company files more and more patents (mainly in China): 2,300 in 2014, 3,600 in 2015, and 28,000 patents in 2020. Ironically, Xiaomi has seen copies of its products appearing on the Chinese market.

(5) Xiaomi's internationalization began with emerging countries. In 2013, the company poached Hugo Barra, one of the bosses of the Android management team at Google, to develop its international activities. In 2014, Xiaomi's market was still 97% Chinese. It then began by penetrating the Indian market, then targeted Latin America by starting with Brazil, then tackled the African continent, i.e. first emerging countries where the company was looking for growth drivers. Intellectual property disputes were less likely there than they might be in the US or Europe (Xiaomi is, however, facing a lawsuit from Ericsson in Indian territory). In 2017, the share of its revenue outside China reached 28%. It was then the turn of Russia and Europe. And Xiaomi was even trying to get into the US from 2018.

(6) Xiaomi undertook diversification toward connected objects aimed at the domestic ecosystem. In the tough world of mobile telephony, the leaders of Xiaomi undoubtedly remember the case of HTC, the Taiwanese manufacturer of smartphones, extolled in the 2000s and collapsing since 2011. They must in particular face the slowdown of the smartphone market in China and even in the world. The sector has indeed reached maturity: The number of smartphones sold fell between 2017 and 2018 (from 1.5 billion to 1.4 billion units). It is unclear if Lei Jun wants to make money on hardware. He is more interested in building a base of customers to whom he can sell Internet service and from whom he can accumulate data (which may one day be able to feed China's generalized surveillance system that is Social Credit). Lei Jun talks about the "triathlon": software, hardware, and Internet services. Lei Jun dreams of founding Xiaomi's own ecosystem; to this end, the company began to develop and market its own television in 2014. Its new products included white goods (pressure cooker, hair dryer, air purifier, fan, etc.) and even scooters. Xiaomi bought its first start-up in the US in 2014, Misfit, an Internet of Things player that produced "activity trackers". Xiaomi then acquired patents held by Microsoft, Philips, and Nokia. In 2017, Xiaomi even released its own processor in an attempt to break away from Qualcomm's domination. Xiaomi entered into partnerships with a large network of start-ups that agreed to join the Xiaomi ecosystem, four of which became technological unicorns (ZMI, Huami, Ninebot, and Smart mi).

(7) The stock market listing took place in Hong Kong more timidly than expected. In 2018, Xiaomi entered the Hong Kong Stock

Exchange and raised \$4.7 billion; the company was valued at \$50 billion (half less than the founder's estimated). Xiaomi products were found to have several flaws. However, the doubts linked to the backdoors do not seem to have had any effect on the development of the company abroad.

(8) Could the winds be turning? The year 2022 was marked by a trend break for Alibaba and Tencent. There was a drop in turnover that the leaders chose to offset by laying off 900 people. There was also a fall in the share price (–40% in the first half of 2022).

Appendix 2: The Evergrande Case Study – Autopsy of a Financial Failure

Evergrande, better known in China as Hengda, is the country's second-largest property developer after China Vanke. The company was established in 1996. It is based in the south of the country, in Guangzhou (capital of Guangdong province). Evergrande's development has been driven by decades of rapid urbanization: Between 1998, the year of the real estate reform, and 2021, China's urban population doubled from 450 million to 900 million. The model is to buy land from the local governments with money lent by banks and start selling apartments before any construction takes place – this is the so-called "pre-sale" model which applies for 90% of the Chinese market. Taking advantage of more easy access to credit, Evergrande has developed strongly: The company grew more than 40% per year between 2004 and 2020. The strategy was first to target the second- and third-tier cities – where the competition was weaker – before attacking first-tier cities (like Beijing or Shanghai).

Evergrande didn't bind its development to real estate. It diversified widely: football with the Guangzhou Football Club, amusement parks, mineral water, telecommunications, insurance, and even electric cars. In 2021, when it hit the headlines because of its financial difficulties, Evergrande had 200,000 employees and generated a reserve of three to four million jobs among its subcontractors. Its founder, Xu Jiayin (Hui Ka Yan in Cantonese – 64 years old as of 2023), a former steel technician from a humble origin, had the largest private fortune in China in 2017 with more than \$40 billion. He became known for his lavish lifestyle: private jets, super yachts, luxurious homes in Hong Kong, etc. He was nicknamed China's Donald Trump for building his empire on a mountain of debt. But, in 2021, he faced a serious reversal of fortune. His assets had shrunk by $25 billion over the year 2020–2021; at $11.3 billion, he was in 2021 "only" the 70th richest person in China (according to the 2021 Hurun Rich List). He was also a member of the Chinese People's Consultative Assembly (but was ousted).

New Rules of the Game Enacted by the Legislator to Deflate the Real Estate Bubble

It all started with the Chinese government's desire to reduce real estate speculation and to introduce more discipline in this sector. The government used the following slogan: "Houses are for living, not for speculating". To this end, government action focused as much on demand as on supply. To curb demand, in 2017, the Chinese government increased the amount of the down payment that buyers had to make for an acquisition. The government was also looking to introduce a property tax payable by owners; it thus launched several trials in a dozen major cities, but these were not extended. Beijing also enacted new rules in August 2020 such as a ban on selling apartments without having completed their construction.

But, above all, prudential ratios – three "red lines" aimed at reducing developers' reliance on borrowing – were imposed by the Central Bank (the People's Bank of China). These were the thresholds imposed: on the debt to balance sheet liabilities ratio (which must be less than 70%), the debt to equity ratio (which cannot exceed 100%), and cash to short-term debt ratio (which must be greater than 1). The regulator decided that real estate developers must reach these thresholds by 2023. The measure had a deleterious effect on developers who found themselves in a liquidity crisis. Evergrande, deviating on two criteria (159% debt to balance sheet liabilities, 83% debt to equity, 0.60 cash to short-term), found itself unable to borrow, and therefore to start new projects. In addition, the banks, on which the government imposed two other red lines, reviewed their loans to the real estate sector.

Evergrande's First Signs of Financial Distress

These new measures made it more difficult for over-indebted developers to gain access to bank loans. In mid-September 2021, Evergrande's liquidity crunch commenced with the company's announcement acknowledging that it might not be able to pay its creditors; the failure to pay an installment of $83 million was confirmed on September 23. Considering the small amount at the due date compared to the size of the company, this was a real sign of difficulty. However, the group was granted a 30-day grace period by the authorities to find a solution with its creditors. Officials from the China Banking and Insurance Regulatory Commission (CBIRC) began to negotiate with Evergrande's directors. New deadlines were not honored at the beginning of October. On October 22, the company honored the deadline scheduled for the end of September in extremis and avoided payment default and bankruptcy. Also on October 29, it executed a $47 million interest repayment. To reassure investors, Evergrande said it had restarted several projects in the Pearl River Delta. A payment of $148 million was honored on the deadline of November 10. But on December 8, Evergrande, still cash-strapped, failed to honor the payment of $82 million in bond coupons when a grace period expired (which should have been paid on November 6). This was the first proven non-reimbursement.

Evergrande Was Officially Found in Default by Two Agencies

On December 9, 2021, the rating agency Fitch placed Evergrande in "restrictive default". Creditors would sue: As of the 10th, a group of lenders seized over $60 million in Evergrande stock held by the President. On December 17, the rating agency Standard & Poor's declared Evergrande in default. The treatment of foreign creditors was closely watched. A repayment of bond coupons of 225 million, scheduled for December 28, was not honored. The company again had a grace period of 30 days. How much longer could Evergrande last?

The Most Indebted Real Estate Developer in the World Owed Money to Chinese Banks

Evergrande's debt was abysmal: $300 billion at the end of 2021 – the equivalent to 2% of Chinese GDP (or the public debt of a country like Portugal). This liability, while substantial, represented less than 1% of bank credit in China. Evergrande's debt was three times lower in 2015, illustrating the overheating of the Chinese real estate sector. As mentioned previously, Evergrande went into debt to buy land from local governments.

The loans were contracted mainly with Chinese banks. Only a sum of $19 billion was borrowed from international markets (so-called off-shore). At the beginning of December 2021, Evergrande announced that it wanted to restructure its debt into international bonds (offshore). A restructuring plan scheduled for July 2022 got postponed to August in a terse update. Assets outside of China could be put to use. These international creditors were ready to defend their rights. In August 2022, the foreign bondholders submitted their own restructuring plan to Evergrande.

American Oaktree Capital had already seized assets from Evergrande on a resort project near Shanghai after Evergrande defaulted on a $400-million loan. In January 2021, Oaktree seized another piece of land north of Hong Kong in the border district of Yuen Long where Xu Jiaying had a construction project after Evergrande defaulted on the repayment of a $600-million loan. This vast land was another symbol of the founder's delusions of grandeur: He wanted to build his own Versailles-style mansion there. The asset in question had been removed from the restructuring project. In October 2022, Evergrande disposed of this undeveloped land for $637 million – land the company had acquired for $1.13 billion.

Evergrande Also Owed Money to Its Suppliers and Contractors

Some suppliers and contractors of Evergrande issued profit warnings. The most fragile would have to close down in the event of bankruptcy of their client. Suppliers like Shanghai Construction Group sued to get paid; in response, a Chinese court froze 100 million assets held by Evergrande (bank deposits and real estate). In July 2022, a collective of suppliers in Hubei Province announced that they were suspending work for Evergrande. It should be noted that construction workers represent 10% of the Chinese labor force. The suppliers were not exclusively Chinese; they included, for example, the Korean Hyundai for construction equipment and machinery and the Swiss Schlinder for elevators. The problem became acute as some suppliers relied heavily on China. If Evergrande failed to pay its creditors, the companies risk liquidation.

Systemic Risk Means That Banks Could Find Themselves in Trouble if Evergrande Were to Fall

Among the banks hit by the real estate debt crisis was China Minsheng Bank, China's first private bank founded in 1996. Minsheng had already seen a 36% drop in profits in 2020. The bank made cuts of its real estate debt holdings its priority for 2022. It would have exposure worth $20 billion to high-risk developers, or 27% of its capital. This bank was one of Evergrande's biggest creditors. It also lent to China Fortune Land Development, another struggling developer. The entry of an outsider into the capital was not denied. Other financial organizations such as Ping An and Everbright Bank were also exposed. On a lesser scale, the Hong Kong-based Bank of East Asia (BEA) reported a 44% decline in first-half net profit in summer 2022 due to increased impairment charges on loans to the mainland China real estate.

The Collapse Also Affected Shareholders

Introduced in 2014 on the Hong Kong Stock Exchange, the Evergrande share had risen to 31.60 Hong Kong dollars in November 2017. It then began to fall in February 2021, reaching HK $17.42. It collapsed in September to hit HK $2.27. Capitalization thus fell from $41 billion in 2020 to $3.7 billion in September 2021.

At the beginning of October 2021, Evergrande decided to suspend its listing in Hong Kong. Trading resumed on October 21 and the stock fell again. It started to rise again on the October 22, after the interest payment was made. Evergrande bonds remained in the 23–29 cent range (down 75% from May). At the end of November, Hang Seng China decided to remove Evergrande from its index. At the end of December, the Evergrande share price fell even further. By 2021, Evergrande shares had lost 89% of their value.

Again, on January 3, 2022, Evergrande suspended its listing. Trading resumed the next day. But shareholders saw rather bad news. Thus, in early 2022, Chinese Estates Holdings, owned by Hong Kong tycoon Joseph Lau Luen-hung, announced a loss of $190 million for 2021 after selling its Evergrande shares.

On March 21, Evergrande again suspended its listing on the Hong Kong Stock Exchange without explaining itself. However, an audit on the 2021 financial year was requested by the Stock Exchange by the end of March. But Evergrande announced that it was unable to produce this report on time. A repayment obligation of up to $2 billion was scheduled for the March 23. And another repayment obligation for 1.4 billion was expected for the month of April. In July, the rating was still suspended.

At the end of June 2022, Top Shine Global, an investor in the Fangchebao (FCB) unit of Evergrande, launched a liquidation petition for a financial obligation of $110 million. And in August, Hong Kong developer Chinese Estate Holdings (controlled by the family of real estate tycoon Joseph Lau Luen-hung) sold half of its shares in Evergrande.

Evergrande Wanted to Deliver Housing

As of the end of June 2021, the company had 778 projects underway in 223 Chinese cities. As of September 2021, Evergrande had 1.4 million uncompleted and undelivered homes; due to late payments, construction on several sites was on hold. At the start of November 2021, the group announced that it had delivered properties to 57,000 owners between July and October. From September to November, only 10,000 homes were delivered each month. At the end of December (the 26th), the founder reiterated his desire to resume construction and deliver new apartments and promised the delivery of 39,000 units; 92% of projects were to be resumed (against half in September). In the end, sales for 2021 fell by 39% over one year amounting to 443 billion yuan ($64 billion).

In February 2022, Evergrande announced that it wanted to deliver 600,000 housing units during the course of the year. And at the end of March, the group claimed that construction had resumed in 95% of its projects. Unfinished work aroused the annoyance of the actors concerned. Centaline, the largest Hong Kong real estate sales agency, initiated legal action in early 2022 against the Hong Kong subsidiary of Evergrande to recover its unpaid commission ($15 million). By 2022, Evergrande was to have resumed work on 732 sites and delivered 301,000 residential units.

The Refund Strike

Buyers were the other stakeholder category particularly impacted. They could not access their property since it was not completed, or even begun in some cases. As the construction of their apartments was no longer progressing, buyers found themselves strangled by repayments having bills to pay aside from their loans. Thus, a growing number of disgruntled owners were refusing to honor their loan payments due to delays in the construction of projects. This refusal to pay started in June 2022 in Jingdezhen (Jiangxi) in a project launched by Evergrande and spread to around a hundred cities. These rebellious buyers began using social media (like the GitHub.com/WeNeedHome platform) to document the extent of the problems affecting real estate and were no longer hesitating from criticizing the government. The pre-sale model worked well when real estate prices were rising rapidly; but this was no longer the case. And unfinished apartments numbered in the millions. These mortgage boycotts forced the authorities to relax the pressure by asking banks during the summer of 2022 to grant more loans to developers. Meanwhile, the revelation of a possible multi-billion-dollar banking scam involving Henan Xincaifu and several rural banks sparked protests in Zhengzhou, the capital of Henan province. The authorities clearly had reason to worry about large-scale social unrest.

Should one fear a large-scale social movement? Probably not. The number of unfinished apartments however – one million – seemed high. If one assumed that it was couples who bought the apartments, then there were two million dissatisfied Chinese citizens. But, compared to a population of 1.4 billion, it was a smaller number than the share of yellow vests (700,000 people) in the French population.

But Evergrande Had to Destroy Housing!

To make matters worse, on December 30, 2021, Evergrande received an order from the city government of Danzhou (northwest of the tourist island of Hainan, in the tropics) to demolish 39 buildings under construction (i.e. 3,900 housing units) due to anomalies linked to the construction permit obtained. The project had been targeted by the Danzhou government since 2017. This was bad publicity at the wrong time. These buildings were part of the Ocean Flower Island ("haihua" in Chinese) complex in Yangpu Bay, the largest group of man-made islets in the world. The group of islands was supposed to mimic a peony. The center of the cluster was built as a commercial and tourist complex. It was an artificial paradise symbolic of the extravagance of the promoter. This vast tourist complex on three islands included 60,000 accommodations, luxury hotels, shopping centers, and amusement parks. The permit for this could possibly have been obtained illegally. The city's former Communist Party secretary, Zhang Qi, was sentenced in late 2020 to a life sentence for corruption. The constructions in question, totaling 435,000 square meters, would cause an environmental problem because of their probable impact on coral reefs. On January 4, Evergrande promised to carry out the demolition order.

Dealing with the Shortage of Liquidity by Selling Assets

In an attempt to secure its repayments, Evergrande embarked on the sale of its own assets. On November 9, 2021, Evergrande sold part of its shares in Heng Ten Networks for $52 million, and finally on November 18, all of its shares for $273 million. In early November 2021, Evergrande sold Protean Electric, a British automotive equipment firm acquired in 2019 for $58 million. In the aftermath, Evergrande announced that it has sold two of the company's Gulfstream private jets for $50 million. Following the resale of three high-end houses located in Hong Kong (including one for $100 million), calligraphy, works of art, etc., Xu Jiayin also sold a London property, the Knightsbridge mansion, which had 45 rooms and overlooked Hyde Park, for more than $200 million.

In February 2022, Evergrande sold four projects to public trust companies for $337 million. In March, Evergrande sold its interests in a massive real estate project in Hangzhou, known as Crystal City, for 3.66 billion yuan ($570 million). In the summer of 2022, the Hong Kong headquarters in the Wan Chai district was to be put up for sale. But Evergrande failed to sell that building, and in September, Evergrande's lenders appointed a receiver to take over the property, valued at $1.27 billion. A new call for tenders conducted in January 2023 was not successful.

The Guangzhou Football Club embarked on budget cuts and started laying off players. The club which had obtained the naturalization of five Brazilian players terminated their contracts in March 2022. In April 2020, Evergrande had spent $1 billion for the right to use a plot in the district of Panyu. The Guangzhou Football Club stadium was to be the largest football stadium in the world (capable of accommodating 100,000 people). It was to be completed in 2022. But its construction was interrupted. Evergrande returned the land-use rights to the Guangzhou government and secured a refund of 5.52 billion yuan ($818 million) to settle its debts. The stadium was taken over by the authorities.

This asset resale program carried the risk of triggering a self-perpetuating downward spiral (this was a "Minsky moment", named after the economist who theorized this phenomenon). Evergrande also resold previously acquired land to the city of Chengdu.

The Dilemma of Diversification in Electric Cars

Other subsidiaries could also be on the list of companies to be sold, such as Evergrande New Energy Vehicle (NEV). Founded in 2019, the company presented 14 projects under the Hengchi brand in three factories (Tianjin, Shanghai, and Guangzhou). Xu Jiayin aimed, without lacking in nerve, to be the first manufacturer of electric vehicles, ahead of Tesla! NEV built a factory for the mass production of electric vehicles in Tianjin in early January 2022. The manufacturer obtained marketing authorization from the Chinese authorities in March (and the buyer's subsidy that came with it). Evergrande applied the pre-sale model again. But, production struggled to take off and customers were annoyed that their vehicle was not delivered. After being repeatedly postponed, mass production of the Hengchi 5 model finally started in Tianjin in September 2022; it was an SUV offered at 179,000 yuan (after government aid) – or $28,000. The first vehicle deliveries took place in October 2022. The product launch of the second model (a "crossover" dubbed Hengchi 6) was due to start in the first half of 2023 and that of a third one (the Hengchi 7 sedan) in the second half. Yet, production of the Hengchi 5 was reportedly halted due to lack of orders. The issue was that such activities consumed cash and were highly competitive, which was a handicap given the financial fragility of the parent company. The solution would undoubtedly be the takeover by another manufacturer.

Delayed Deadlines

In addition to selling its assets, Evergrande sought to renew or extend outstanding loans. Thus, in mid-January 2022, the company managed to convince local bondholders (onshore) to postpone the payment of $707 million for six months. Another developer, Guangzhou R&F Properties, similarly avoided a $725 million default by successfully convincing its creditors to extend a term. Evergrande was also being examined over its relationship with a regional bank, the Shengjing Bank (8,000 employees), based in Shenyang (Liaoning) and listed in Hong Kong. Potential violations were reported. Evergrande held a majority stake in the bank. But the promoter had sold a stake for 10 billion yuan in 2018. Then, Evergrande sold 20% of the bank's capital in 2019 for 10 billion yuan ($1.5 billion) to the public investment group Shenyang Shengjing Finance. Evergrande then sold its remaining 14.7% stake in September 2022 for seven billion yuan ($1 billion) to a group of state-owned companies in the city. The founder, who had nothing to fear, did not hesitate to announce in January 2023 that he would repay his debts that year. Yet, as of February 2023, Evergrande had still not reached an agreement with major creditors on a framework for restructuring its debt to evacuate a possible court-ordered asset liquidation.

The Chinese Authorities Got Involved

Will the Chinese authorities come to the rescue and save the private company Evergrande – considering it is "too big to fail"? Beijing seems reluctant to bail out the company – especially since the head of the Central Bank of China (PBoC) announced that Evergrande's problems would be solved through the market. Will the Chinese authorities let it go bankrupt like they did with HNA or will they orchestrate a restructuring like what was done with Anbang? Will they dismantle Evergrande by having its assets taken over by other companies? Will they convince public companies to buy parts of Evergrande? Will the regulator let the bankruptcy of the group take place, which could become a threat to the Chinese economy through a domino effect?

At the end of October 2021, the Chinese state suggested that the founder should tap into his personal reserves to pay future reimbursements. Between July and November, Xu Jiayin actually personally cleared one billion shares of the group. At the end of November, he sold off 9% of shares that he personally held in Evergrande for $340 million at 2.23 Hong Kong dollars per share. But his personal fortune of $11 billion will not be enough to repay a debt of $300 billion. Other billionaires also dipped into their pockets to save their companies (including Guangzhou R&F Properties, Yango, Sunac, Cifi, and Shimao). The separation between personal and business assets is not as clear in China as in other countries. On December 6, 2021, to calm things down, the PBoC lowered the reserve requirement rate for banks. It also lowered the prime rate on one-year loans.

The Turnaround of the Chinese Government in 2022

Faced with difficulties of the real estate sector, the Chinese regulator decided in January 2022 to relax the rules of the three "red lines": The debts contracted by a developer to acquire the assets from another developer in difficulty were now to be excluded from the calculation. In November 2022, the Chinese State decided to support the sector – no more strict regulation. The PBoC published a 16-point plan calling for easier funding for healthy developers. The main measure requested Chinese banks to grant "special loans" to real estate players to help indebted developers and to complete ongoing projects. It was equivalent to helping good students. The main Chinese banks thus promised to lend 1.28 billion yuan ($186 billion) to Chinese promoters. This was followed by a rebound in the stock market listing of several companies in the sector: Country Garden's shares on the Hong Kong Stock Exchange gained 190% between the beginning of November 2022 and mid-January 2023 (Longfor is also among the winners).

That is another illustration that, in China, it is the government that makes the rain or the sunny weather. Another dramatic reversal was when the government decided in December 2022 to stop the zero-COVID strategy, leading to widespread infection of the population and a deterioration in the economic situation, which stifled the stimulus measures. Locally, in early 2023, Wuhan (capital of Hubei province) took the initiative to completely remove home ownership limits (which had been imposed in 2017) to help revive property sales. It became possible to buy a second apartment again. No other community had made such a decision before. In February, the China Securities Regulatory Commission (CSRC) detailed a program allowing private equity funds to invest in the real estate market. This is a new source of cash for developers. The program is open to foreign funds wishing to tap into the mainland China market.

Xu Jiayin Lost Control of His Group

In early December 2021, after he publicly announced that there was no guarantee that the group would have sufficient funds to repay its debts, Xu Jiayin was summoned by the Guangdong province authorities. The local government, in agreement with the PBoC, decided to set up a task force within the company to meet the creditors, coordinate the payments, and restructure the debt. This working group was mainly made up of representatives of state-owned companies. Their first task was to assess the assets of the group and of the founder. At the beginning of 2022, the provincial government wanted to separate the offshore assets of the company and sell them to repay the foreign debt. Evergrande asked foreign holders to identify themselves to compile a list. In mid-January 2022, Liang Senlin, an executive from Cinda Asset Management, was appointed to Evergrande's Board of Directors; Cinda was one of the structures created especially at the end of the 1990s by the Chinese Ministry of Finance to take over the bad debts of the four largest Chinese banks. At the end of January 2022, the restructuring road map was presented in a conference to creditors who were disappointed.

In July 2022, Xia Haijun, vice chairman of the board and chief executive officer, was forced to resign; he was replaced in by Siu Shawn, former president of the Evergrande New Energy Vehicle subsidiary, who meanwhile became executive director. Pan Darong, chief financial officer, also resigned. Xu Jiayin was losing control of his group.

The Shock Wave Propagated to the Sector

Evergrande was just the epicenter of a wider malaise among Chinese promoters. The contagion was affecting a growing number of companies in the sector – and not just those that appeared to be fragile. More than a dozen names emerged since September 2021.

Fantasia: At the end of September 2021, the listings of the property developer Fantasia were suspended in Hong Kong. The company was founded in 1996 in Shenzhen (the city created from scratch, north of Hong Kong) by a niece of Zeng Qinghong (a former vice-president of the PRC). It is, however, much less important than Evergrande. In October 2021, Fantasia was unable to honor repayments of $206 million within a deadline. Two of its directors decide to leave the company. At the end of November, the company obtained the agreement of investors to delay for two years the repayment of bonds for $100 million.

Sinic: The promoter Sinic (based in Shanghai), which had collapsed in September 2021 and lost 87% of its value on the Hong Kong Stock Exchange, announced in October that it would not be able to honor the repayment of a loan (of $250 millions). Its listing was suspended. Another reimbursement should have taken place in January (for the same amount). An order to wind up Sinic Holdings came from a court hearing in December; a provisional liquidator was to be appointed to take control of the debtor's assets.

China Modern Land: At the end of October 2021, China Modern Land did not honor a refund. Its listing in Hong Kong was suspended on October 21 before resuming in early January 2022. The company was established in 2000. It is 66% owned by Zhang Lei, founder and chairman of China Modern Land. The company is based in Beijing, but has been listed in Hong Kong since 2013. The company has engaged in the search for a solution with its creditors and has initiated a restructuring of its offshore obligations. In November 2022, the founder Zhang Lei resigned from his positions at the company.

Kaisa Group: Kaisa is the 25th Chinese promoter in terms of sales. It is based in Shenzhen, listed in Hong Kong, and chaired by Kwok Ying Ching (59 years old as of 2023, originally from Guangdong province). It had 17,000 employees at its peak with construction projects in 51 Chinese cities, many in Guangdong, and 200 renovation projects. It acquired the Shenzhen Football Club in 2016 and diversified into medical services and shipping. It is the most indebted Chinese promoter abroad (about $3.2 billion) after Evergrande. Kaisa was the first Chinese property developer to default in 2015 on a foreign bond. On November 4, 2021, Kaisa missed a payment. In the aftermath, on November 5, Kaisa suspended its listing in Hong Kong. Its shares had fallen by 70% in 2021. Its recovery tactic involved, like Evergrande, the selling of assets. The developer auctioned 18 of its real estate projects in Shenzhen (for $12.8 billion) to try to meet upcoming deadlines. On November 9, it made a desperate plea for help. Fitch downgraded the company, lowering its credit rating from C to CCC–. In mid-November (the 11th and 12th), it defaulted on an interest payment of $88 million – within a 30-day grace period. At the end of November (the 25th), Kaisa sold its share in a development on the site of the former Hong Kong Kai Tak airport (in Kowloon Bay) and proposed a debt restructuring by exchanging $380 million of offshore bonds (due December 7) against new notes due in June 2023; its future hangs on the response of the bondholders. On December 8, Kaisa suspended its listing in Hong Kong. The promoter was downgraded by Fitch – which finally decided to withdraw its ratings in January 2022. Kaisa had its listing suspended on the Hong Kong Stock Exchange in April 2022 for failing to release them on time. Kaisa announced in April that it had established a link with the China Merchants Shekou Industrial Zone (a manufacturer controlled by China Merchants Group) and China Great Wall Asset Management (one of China's bad debt managers, like Cinda), opening up new avenues of refinancing. Yet, after 11 months of suspension of trading, when Kaisa went back to Hong Kong Stock Exchange in March 2023, its stock price hit its lowest (HK $0.5 per share). The company reported losses of $1.8 billion in 2021 and $1.1 billion in the first half of 2022.

Sunshine: At the beginning of December, it was the turn of the promoter Sunshine 100 China Holdings, listed in Hong Kong and chaired by Yi Xiaodi, to announce that it had liquidity problems. It defaulted on December 5 on $179 million in bonds. The promoter had already defaulted in August.

Shimao: Shanghai-based Shimao was a higher-rated promoter than either Evergrande or Kaisa. Shimao had not crossed any of the three red lines set by the regulator. The company borrowed $7 billion on offshore bond markets. Hui Wing Mau, the founder of Shimao, also managed hotels; he was a member of the Chinese People's Consultative Assembly. Standards & Poor's placed Shimao at a lower B+ rating in December (a B-rating means there is significant default risk but a limited safety margin remains). Subject to the slowdown in apartment sales in early January, Shimao failed to repay bonds listed in renminbi amounting to $103 million. Standard & Poor's again downgraded Shimao to B–. The company then decided to put all its real estate projects – residential and commercial properties – up for sale. This did not prevent Shimao from being the target of the bank of Singapore (OCBC) which filed a complaint for a loan repayment request. In 2022, Shimao saw a significant drop in sales. In July, cash-strapped, Shimao failed to repay a billion-dollar bond.

Country Garden: Country Garden was created by Yang Guoqiang in 1992. It went successfully on Hong Kong Stock Exchange in 2007. At the start of November 2021, Country Garden suffered declines but then caught up around mid-November. The promoter planned to issue short-term securities based on supply chain assets. At the beginning of January 2022,

Country Garden announced that it was abandoning an issue of convertible bonds in dollars. During the summer, the Hong Kong stock market reacted badly to the group's sale of new shares to raise funds – Yang Huiyan, daughter of the founder, majority shareholder of Country Garden, and also the richest woman of Asia ($23.7 billion in 2021), saw her fortune melt by half. In August, the company announced a fall in its half-year profits from 15 billion yuan ($2 billion) to 600 million ($88 million). From September 2022, Country Garden could issue five billion yuan of bonds guaranteed by China Bond Insurance (following a request from the Chinese regulator). In October 2022, Fitch downgraded its rating from BB+ to BB–.

Yuzhou: In early January 2022, it was the turn of Yuzhou (based in Xiamen) to face a liquidity crisis. The company, established in 1994, was seeking to delay the payment of obligations amounting to $582 million. Yuzhou had made extensive use of offshore loans. Yuzhou was seeking to delay the deadline for a year. The payment default was confirmed at the end of January (the 23rd). Fitch downgraded Yuzhou's rating from RD (restricted default) to C. In the aftermath, Ernest & Young decided to sever ties with Yuzhou, not feeling sufficiently comfortable with the company's accounting processes.

Aoyun: At the end of January, Aoyun, much smaller in size than Evergrande, announced that it was unable to repay two interest payments on dollar bonds.

Zhenro: In mid-February, the promoter Zhenro Properties collapsed after announcing that it could not meet its obligations. The company, the 30th Chinese developer, was nevertheless perceived as financially solid. It was facing a shortage of cash. It saw a 30% drop in sales in January 2022 compared to January 2021. Fitch lowered its rating from B to C and Moody's similarly downgraded Zhenro.

Yango: In March 2022, Yango defaulted on an offshore bond repayment of $95 million. The developer had already defaulted in February. It was ordered to wind up in October by a Hong Kong court. That was the first time such a decision was made against a major builder during the country's property debt crisis. This opened the door to more such decisions.

Sunac: In May 2022, facing a collapse in sales, it was Sunac (based in Tianjin and the continent's third-largest promoter, chaired by Sun Hongbin) which defaulted on a repayment of $30 million in interest. The company was fighting to obtain a rescheduling of its debts. It was downgraded by Fitch Ratings and Moody's. At its peak in 2019, Sunac employed 50,000 people. In 2017, the Sunac group diversified into hotels and resorts by buying assets from Wanda, spending 63 billion yuan for this purpose. The debt was nine billion US dollars. Quotation on HKSE, which was suspended in April 2022, was restated in April 2023, but the share plummeted in one day by 59%.

CIFI Holdings: In October 2022, it was CIFI Holdings, based in Shanghai, which faced a deterioration in its sales and declared that it was suspending the payment of all its offshore obligations after failing to reach an agreement with its creditors. The company defaulted on a bond payment of $318 million. A restructuring of offshore debt was then launched.

Longfor Properties: In October 2022, Wu Yajun, the billionaire founder of Longfor Properties, left the company's presidency after announcing health problems. Shares in the company lost 70% of their value since the start of the 2023.

Who will be the next property developer on the list? These are all the developers who will not be able to meet the three "red lines" requirement. Promoters like Tianji, Logan, Risesun, and Ronshine have shown signs of weakness. This turmoil in the industry is not a nightmare for all the developers because there are also many opportunities for mergers and acquisitions for promoters.

A Record of Downgrades by Rating Agencies

The rating agencies (Standard & Poor's, Fitch, and Moody's) have all downgraded ratings of developers – the sector has been hit in 2021 by a record number of downgrades. At the end of October, Standard & Poor's suggested that a third of Chinese promoters could be in difficulty. Fitch came to the same conclusions in December. In addition, the hypothesis of hidden debts (to circumvent the three "red lines") has been mentioned more and more frequently.

However, Evergrande Will Not Be the Chinese Lehman Brothers

Real estate activity and construction officially represent almost 14% of Chinese GDP (7% for construction and 6.8% for real estate). Construction alone represents 15% of urban employment. But those numbers could be higher. In 20 years, prices per square meter have increased considerably. And in less than 30 years, China has become a market for owners. Oversupply is however a problem. There are three billion square meters of unsold apartments in China, enough to house 30 million three-person families, i.e. enough square meters for 90 million people to live there (according to the consultancy firm Rhodium). If the sector is to deflate, there will be significant adjustments ahead in the Chinese economy. The fall could also have an impact on commodity markets (aluminum, copper, coal, etc.).

Evergrande's case could also affect projects led by Chinese developers outside of China – such as Guangzhou R&F Properties' projects in London. Although the US Federal Reserve (the FED) issued a first warning in November 2022 of the risk of contamination on a global scale, it is unlikely that a fall of Evergrande could have the global impact that the bankruptcy of the investment bank Lehman Brothers had in 2008, as the activities of the promoter are essentially Chinese. And as previously indicated, it is primarily Chinese banks that are exposed. Moreover, in this fragmented sector, Evergrande's market share does not exceed 5%. Still, its auditor, PwC, had not issued any warning signals when, as early as 2016, analysts at GMT Research (Hong Kong) revealed questionable accounting practices.

Downward Adjustments

Under the effect of the real estate crisis, the slowdown in urbanization, the fall in the birth rates, the general decline in the population, and the wait-and-see attitude after the COVID crisis, the demand for new housing and land is down. In fact, real estate and construction experienced a contraction in the third quarter of 2021. The mistrust of buyers resulted in a drop in new home prices of a modest 1% (according to the National Bureau of Statistics), but this was the first decline since 2015. The risk of loss of consumer confidence was great. October in turn marked a drop in real estate prices. New housing prices continued to fall (–0.3%) for a third consecutive month in November 2021 (according to the National Bureau of Statistics). However, the trend was partially reversed in February 2022 when the prices of new homes rose in 100 Chinese cities. The ratio of housing prices to annual income reached 43 in Shenzhen, 42 in Beijing, and 33 in Shanghai, while the same ratio was 13 in London and 9 in New York. In September 2022, prices were still falling for the 13th consecutive month. Prices fell at an accelerated rate in December 2022. In the first eleven months of 2022, deals for China's top 100 developers fell 42.6% from 2021 and 31% in December from 2021 (according to China Real Estate Information Corp.).

Appendix 3: Brief Profiling of Large Companies Cited in the Book

The Chinese companies presented in Appendix 3 are quoted in the text. The aim of this appendix is to help the readers who are not familiar with these companies get a brief description of their profile. This sample covers different cases. It includes privately owned companies like Haier or Renren and also state-owned companies like China Mobile or Sasac. We have B2B companies like Sany and B2C companies like Lenovo. We have industrial companies like Sany and financial companies like Sasac. We have companies focused on China like China Mobile and companies with significant positions abroad like Haier.

ByteDance

It is a private unlisted, Internet company created in 2011 by Zhang Yiming. The founder studied computer science and was inspired by American Internet entrepreneurs. When ByteDance was created, the founder bet that the Internet of the future would give priority to platforms offering content that would draw in the users (and not the other way around). In 2012, he launched Jinri Toutiao (literally, "news of the day") on the information market. The Chinese equivalent of Yahoo News, the start-up aggregates news content using artificial intelligence by using personalization. Its users number in the tens of millions. It was valued at more than $10 billion in

2017. In 2018, however, it was called to order by the Chinese authorities to be more respectful of socialist values. ByteDance has branched out into e-commerce, music streaming, and mobile video game publishing. The platform has developed in more than 150 countries – in particular after the acquisition in 2017 of Musical.ly, a network focused on dance and playback. ByteDance was valued at $75 billion in 2019. But above all, ByteDance has achieved a genuine breakthrough outside of Chinese territory with TikTok. The platform doubled its revenue in 2020 to $34 billion. In 2021, ByteDance started selling artificial intelligence technology applications to Internet companies in China and outside China – competing with companies like Amazon Web Services, Google, and IBM. Also in 2021, when the Chinese government was initiating regulatory tightening aimed at the digital giants, the founder Zhang Yiming chose to resign. In 2022, ByteDance continued to rise with revenue exceeding $80 billion (up 30% from 2021) with high profitability. An IPO has been planned. In 2023, with 34 billion euros (in the Hurun ranking), Zhang Yiming became the second richest entrepreneur under 40 in the world (after Mark Zuckerberg).

China Mobile

The company is the largest mobile phone operator in the world. It exceeded 900 million subscribers in China in 2018; the figure reached 975 at the end of 2022. China Mobile overwhelmingly dominates its two competitors, China Unicom and China Telecom, which have 324 and 242 million subscribers, respectively (in 2018). At the beginning of 2022, they add, respectively, 401, 160, and 196 million 5G subscribers. With China Mobile at 61% and its two competitors at 22% and 16%, the Chinese market of telecommunication services is incredibly concentrated: The Herfindahl index of industry concentration (sum of the squares of market shares) is close to 0.50. The company employs about 400,000 people. It covers all market segments. It operates within a gigantic ecosystem with the blessing of the Chinese state. The company was listed in New York (until 2021) and is still listed in Hong Kong, but it remains 74% owned by the Chinese state. Driven out of Wall Street by the US administration, China Mobile successfully entered the Shanghai Stock Exchange in early 2022 with the aim of raising $7.5 billion to finance the development of 5G. China Mobile had historically deployed a Chinese 3G system called TD-SCDMA. The company is highly decentralized; the subsidiaries in the provinces are all responsible for their own income statement. China Mobile is mainly active in China alone. The only two exceptions are the acquisition of Paktel, the Pakistani mobile operator in 2007, and the acquisition of an 18% stake in the capital of the Thai operator True Corporation in 2014 (third in its country).

Haier

The company is the Chinese home appliance and consumer electronics giant. It originated from a joint venture with the German company Liebherr (transliterated at that time as li-bo-hai-er). The company was created in Qingdao (Shandong) in 1984 by Zhang Ruimin (74 years old as of 2023). Unsurprisingly, the founder is also a member of the CCP Central Committee. He transformed a state company producing refrigerators, close to bankruptcy, into a company producing white and brown products at a global level. He is said to have asked employees to publicly destroy a few dozen defective refrigerators with the idea of pushing staff toward quality. More recently, he championed the concept of dynamic capabilities (from Professor David Teece) and his own model called "ren dan heyi": The model is based on employees (ren), user value (dan), and the integration (heyi) of employee achievement values and user value creation. He wanted to put the employee at the center of the organization to encourage him/her to produce innovation. The group became the Chinese giant of household appliances and consumer electronics with 100,000 employees and more than 350 billion yuan in turnover in 2022 ($52 billion). The company is owned by its employees. Its range of offerings is wide: Haier offers products for rural people (potato washing machines), low-income people (mini washing machines) or high-income people (wine cellars). Haier competes with locals companies like Hisense, TCL, Gree, and Midea and also with foreign competitors like Philips, Whirlpool, Samsung, and Electrolux. It also has listed subsidiaries in Shanghai and Hong Kong. Haier has a strong presence abroad both commercially and industrially. For example, the company entered the US market in the 1990s; the brand is now part of the landscape. Its competitor Hisense – also based in Qingdao – is present industrially in Mexico, Europe, and Africa and has also invested significantly in R&D. One of Haier's big hits was the 2016 takeover of the home appliance division of General Electric for $5 billion. A third of its revenue comes from products made and sold in China; another third of products are made in China and sold overseas; and the final third comes from products manufactured and sold abroad. Haier puts particular emphasis on innovation. The company devotes more than 6% of its turnover to R&D with 22,000 employees working in R&D. Haier has 10 R&D centers not only in China but also in the US, Europe, and New Zealand. The company is known for its frequent organizational changes. It is now looking for technologies to buy.

Lenovo

Lenovo is one of the Chinese companies that exemplifies China's ambitions in global markets. Initially, it was established as a spin-off from the Chinese Academy of Sciences. The company was founded in Beijing in 1984 by Liu Chuanzhi, an electronics engineer. Lenovo quickly became the number one seller of personal computers in China. The company went public in Hong Kong in 1994. In 2004, it employed 10,000 people and achieved a turnover of $3 billion. The Lenovo name became famous worldwide in 2005 when the company took over the "personal computer" (PC) division of IBM for $1.25 billion. Upon completion of the takeover, nearly 10,000 IBM employees joined the Chinese company; it was a little fish that swallowed the whale. The integration of the American entity was eventually conducted without too many clashes – in any case, much less than one could have imagined. Lenovo has since surpassed the world's top personal computer manufacturers one by one. In 2010, Lenovo was the world's fourth-largest PC manufacturer. In 2011, the company moved to the second step of the podium; it overtook the American Dell and the Taiwanese Acer, but remained second after Hewlett-Packard. The year 2011 also marked the end of the career of the founder: At 67, Liu Chuanzhi left with his head held high. He was replaced by Yang Yuanqing. In 2013, with 55 million machines sold, Lenovo ended up snatching the first rank from Hewlett-Packard as world leader on the market (which Hewlett-Packard had held since 2006) while retaining total control of its production chain. Unlike its competitors HP and Dell, Lenovo produces most of its products by itself; it buys its components from Intel, Nvidia, AMD, Samsung, and SanDisk. The company is the king in China, in particular thanks to a successful distribution network in the territory. However, PC is a sluggish market affected by the development of digital tablets. Lenovo has developed an extensive line of servers, smart TVs, peripherals, handsets, and mobile phones (as of 2010). The company has thus pushed pawns in smartphones and tablets with, respectively, 50 million and 10 million units sold in 2013. In 2014, it acquired the mobile telephony division of Motorola for $3 billion; it is thus relying on the international market to compensate for a decline in the Chinese market where it is experiencing growing competition from Xiaomi (see Appendix 1). Also in 2014, Lenovo bought part of its server division (entry-level servers) from IBM for $2.3 billion. The company is now owned by Legend Holdings and the private company of Yang Yuanqing (the chairman of Lenovo); more than 50% of its capital is listed on the Stock Exchange. Lenovo today employs more than 60,000 people. The turnover has stabilized around $60 billion. It devotes a small 2.6% of its turnover to R&D. However, the tensions between the US and China will not help matters knowing that Lenovo makes a quarter of its turnover in the US.

Renren

Not all start-ups are "success stories" in China: Renren is an illustration of a failure. It was the alter-ego of Facebook – which has been inaccessible in China since the 2009 riots in Xinjiang, except through a virtual private network (VPN). This Chinese clone was launched in 2005 under the name Xiaonei by Chinese students from Tsinghua University and Tianjin University. The Japanese telecommunications operator Softbank owned a third of the capital of the company. Renren was similar to Facebook, but it differed from it by a more restrictive application platform than that of the American (for example, it offers its own games under the Mop brand). Renren had 160 million registered users in 2011 (its competitor Kaixin 001 was said to have 120 million) in a country where the number of Internet users was approaching one billion. The first Chinese social network therefore had a good margin of progress (in comparison, Facebook had 2.2 billion monthly active members). Renren illustrated both the rise of private companies in China and the Chinese government's desire to facilitate the emergence of national champions. Thus, Chinese firms operating on the Internet are lucky not to have to face competition from foreigners, with Facebook, YouTube, and Twitter being banned, and Yahoo and more recently Google having thrown in the towel. Although its activity was limited to the Chinese market, and it was not listed in China,

Renren went public in the US in New York in 2011. However, since this listing, Renren's share value plummeted: Initially quoted at $16.80, the share evolved to around $15, until 2016 when it fell below $10. It dropped to $2 in mid-2018. After taking too long to switch from desktops to smartphones, Renren seemed to be losing the game. Renren was trying to enhance its portfolio of holdings in around fifty companies. The company was sold in 2018 for $20 million. Prospects vanished with young Chinese people now on WeChat, QQ, Weibo, and TikTok.

Sany

It is the "Chinese Caterpillar"; the company manufactures lifting equipment, cranes, excavators, rollers, concrete pumps, asphalt spreading plants, etc. Beside Caterpillar, Sany's foreign competitors are the South Korean Hyundai or the Japanese Komatsu and Hitachi. In China, Zoomlion is its strongest competitor. Sany was founded in 1986 in Changsha (Hunan) by former executives of public companies. The company was driven by the development of construction in China. At the beginning of the 2010, the workforce went up to 50,000 people. It went down over the following years because of China's slowdown and has now stabilized around 20,000 employees. The company has also expanded internationally. Sany is targeting overseas markets. In 2017, the company managed to export 40% of its production. Sany is frequently cited for its takeover of the German concrete pump manufacturer, Putzmeister (a family company with 3,000 employees based in Stuttgart), for $320 million in 2012. Contrary to stereotypes, Sany's strategy is not to produce machines at low cost but to make a difference with innovation – like Chinese companies Huawei, ZTE, Lenovo, Haier, Hisense, or even BYD. During the good times, up to 7,000 people worked in R&D and 5% of the turnover was devoted to R&D. R&D is analyzing, for example, the use of new materials or the introduction of assistance for the operation of machines by computer. The company prides itself on having a portfolio of over 5,000 patents. Sany was honored by Fortune China magazine in August 2012 for the technological innovations in its products. It should also be noted that the Boston Consulting Group placed Sany in the top 10 most value-creating companies in 2010. The group has R&D sites in China, but also in Germany, the US, and Brazil for the localization of its products. Liang Wengen, the founder, is now one of the richest people in China.

State-Owned Assets Supervision and Administration Commission (Sasac)

Sasac is the world's largest public holding company. It was created in 2004 by consolidating several activities. It controls the following: in energy, China National Petroleum Corporation, State Grid Corporation of China, and China Three Gorges Corporation; in steel, Ansteel, Sinosteel, and Baosteel; in automotive manufacturing, First Automotive Word (FAW) and Dongfeng Motor Corporation; in air transport, China Eastern Airlines and China Southern; or even Aviation Industry Corporation of China, China Mobile, Sinochem, or Cofco. These companies operate in highly oligopolistic sectors deemed essential for national security and economic development. Sasac is placed under the direct control of the State Council (in other words, the Council of Ministers). It is piloted by an office of nine people, all members of the CCP. It is this body that appoints the leaders of these companies. Sasac is not only central but also has its regional relays. This supervisory authority initially held 185 companies, representing a portfolio of $800 billion: It is a state within the state. Driven by a desire for concentration, the number of companies was reduced to 150 in 2007 under the effect of mergers. Companies in the same sector have been brought together to reduce excess industrial capacity, to generate scale effects, and to reduce competition in China. It may also have involved strengthening vertical relationships. The ambition is to create national champions with a stronger international profile. Baosteel thus merged in 2016 with Wisco (Wuhan Iron & Steel Corporation) to form Baowu Steel, becoming the second-largest steelmaker in the world. The objective was to reach the figure of 80 to 100 at the beginning of the 2010s. In fact, the figure was 100 in 2017. And the movement continues. It is Sasac that could decide on the merger between Dongfeng and FAW – which would make the merged entity the sixth-largest manufacturer in the world (the example is not taken at random but based on rumors of a merger). Chem China and Sinochem could also be merged to form a single chemical group. There is a potential consolidation of the energy "big five" – China Datang Corporation, Guodian, China

Huadian Corporation, China Huaneng Group, and China Power Investment Corp. – to build a trillion pool of assets: The operation aims to better control the installation of new production capacities (in fact higher than demand). However, this race for size also amounts to creating mammoths that could prove difficult to maneuver, or worse, generate diseconomies of scale.

Index

Printed in the United States
by Baker & Taylor Publisher Services